CITIZEN SHAKESPEARE

EARLY MODERN CULTURAL STUDIES

Ivo Kamps, Series Editor

PUBLISHED BY PALGRAVE MACMILLAN

CITIZEN SHAKESPEARE

FREEMEN AND ALIENS IN THE LANGUAGE OF THE PLAYS

John Michael Archer

CITIZEN SHAKESPEARE
© John Michael Archer, 2005.

First published in 2005 by
PALGRAVE MACMILLAN™
175 Fifth Avenue, New York, N.Y. 10010 and
Houndmills, Basingstoke, Hampshire, England RG21 6XS
Companies and representatives throughout the world.

PALGRAVE MACMILLAN is the global academic imprint of the Palgrave Macmillan division of St. Martin's Press, LLC and of Palgrave Macmillan Ltd. Macmillan® is a registered trademark in the United States, United Kingdom and other countries. Palgrave is a registered trademark in the European Union and other countries.

ISBN 1–4039–6666–4

Library of Congress Cataloging-in-Publication Data is available from the Library of Congress.

A catalogue record for this book is available from the British Library.

Design by Newgen Imaging Systems (P) Ltd., Chennai, India.

First edition: August 2005

10 9 8 7 6 5 4 3 2 1

Printed in the United States of America.

To the memory of my father,
Alfred Archer

CONTENTS

ACKNOWLEDGMENTS

My thanks to the University of New Hampshire, which provided me with financial support through the Hortense Cavis Shepherd Professorship and a Senior Faculty Fellowship at the Center for the Humanities during the completion of this book. I would also like to thank my former colleagues in early modern literary studies at the University of New Hampshire: Elizabeth Jane Bellamy, Elizabeth H. Hageman, Douglas M. Lanier, and Rachel J. Trubowitz. I owe a particular debt to Jean E. Howard, a former colleague at Columbia University, for many fruitful conversations on the topic of this book over the years. I am grateful to Richard Helgerson, who read the manuscript for Palgrave and offered some indispensable suggestions about the ends of *Citizen Shakespeare*. And a special thanks goes to Ivo Kamps, my series editor, who saw the project through to completion from an early stage.

Editor's Preface for John Archer's *Citizen Shakespeare: Freemen and Aliens in the Language of the Plays*

"The subject" has been the focus of an enormous amount of early modern literary criticism in recent decades. The influence of such thinkers as Foucault, Derrida, Althusser and other theorists on the human "subject" is probably largely responsible for initiating this trend, and for displacing the concept of the "individual." But it is of course not only the vogue of continental theory that swayed North American and British critics to examine early modern culture through the lens of the subject. "Subjection," a prominent feature of recent discussions of the "subject," seems also to be an integral part of that culture and its literature. When Shakespeare's Henry V bitterly complains that he is "subject to the breath of every fool," he is simultaneously asserting the king's subjection and declaring such subjection to be absolutely against the social and natural norm. As we are so often reminded by a wide range of early modern texts, it is the head that should rule and subject the body, and not vice versa. But has the critical pendulum swung too far in the direction of subjection?

John Archer's *Citizen Shakespeare: Freemen and Aliens in the Language of the Plays* can be viewed as a move away from the emphasis of subjection in favor of a consideration of identity formation in the context of urban life. Despite the often-noted close association of Shakespeare's plays with the Elizabethan and Jacobean monarchies, Archer demonstrates that the plays are also rife with the language of urban *citizenship*, and that such language positioned many Londoners not only in opposition to the aristocracy but also to "urban non-citizens, especially immigrants from continental Europe." The "citizen" of Archer's title does have certain affinities with the "subject" of recent criticism, but the appellation of "citizen" does, for those who were entitled to it, tout a number of classical, republican, and civic qualities that notably diminish the degree of their "subjection" implied in the term "subject." The vocabulary of citizenship allowed specific groups of early modern Londoners to shape their identities vis-à-vis the crown and "strangers" in ways that underscored their status as freemen who belonged to "a body or corporation of citizens that had been granted certain rights."

Archer's decision to study the *language* of citizenship in Shakespeare's comedies, histories, and Roman plays is a subtle move away from the preoccupation with questions of representation that has marked the work of cultural materialists, new historicists, and historically oriented feminists in recent years. It is not so much that Archer finds fault with a focus on the drama's representational aspects—he calls "the despotism of *mimesis* over drama . . . absurdly benign"—but he does insist that we reinvigorate our concern with the *language* employed in the exchanges between stage and world, because language too often "resists representation to effect new realities in the productive field of the dramatic event." The vocabulary of citizenship is crucial to our study of the early modern period, Archer argues, not only because it contains "urban meanings now mostly lost to us," but also because those meanings may not be retrievable from other sources. Archer's *Citizen Shakespeare*, therefore, offers its readers a lexical archive—"an underworld of citizen speech," Archer calls it—that sheds light on the meaning of a wide range of early modern subject positions such as citizen, freeman, citizen-soldier, city-wife, stranger, alien, livery-company member, and the "middling sort," and a counterweight to the widely held notion that Shakespeare's plays are "overwhelmingly concerned with aristocratic-monarchic life in mostly rural settings." Archer aims to do nothing less than approach the vexing question of the "subject" through a "historical semantics" of citizenship, thus altering both our view of early modern urban identity formation and our understanding of Shakespeare's plays.

Ivo Kamps
Series Editor

INTRODUCTION

Was Shakespeare a citizen? Yes, if we use this word in its everyday sense of "inhabitant of a city," for he spent much of his life in London. But Shakespeare was not admitted to "the freedom" of the city, and thus he never became a "citizen of London" in the accepted legal and political sense of his time. He was both a civic outsider and an urban insider. The discourse and disposition of London citizens imbue his plays, although citizens proper are seldom represented directly on his stage, and when they are they usually appear anxious and inconsequential. The *Citizen* of my title is meant as an adjective, and its *Shakespeare* employs the conventional metonymy by which we designate a collection of texts and all that pertains to them by the author's name.

I shall recur briefly to the question of Shakespeare's own citizenship below. The burden of this book pertains to the language of the plays. Citizenship carried with it a particular stock of words and turns of phrase, often inflected by topical events and issues. In this way, citizens anxiously defined themselves, against the aristocracy to be sure, but more pressingly in opposition to urban noncitizens, especially immigrants from continental Europe. *Citizen Shakespeare* answers Patricia Parker's call for a "historical semantics" in the mode of Leo Spitzer that traces the manifestations of material life as well as philological change in literary language.[1] In the following pages, I shall consider some recent approaches to the idea of citizenship, and then describe London citizenship as an institution and Shakespeare's relation to citizen identity and noncitizen status. A survey of recent criticism that takes Shakespeare's urban and artisanal milieu into account follows: how does the category of citizenship challenge this work, and how might it alter our understanding of the way political power operates in and around his plays?

Let me turn first to an influential theorist of citizenship in general. Etienne Balibar states that the citizen *comes after* the subject; that is, "citizenship" is a philosophical as well as political category of being that has succeeded *being subject to* a sovereign or ruler as a model for individuality.[2] He is thinking of the revolutions in the Atlantic world of the late eighteenth century, and particularly of the French Revolution, which replaced the monarchical subject with "the citizen." Yet citizenship did not cancel out subjecthood in a linear fashion, for the monarchical subject survived "within" the citizen as self-control and self-awareness, lending its root to the words *subjection* and *subjectivity*. Instead of an evolution from subject to citizen, we have alternations, overlappings, and doublings-back in the history of what Balibar, following Michel Foucault, calls "subjectivation."[3] From early modern to modern Europe, the relay of terms runs from monarchical subject, to citizen, to "citizen of the world" in Immanuel Kant's sense, and then to the "free and autonomous subject" of philosophy that grounds the global claims of citizenship that citizen status in particular polities is supposed to fulfill.[4] The subject also comes after the citizen, then, and one cannot understand subjectivity without a knowledge of the forms of citizenship that both preceded subjecthood and fulfilled its potential as philosophical and political subjectivity.

The prehistory of modern citizenship goes back to Greek and Roman institutions, and to their uneven revival in the Middle Ages. For Aristotle, the democratic citizen knew both how to rule and how to be ruled; citizenship required dedicated participation in the government of the *polis* through deliberative offices, so full-time workers, artisans, and merchants could not be citizens. Women and slaves were not citizens either, although they were disqualified for vastly different reasons. Resident aliens and visitors were also excluded; Aristotle cites Homer in comparing noncitizens to alien vagabonds without honor.[5] Aristotle's citizen as philosophical and political subject is masculine, adult, free, born into the community, and active without being economically productive. Although Aristotle's insistence on political activity was the single greatest influence on later citizenship theory, his citizen remains a paradoxically static being. Perhaps this is why Balibar locates the first stirrings of citizenship-as-subjectivity much later than Aristotle, in the intersection of Roman law with a Christianized empire. Subjects of *imperium*, Roman-born and conquered men alike, attained citizenship as a personal status within the empire. Although subject to the emperor, the citizen was classified as a *subditus* rather than a *servus* or slave. Aristotle's dictum was implicitly revised: the citizen-*subditus* knew how to obey and be obeyed down a chain of command whose apex was the emperor and ultimately God, not how to rule and be ruled within an elite circle of equals. The internalization of obedience required a concept of the soul that was alien to the Greek tradition;

premodern, it prepared the way for the more complex internalization of subjection within the citizen of the eighteenth century.[6] In between, Balibar pauses to sketch the philosophical and institutional contribution of the medieval period. He attributes to Thomas Aquinas a conception of the citizen as the holder of a neutral freedom before secular sovereignty. The citizen-subject submitted to sovereignty, but as a member of a body or corporation of citizens that had been granted certain rights. The citizen's subjecthood was gradually revealed as the effect of an artificial political order. Thus, "Intellectual reasons as well as material interests (those of the lords, of the corporations, of the 'bourgeois' towns) provide an incentive for thinking the freedom of the subject differently, paradoxically combining this concept with that of the 'citizen,' a concept taken from Antiquity and notably from Aristotle." Later, the revolutions against absolutism exploited the mounting tensions of the classical and medieval inheritance. The monarchical subject became the citizen, and in turn the philosophical subject, by claiming the right to govern as the only means to good government—"The comparison with the way in which medieval politics had defined the 'citizenship' of the subject, as the right to be well-governed, is instructive."[7] It was only at this moment that the notion of passive citizenship became a contradiction in terms.

My intent is not to provide an authoritative history of the idea of citizenship, but simply to place certain terms in play while outlining Balibar's useful account of the ontological and temporal dialectic of subject and citizen. Broad surveys such as his have inherent problems of omission and condensation. It must be said that Balibar's account of the medieval and, by extension, early modern periods leaves out the "civic" or "classical republican" tradition of the Italian city-states. Niccolo Machiavelli codified earlier writers' reclamation of the political thought of Aristotle, Cicero, and others, with its stress on active involvement in public affairs, the *res publica*. Quentin Skinner has outlined the principal tenets of classical republicanism: the citizens' devotion to the "common good," their *virtù* in both military and public service, and thus their active defense of the greatness of the community and the liberty of its members.[8] According to J. G. A. Pocock, the figure of the citizen-soldier was especially important in Machiavelli's definitive version of republicanism. In his *Discorsi* on Livy, "The plebeian as Roman citizen is less a man performing a certain role in a decision-making system than a man trained by civic religion and military discipline to devote himself to the *patria* and carry this spirit over into civic affairs."[9] Skinner emphasizes civic participation in elective government, noting that the *Discorsi* connects "the capacity to achieve civic greatness with the enjoyment of 'a free way of life.' " He demonstrates that even before Machiavelli, the merchant-citizens of medieval Italy had developed the ideal of an active public life dedicated to the common good of their republics by recourse to the political thought of ancient Rome.[10]

Chantal Mouffe, another theorist of citizenship whose analysis in some sense parallels Balibar's, refers to Skinner's treatment of classical republicanism in her attempt to rehabilitate citizenship as a political category. She follows a common division in current citizenship theory in remarking the split between "liberals," whose focus on the individual postdates the early modern period, and "communitarians," who often trace their ideas of an organic society with a common purpose back to republicanism in classical antiquity and Italian humanism.[11] Communitarian republicanism offers a necessary corrective to a somewhat passive liberal notion of citizenship, precisely by returning to the participatory model of classical Greece and Rome, and the Renaissance.

As Mouffe insists, however, with classical republicanism "there is a real danger of coming back to a pre-modern view of politics," for "a modern democratic political community cannot be organized around a single substantive idea of the common good."[12] Longing for the supposedly unified and organic communities of the past leads citizens to reject anyone who challenges the enjoyment of a free and common "way of life" that such nostalgia retrospectively enshrines. Mouffe cites the psychoanalytic perspective of Slavoj Zizek, who argues that "hatred of the enjoyment of the other" lies behind ethnic rivalry and racism in the nostalgic community. Aliens are cast as "thieves" of enjoyment, as if their anti-community saps the pith of the nation that hosts them. This is because the others' enjoyment, which includes their sociability, work-habits, and the like as Zizek indicates, is always the nation's *own* enjoyment in a misrecognized and excessive form.[13] The oddly static activism of the Aristotelian citizen turns on others rather than consuming itself as the communitarian myth breaks down.

In reconsidering classical republicanism, Mouffe would preserve the openings that liberal individualism has tentatively made for identities based on gender, sexuality, and especially race or ethnicity in the political field.[14] Less optimistic about the prospects for the renewal of citizenship in Europe today, Balibar nevertheless places a similar stress on the need to recognize immigrants, particularly former colonial subjects, as citizens if the citizen is to survive as an ideal. "To put it in a word," he writes, "the colonial heritage is the persistence of the empty place of the *subject*, forming the shadow cast by the *citizen* in the space of sovereignty."[15] As we shall see, apprehensions about otherness were already part of citizenship in the para-colonial and early modern past. Like Balibar, Mouffe dates the full realization of citizenship to the eighteenth-century revolutions. Both theorists underscore the "indeterminacy" of the Enlightenment citizen, "the possibility," as Balibar puts it, "for any given realization of the citizen to be placed in question by a struggle for equality."[16] And, recently: "it is always the practical confrontation with the different modalities of exclusion (social, and thus political, for the two notions have never truly been separate) that constitutes the founding moment of citizenship, and thus of its periodic test of truth."[17] Mouffe defines citizenship as an "articulating principle" among different subject-positions and allegiances, "not as a legal status but as a form of identification." Fundamentally it is inclusive and expandable, but only through constant struggle and antagonism.[18] We arrive, again, at the notion of citizenship as a form, perhaps the chief form, of philosophical and political subjectivity in action. Yet it is wrong to find its moments of truth only in Aristotle, Roman law, or the great revolutions of the eighteenth century and their aftermath. Between classical antiquity and the classical age of reason and revolution, citizenship was put to the test many times (and not only in Europe and the Americas). This book contends that late-sixteenth- and early-seventeenth-century London is a key case in point. The tension between exclusion and inclusion in citizenship, indeterminacy, struggle, and even ethnic antagonism were all on the early modern scene in an exemplary but now partly invisible way.

Shakespeare's plays, after all, helped make the word *citizen* part of the everyday vocabulary of English in their own time and thereafter. His English histories and Italianate comedies were instrumental along with the Roman tragedies here. Although they have since been read through the lens of an anachronistic liberal individualism that extends from their supposed politics to the aesthetics of their characterization, the plays are best seen in a communitarian mode. Communal and civic concerns animate their dramatic language in a manner that liberal interpretations, largely characterological and plot-based, have obscured. The classical republican tradition of the Renaissance would seem to offer an immediate context for Shakespeare, then. Pocock argues, however, that Machiavellian ideas about armed *virtù* and the common good had yet to infuse a monarchical frame of mind "in no way disposed to require the definition of England as a polis or the Englishman as a citizen." As he rightly notes, citizen and soldier were not linked until the Civil War period—as we shall see, indeed, these figures were often cast as opposites in England. "In an important sense," Pocock concludes, "post-Elizabethan England lacked a fully developed civic consciousness," or rather, "there was an excess of it, more than the available institutional and conceptual schemes could contain."[19] The "excess" of civic consciousness that Pocock refers to comprised diffuse notions of authority, custom, fortune, and virtue that failed to cohere in relation or resistance to sovereignty. But he leaves out an important component: in London and other English towns there were citizens, usually labeled as such, who possessed precisely a "civic," if not a republican or national, consciousness of a specific kind.

According to the political scientist Antony Black, "State and nation were conceptualized not only, as Pocock and Skinner have rightly emphasized, in terms of classical humanism, but also in terms of corporate, sometimes explicitly guild, values, and . . . in terms of the values of market exchange."[20] We must return, then, to Balibar's evocation of the corporate cities of premodern and early modern northern Europe, while realizing that they displayed exclusionary forms of civic consciousness and violent struggle over citizenship as an economic right that later communitarian and liberal ideals alike have yet to escape. The very concept of citizenship in English towns lay in exclusion: of women in fact if not by law, of adult craftsmen from the countryside, and increasingly of aliens from abroad, like the French Huguenots and refugees from the Netherlands. This was because of its function as a protective barrier for established artisans and merchants against commercial competition of all sorts. Yet citizenship was usually earned through apprenticeship, even by the sons of immigrants, and could be bought outright by Englishmen. Renaissance republicanism shared common roots with the guild model of the north and England, despite its elaboration of citizenship as an abstract and participatory identity.[21] Aristotle, its major influence, would have excluded artisans and merchants themselves. In England, the figure of the citizen reveals the exclusionary yet indeterminate character of post-Aristotelian citizenship in general more clearly than classical republicanism does. Furthermore, despite its demise in the eighteenth century, London citizenship clearly bequeathed something of its restrictive and commercial disposition to British subjecthood later on. My principal purpose here, however, is not to decry exclusion. Instead, I want briefly to consider the institutions that managed citizenship and alienage in Shakespeare's London as both economic categories and as forms of identification and subjectivation.

The status of citizen during the sixteenth and seventeenth centuries in England conferred an urban rather than a national identity. Moreover, only a select group of people who lived in cities could be citizens as well as subjects of the Crown. In London, as in many other English cities and towns, citizenship was constituted by possession of "the freedom," derived from the borough franchise of the Middle Ages.[22] London freemen generally called themselves "citizens" in their wills, and both the term and the identity of citizen were familiar and valued during the sixteenth century.[23] Admission to citizenship or the freedom was in practice controlled by the livery companies or crafts, descendants of medieval guilds. There were roughly one hundred associations that could be described as companies, but the twelve "great companies," among them the Merchant Taylors, Clothworkers, and Grocers, dominated civic life. The livery companies provided Lord Mayors, aldermen, and a host of minor officials; they had their own courts of law; they often ran schools for their members' sons, and they administered a range of charities for their poor brethren. In order to become a citizen and gain the freedom, one had first to be admitted to membership in a company. This usually meant serving out a term of apprenticeship to a company member; only then could one gain admission to the craft at the level of journeyman or wage-laborer. Most journeymen became householders and opened their own shops a few years later. Some candidates claimed company membership and the freedom by patrimony, a right granted to all London-born children of freemen; fewer purchased membership outright by "redemption," or were granted it by royal or city patronage. The oath of citizenship was often sworn the same day as the oath of the company, in the Guildhall.[24]

The historian Steve Rappaport has shown that the number of company members, and thus of citizens, was much larger than used to be thought. In the mid-sixteenth century, some three quarters of men over the age of 26 living in London possessed the freedom; by the end of the century this proportion had shrunk to two-thirds, but is still considerable.[25] Ian W. Archer builds on Rappaport's research, but disputes the picture of an inclusive and harmonious London citizenry.[26] Women were not formally banned from company membership and the freedom, yet as Rappaport himself has described in detail, they were rarely admitted to companies whatever rights they may have practiced as wives and widows of freemen. The "city wife" was an anomalous figure in early modern London. One half of the English-born city population was customarily denied citizenship.[27] "Strangers" and "foreigners" were two other noncitizen groups: the terms were sometimes used interchangeably, but for the most part strangers or "aliens" were born outside the British Isles, and foreigners, despite the modern connotations of the name, were native-born English, who had newly come to the city as adults, rather than as young and assimilable apprentices.

Strangers were the more troubling group to sixteenth-century London freemen, jealous of their privileges. It has been estimated that in the mid-sixteenth century, there were 4,000–5,000 aliens residing in the city; the total population of London was somewhat over 70,000 at that time, and would reach 200,000 by 1600. A small population of German merchants gave way to French Huguenot and especially to "Dutch" immigrants as the century progressed. This term referred to both immigrants from Holland and other northern provinces of the Netherlands, and to aliens from Flanders and the southern provinces, also called Flemings. French-speakers among this group were called "Walloons." About 75 percent of the alien population in London at mid-century was "Dutch" in this sense. The Spanish response to the Dutch Rebellion against Hapsburg rule drove still more refugees to England after 1567. Citizen resentment against strangers had already led to the "Ill May Day" riots of 1517, and although London never saw another exclusively antialien riot during the period, company complaints about the employment and trading practices of aliens, as well as covert threats or "libels," continued into the early seventeenth century.[28]

In 1593, a long piece of ragged verse was affixed to the Church frequented by the Netherlandish communities at Austin Friars in London. The Dutch Church Libel, as it is known, led to the arrest of Thomas Kyd, who implicated Marlowe in another, heretical matter. But it is the content of the libel itself that is of interest here. Reflecting fears that strangers, especially the Dutch, engage in illegal manufacturing and trade, this document threatens alien men, their wives, and their children with death. The strangers are mostly indicted along economic lines: their craftsmen produce cheap wares in competition with citizen artificers, their merchants corner the market in certain goods, and engage (improbably) in usury. The libel continues:

> That Egipts plagues, vext not the Egyptians more
>   Than you do vs; then death shall be your lotte
> Noe Prize comes in but you make claime therto
>   And every merchant hath three trades at least,
> And cutthrote like in selling you vndoe
>   us all, & with our store continually you feast:
>   We cannot suffer long.
> Our pore artificers doe starve & dye
>   For yt they cannot now be set on worke.

Twenty strangers live in one house, and help drive up rents. Meanwhile, English soldiers fight the Spanish on the continent in religious wars on behalf of hypocrites who escaped the fight to profit from their protectors.[29] Citizenship primarily concerned the control of access to economic rights, the right to work for wages, to trade for materials, and to produce and sell one's own products. Although competition from strangers presented a negligible economic threat, freemen feared the advantage aliens would gain if allowed to operate outside company rules. In the late 1590s and early 1600s, the Merchant Taylors' company pressured the aldermen to expel all strangers from the city of London, a move they resisted at the behest of Queen Elizabeth, who feared an alien mutiny.[30] It is not a coincidence that in 1596 and 1601 the Crown did sanction the expulsion of a much smaller number of "blackamoors," who had recently entered the kingdom and were seen as taking work and charity away from native-born inhabitants.[31] All strangers were accused of keeping to themselves in sealed off communities with unknown languages and customs, a charge that led to a growing sense of ethnic difference.[32]

In London, William Shakespeare was technically a foreigner, and he lived among aliens in the peripheral wards and neighborhoods noncitizens tended to inhabit. At the same time, as Louis Montrose has observed, many of his associates in the theater were London artisans and freemen, and his interests were allied with theirs because of his own craft background in an English town.[33] The story of Shakespeare's Stratford life is a well-known one, but some of its episodes bear reexamination in the reflected light of London citizenship. He was educated at the borough or free school, above the Guildhall, at the corporation of Stratford's expense. His father John was a burgess, and he worked as a glover and whittawer or dresser of white leather. Shakespeare may have apprenticed at these trades; the glovers were not a proper guild in the town, but if they bound apprentices the indentures probably forbade marriage, and this may have contributed to Shakespeare's eventual departure from his new wife and children.[34] Stratford was chartered by the Crown in 1553; the corporation was administered by a bailiff or mayor and 13 other aldermen, and by 14 principal burgesses. John Shakespeare became one of the latter, then an alderman, then bailiff in 1567, serving in the lesser capacity of chief alderman a few years later. In 1576, he stopped attending council meetings, and he was replaced as alderman and council member in 1586. Financial problems and illegal wool-dealing led to his fall.[35]

William Shakespeare left a formal civic career in Stratford behind him, but returned to the town frequently as a businessman, buying New Place, its second largest house, for his family in 1597 and a share in a lease of tithes from the town in 1605. This was an investment, but as Park Honan has shown it also helped the corporation fund its charitable obligations with short-term cash. The tithes lease may be evidence of a sense of civic duty—a prudential one, perhaps, at a time of growing anti-theatrical sentiment in Stratford.[36] When the playwright began spending more and more time in the town during his final years, he displayed good "citizenship" in this loose sense on at least two other occasions. Shakespeare gave money to a campaign for the passage of a road-improvement bill in Parliament in 1611, and he put up the visiting preacher of a foundation sermon at New Place in 1614. Yet he remained somewhat at odds with the burgesses over proposed enclosures of common lands, which was a hot issue.[37] It is tempting to suppose that Shakespeare wanted some of the status that came with being a town magnate but wished to minimize the administrative, economic, and social obligations that citizenship properly entailed.

When we turn to his career in London, we find Shakespeare living a similar half-life. His brother Gilbert also traveled to the city and seems to have become a member of the Haberdasher's Company by 1597, before returning to work in Stratford once more.[38] Shakespeare never became a company member or gained the freedom: apprenticeship would have been awkward at his age, even early on, but he might have sought the freedom through redemption. If so (and it seems unlikely he tried), he did not succeed. After the mid-1590s, he is always described as a "gentleman" in the documents we have.[39] In 1596, he succeeded in obtaining a coat of arms for his father and hence himself, taking up a scheme that John Shakespeare had first proposed in the wake of his bailiwick.[40] As this shows, gentry status could be seen as complimentary to citizenship and civic identity, and not necessarily their opposite. This was true in a different way for John's son, the Londoner.

When he bought the Blackfriars Gatehouse with three co-purchasers in 1613, the indenture describes the seller, Henry Walker, and the buyers as follows:

Henry Walker citizein and Minstrell of London of th'one partie; And William Shakespeare of Stratford Vpon Avon in the countie of Warwick gentleman, William Johnson, citizein and Vintener of London, John Jackson and John Hemmyng of London gentlemen, of th'other partie.[41]

Walker and Johnson are identified as citizens of London and by their occupations, as was customary, while Shakespeare and the two remaining purchasers are "gentlemen," the one of Stratford and the others of London. I would suggest that one reason Shakespeare pursued the coat of arms was to acquire the right to sign himself (in effect) as a "gentleman" in deals such as these. Moreover, he did so not to outdo citizens but simply to manifest an identity that might match theirs and make up for his lack of burgess or citizen status in Stratford or London.

Shakespeare does not seem to have evinced the same degree of good citizenship in London that he did at Stratford. He was a rate-payer in London, but he was cited for nonpayment of the subsidy three times.[42] Tax documents also reveal where he probably lived in, or rather about, the city between 1596 and 1599. He is first called to account in St. Helen's parish, Bishopsgate ward, and later his case is referred to the liberty of the Clink, in Southwark. Strangers, especially French and Dutch aliens, dwelt in Bishopsgate as well as Southwark; by 1604, we know from other sources that Shakespeare stayed with the Mountjoys, a naturalized Huguenot family in St. Olave's parish in the northwest corner of the city. As Honan has recently emphasized, "an unusual number of those in Shakespeare's circle . . . were of Dutch, Flemish, or French origin. Coincidence does not quite account for this."[43] In addition to the Mountjoys, he certainly or most likely knew Jacqueline Vautrollier, a widow who married the printer and fellow old-Stratfordian Richard Field, Peter Streete, the Dutch joiner who built the Globe theater, and Gheerart Janssen, the Southwark stonemason responsible for his own funeral monument in Holy Trinity Church, Stratford, and for an earlier Stratford tomb, perhaps after Shakespeare's recommendation. The frontispiece portrait of the first Folio, of course, was engraved by a Fleming, Martin Droeshout, either the painter or his nephew of that name. In noting some of these connections, E. A. J. Honigman finds it remarkable that the two most authoritative likenesses we have of Shakespeare proceeded from the hands of alien craftsmen.[44] To the extent that he distinguished himself from London freemen in his daily life, then, Shakespeare the "foreigner" may have aligned himself with aliens more than with the aristocracy. But he seems to have consorted with citizens and strangers alike, depending on the occasion.

Rarely is Shakespeare's city experience made the explicit subject of current criticism. Like Montrose, Richard Helgerson duly notes in *Forms of Nationhood* that "Shakespeare was the son of a small-town glover," just as other leading playwrights were the sons of craftsmen.

He adds: "The Burbages, who built the Theater and eventually supplied Shakespeare with his leading actor, had been joiners. Philip Henslowe, landlord and manager of the Rose, began his London career in the service of a dyer."[45] It was Henslowe, however, who would capitalize upon the urban craft identity he shared with much of the public theater audience. The resourceful impresario mounted a series of chronicle histories at the Rose playhouse and elsewhere that vividly depicted the sufferings of simple subjects like the citizen Matthew Shore and his wife Jane at the hands of monarchs and the aristocracy. "The central problematic of Shakespeare's history plays," by contrast, "concerned the consolidation of monarchic rule." Shakespeare left out the subject in his obsession with the sovereign:

> The situation of the citizen and the Protestant—both figures who identify strongly with the nation and its ruler but both of whom are intent on keeping some part of themselves and their community free from the encroachment of national power—is central to the Henslowe version of English history. Neither of these figures is of much interest to Shakespeare.[46]

Helgerson allows for festive "popular revolt" in comedies like *A Midsummer Night's Dream* and *Twelfth Night*, but he does not discuss the presence or absence of citizens and Protestants in these plays or the tragedies, presumably for the very sound reason that we should hardly expect to find many such figures represented in these genres (Bottom, Malvolio, and the Cobbler in *Julius Caesar* notwithstanding). "Between the extremes of high and low, noble and base" in the streets outside the theater, "there was only semiotic vacancy, a noplace without meaning."[47]

Helgerson makes a plausible case that Shakespeare distanced himself from his low origins by identifying his theater with sovereign power and aristocratic prestige, gaining for his plays the "canonical exclusivity" they have yet to relinquish.[48] Similarly, Leah S. Marcus—one of the few critics to discuss some of the plays' London atmosphere in detail—relates Shakespeare's pursuit of the coat of arms to both his design of an impresa for the Earl of Rutland and the royal iconography of *Cymbeline*.[49] The manner in which gentry symbolism and loyalty to the Crown supplement rather than completely cancel urban identity is not the only curiosity of status that such accounts neglect. On the upper end of the scale, aristocrats were often at odds with their sovereign; on the lower, citizens were more likely to set themselves against strangers and foreigners than against the nobility and tranquility (to recall Gadshill's jest in *Henry IV, Part 1*). Jean E. Howard offers a nuanced view when she discusses *Measure for Measure*, which she reads in context with the "city comedies" of the early Jacobean period. Shakespeare "is both the same and different" as the city comedy authors, for he sees a city in need of regulation while "creating an urban representation that elides the middling sort and their marital and civic regimes." Howard takes no position on Shakespeare's representative omissions and his possible identification with the aristocracy.[50] The notion of "the middling sort" itself deserves scrutiny. In an article in *Shakespeare Quarterly* from 1993, Theodore B. Leinwand makes it the opening point in a major counterstatement to the stark view of an England split sharply between high and low. He proposes a "reconfiguration of the socioeconomic and political map" upon which Shakespeare and the theater are placed.[51] Leinwand's map is confined to London, as he admits, but it is all the more useful in redressing the virtual omission of the city and its "middling sort" from past critical cartography. As Leinwand states in his introduction, Stephen Greenblatt, the representative new historicist, and Phyllis Rackin, a leading feminist and cultural materialist, have equally perpetuated a two-tier model of class, in which the elite possessed power, knowledge, and wealth while, as Greenblatt puts it, "the overwhelming majority of men and women had next to nothing." Although his assessment of current class analysis in the field is a little stark itself, Leinwand's forceful and well-reasoned insistence on "a third, or intermediate group" in the theater of social relations is a new contribution that should change the way we understand political power in Shakespeare studies.[52]

Taking full account of the poor in early modern England, Leinwand nevertheless revises our sense of Shakespeare's rural and urban characters: Bottom, the Cobbler, and Constable Elbow in *Measure for Measure* would not have been seen as poor by the contemporary audience. In the amphitheater playhouses, this audience comprised a similar mix of middling people of different incomes and degrees, as did the acting companies, composed in part of "honest householders and Citizens," as even Gosson admitted. Burbage and Henslowe figure in the argument once more, but again, when we come to Shakespeare, a note of hesitation sets in. In Sonnet 111, the poet worries about the dyer's hand being subdued to its "publick" work (perhaps an apotropaic recollection of his employment by the dyer Henslowe, I could add). Leinwand thoughtfully scans the coat of arms and the subscription as "gentleman" along with the business dealings in Stratford and London. "Shakespeare was himself one of the middling sort," yet finally "Shakespeare's precise socioeconomic position seems both securely among the middling sort and anything but precise." Like the theater itself, he embodied the contradictions of his society without resolving them.[53]

My own assessment of Shakespeare's complex relations to urban modes of belonging is indebted to Leinwand's statement of the problem. And a problem with the phrase "middling sort" remains. The term is hard to define, as he goes on to concede: it is a "status group" that is somehow linked with wealth and land, including nontaxpayers at one end and lesser gentry at the other; its members, like Shakespeare, slide up and down and perhaps off this scale depending on where they live or who they deal with at different times. Leinwand claims that this indefinition does not weaken the category, for it provokes "greater specificity below the metadefinitional level." But where is such specificity to be found?

> It becomes clear that the middling sort was a most heterogeneous lot if we consider that many apprentices (in high ranking trades, at least) were younger sons recruited from gentry families or from the families of comfortable merchants, and that even well-off merchants were not quite of the gentry. Among them we might find people identifying with their own sort, with their betters, or with their inferiors.[54]

Keith Wrightson, as Leinwand notes, finds in any case that phrases like "middling sort" were not applied to a social grouping much before the mid-seventeenth century. Leinwand seems to be making Helgerson's point about the "semiotic vacancy" of the absent middle, which he quotes disapprovingly, for him.[55]

Helgerson is right about the "noplace" of the middling sort, but only if we cast social relations in terms of place and space to begin with. High, low, and middle are unalterably spatial terms, and the project of recasting our idea of what might succeed them is a large one. As a humble beginning, I suggest that we might find a measure of "specificity" in the complicated but manageable category of citizenship, particularly in the dual form of burgess freedom and livery company membership in early modern London. Leinwand's chief example of his key phrase comes from Richard Mulcaster's *Positions* (1581), where we read that the best candidates for service to their country come from "the midle [*sic*] sort of parentes," neither too wealthy nor too wanting. As headmaster of the Merchant Taylors' School, Mulcaster was intimately bound to one of the Great Companies and to a principal nursery of citizenship. Citizens, however, are not identical with the middling sort.[56] Journeymen trade-fallen into poverty, gentry younger sons who have taken up a craft, and aristocratic magnates with commercial ambitions could all possess the freedom.

In an inaugural statement, Marx and Engels chose to exemplify "class struggle" in the opposition of "guild-master and journeyman," that is, householder and wage-laborer in a company, both citizens, and not in the conflicts of noble and peasant or noble and citizen.[57] Citizenship is both larger and smaller than class, which nevertheless remains a referent for it. It is defined not by its middling place on an imaginary (that is, picturable) scale, but by language, education, laws, rules, customs, ceremony, participation, and social antagonism.[58]

Antagonism delimits urban selves and bodies through relational processes of opposition to others and identification with groups, not through given identities. Citizen "identity" was highly differentiated in early modern London: freemen were both citizens of London and members of their company, and also belonged to either the elite livery or rank-and-file "yeomanry" within that company; yeomen might be householders or journeymen; in many companies, elite merchants set themselves apart from artisans, and were resented for it, although individual artisans could rise to the livery and help run companies alongside merchants, too. There was indeed tension between guild-masters and journeymen. Yet, solidarity was reestablished in the shop when companies competed with each over similar trades and raw materials, or fought with the city government partly composed of their own liverymen. Guild members did not have to practice their company's trade—a Cutler or knife-maker might work as an armorer, for instance, or a Grocer might trade in textiles, to the chagrin of the Clothworkers and Merchant Taylors. City wives were oppressed by patriarchal expectations and laws, but a wife sometimes ran the household in her husband's absence, commanding its apprentices and journeymen, and she often retained her deceased spouse's shop and his company privileges as a widow. In the luxury trades, women seem to have affected the expensive tastes of their wealthy and noble customers. As Leinwand shows, then, multiple identifications up and down the hierarchy were possible. He disputes the notion that middling people came to see themselves in opposition to "the meaner sort" by citing their inclination to join with the low against elites when it suited them.[59] It becomes possible to specify the how, what, and why of such alliances when we separate citizens from the amorphous middle in London society, and look at particular strata in particular companies during times of crisis as well. But the principal object of antagonism, and thus of identification, antagonism's back-formation, is left out of both the Helgerson and Leinwand models of hierarchy—the figure of the alien.

Citizen constituencies were disposed to define themselves against strangers or aliens, and by extension against foreigners or English non-Londoners, rather more than against any other group within or without the freedom. Economic, and then ethnic, identities were at stake. The sheer weight of antagonism with noncitizens skews our persistent, if supposedly unfashionable or outdated, tendency to read plays' relation to political power through the critical paradigm of subversion and containment. Helgerson's two-tier society opens and then forecloses the possibility of overturning power from below. Shakespeare's replacement of suffering subjects with triumphant monarchs on stage puts the spotlight on the upper tier, but not necessarily to its advantage: "The exposure of kingship in a narrative and dramatic medium that not only displayed power but revealed the sometimes brutal and duplicitous strategies by which power maintained itself might be thought to subvert the structure of authority it ostensibly celebrated." Despite their "subversive potential," Helgerson concludes, Shakespeare's plays simply did not have this effect; moreover, they bequeathed a ruling-class Britain to the modern successors of the early modern ruling class.[60] Leinwand launches his paper with the artificial split between rich and poor in current criticism, evoking patriarchal privilege and the new historicist monolith as illusions at the outset as if he intends to contest the recuperative image of power we find in critics like Helgerson. Although Leinwand never makes this argument about new historicism, the Greenblatt passage he cites comes from an analysis of the "sleepless monarch" commonplace in Shakespeare, by which the audience is made privy to the inequities of sovereign power in order to manage their anger by subjecting the monarch himself to power's quotidian repercussions.[61] According to a certain misreading of Michel Foucault, of course, this is how power operates. It allows awareness, creating identities or specific nodes of opposition down below in order to control the mechanism of identification and thus of opposition in general from above. The uncovering of a burgeoning middling sort, or rather a category of multilayered belonging called citizenship, should indeed challenge, if not overturn, this high–low way of thinking about power.

Foucault had already mounted such a challenge to what he called "the repressive hypothesis." Power does not repress abject individuals or groups; instead, it is productive. It produces identities and points of "resistance," not in the interests of rulers but as a way of extending its anonymous potential. The results can be either oppressive or liberatory. "Power" is not an intelligence or even a social energy, but a lexical convenience that designates the shifting field of relationships among people. In the history of sexuality, what else was the bourgeoisie but the multiform creation of this field, a cluster of perversities whose exponents learned to speak for themselves under a regime of ostensible normality?[62]

The burgesses who preceded the bourgeois in the narrower histories of urban economies and political organization were a less grand but equally complicated creation. In recovering their traces within the canon even of so putatively aristocratic (and, later, bourgeois) an author as Shakespeare, we will mark the importance of citizens to his theater and finally confirm some productive alternatives in the criticism of power within it.

This is not to say that *Citizen Shakespeare* reveals the plays to be purely resistant to sovereignty within the larger field of power relations. Freemen and the city government that represented them jealously guarded their privileges against encroachments by the Crown and its clients, albeit in loyalist guise and through the charters granted to London and its various companies by the monarch. The rights and wrongs of noncitizens were a major topic of contention. Aliens had been protected by successive rulers, for religious reasons and for their technical expertise in the manufacture of armaments and textiles. They often dwelt in suburbs and liberties beyond city jurisdiction and notionally under the Crown's protection. Furthermore, in mandating the strict regulation of strangers' shops and even campaigning for their expulsion, companies like the Merchant Taylors and the city government they influenced were exercising power "from above" in one sense while resisting it in another, antimonarchical, manner. The aliens had their sponsors at court and "subverted" the citizens, paradoxically from above, themselves. They also disciplined their own members, exercising power from within largely through the separate French and Dutch churches, potentially at odds in turn. "Foreign" English, needless to say, had separate interests from continental strangers although often lumped together with them by citizens; Shakespeare, on the other hand, seems to have lived comfortably enough among aliens in London as a foreign gentleman of Stratford and an actor–playwright, who on occasion made fun of their accents, their diet, or their insularity. The familiar pattern of people or texts covertly undermining sovereign orthodoxy, or of sovereignty instilling, managing, and finally quelling such social pressure, is inadequate to the multivalent antagonisms and alliances in London during the period.

The critical paradigm of pseudo-productive sovereign power has a provenance that precedes the early stages of new historicism and its cultural poetics. Long before Foucault, the top-down conception of authority appears clearly in studies that treat the representation of urban life in early modern drama. Over the past forty years a number of influential books—about one or two a decade—have appeared on city comedy, city dwellers, or the city itself, often with "the Age of Shakespeare" in their subtitles, but with relatively little reference to Shakespeare in their texts. Brian Gibbons's *Jacobean City Comedy* (1968) is generally recognized as the book that put its titular genre on the map, although not firmly—the definition of city or "citizen" comedy remains unstable and controversial. Gibbons anxiously distances urban dramatic satires like Marston's *The Dutch Courtesan* and Middleton's *A Chaste Maid in Cheapside* from the historical and political conditions he nevertheless casts as their background. But he opens his argument by appealing to the "critical realism" of Georg Lukacs: "the critical realist writer is primarily concerned to shape character and incident in order to bring alive the underlying social and moral issues *through* the specific and local experience." The city authors "dramatized conflicting forces" in the transition to the seventeenth century, but to dramatize is not, as he realizes, to reflect, especially where forces and relations are concerned.[63] A brilliant insight, too much so for subsequent critics to fix their eyes upon it for long.

Alexander Leggatt stressed the ethical side of Gibbons's exploration of the genre a few years later. "The assertion of morality," he writes, "and the subversion of morality are the poles between which citizen comedy moves." Subversion has entered the garden of moral vision. But citizen comedy (not "city" comedy, for the stress is on character and on the will) ultimately works to reinforce the audience's sense of "social stability" by channeling the "amoral energy" of its material investments in property and sex. The demands of the community and the individual can be comically "harmonized." Shakespeare, who stabilizes attitudes toward romantic love rather than society, is mostly insulated from the "tension" between moral assertion and subversion.[64] Gibbons's analysis of social and moral contradictions has lead to something not unlike the arousal of amorality for a broader, more humane moral purpose; an earlier literary criticism's moral harmonies have a lot in common with the containment strategies first proposed by the political and cultural schools whose onset it resisted. Sovereign power entered as morality took its bows.

Leinwand's book *The City Staged* (1986) presents an earlier version of his view of the "merchant–citizen" as an intermediary social figure. He calls for a departure from the moral and generic criticism of Gibbons and Leggatt, emphasizing the activation of stereotypes about merchants, their wives and aristocrats in social roles and situations that present a highly stylized image of the London world. Leinwand quotes Harry Berger, Jr. on how Shakespeare's drama invests the "charismatic representation of a world with verbal traces of the hidden processes by which the communities of the play and the theater join in producing the world." Leinwand suggests that city comedy offers exaggerated characters instead of verbal traces to a similar end.[65] It is vital to keep Berger's formulation in mind, however, for it works particularly well in the case of city comedies and other plays with citizen subjects or subtexts. The magnitude of language must not be forgotten.

Leinwand's focus on what Gibbons calls "character and incident" is traditional in discussions of the genre, and of the period's drama as a whole. The staging of the city through these elements also foregrounds setting over language. "The place of the stage," in the words of Steven Mullaney's title, ultimately governs the theater of representations. Leah S. Marcus's "local reading" is precisely about parallels between the action of plays and situations linked to particular places (and times), including Jacobean London.[66] Gail Kern Paster's *The Idea of the City in the Age of Shakespeare* (1985) makes the city the versatile subject as well as the setting for a wide range of masques and civic pageants, as well as for Shakespeare's Roman plays and his few urban-centered comedies. Douglas Bruster cites Paster's slippery idea of the city in questioning the relevance of place to the now traditional notion of city comedy: early modern London is everywhere and thus nowhere in its theater. Similarly, character is no index to social class, or even social type, in a period of extreme social mobility. Bruster proposes that we do away with the term "city comedy." I feel he is too hasty, although the suggestion accords with my own sense that Shakespeare's mostly pre-Jacobean and thus pre-"city comedy" comedies, not to mention his non-comic plays, have more in common with the surrounding drama than has been recognized. Bruster's bold intervention is welcome, then, because it suggests an alternative to the diegetic way drama is universally regarded: "I argue that the concept of *place*, once crucial to a social analysis of the plays, is ultimately less important in Renaissance drama than a concern with material life which underlies the themes and structures of the drama."[67] Yet what lies between structure and material life? How is language critical for the "material-ization" of things and relations on stage?[68]

All of these studies are attentive to language as well as moral tone, material power, character, plot, and *mise-en-scène*; I have profited from all of them, and specific debts will appear in the text and its notes. An overwhelming disposition to understand drama mainly in terms of representation rather than language characterizes many books in the field, however. Plot, character, and place have conspired to install a totally mimetic theater. The despotism of *mimesis* over drama seems absurdly benign, of course. But Aristotle's *lexis*, Spitzer's historical semantics, and Berger's "verbal traces" all address the way language resists representation to effect new realities in the productive field of the dramatic event.

Although concerned with the city and with city-dwellers, previous critical work in the field neglects the specific categories of London citizenship and livery company membership that I have described earlier. A definite vocabulary went along with the freedom, one in which common words (like "freedom" itself) took on technical significations, as did particular terms for titles, offices, and procedures. Broadly, linguistic traces of topical incidents in the city and fragments of everyday life, even certain vegetables, as we shall see, were inflected in the citizen imagination with urban meanings now mostly lost to us. Metaphor and metonymy extend urban allusiveness across the surface of each play. References to aliens and their ways formed a large chapter in this often obscure lexicon (the word "alien" fully assumed its legal sense of "immigrant" in the mid-sixteenth century). None of the books mentioned above discusses strangers in the city.[69] Yet as we have already glimpsed, the alien was the definitional opposite to the citizen, and this close if antagonistic relation is borne out in citizen vocabulary: *citizen*, from Old French *citeain*, was itself probably formed after *denizen*, a word of Anglo-Norman origin that designated an alien who was granted the rights of a subject by the monarch, and not by a town.[70]

Citizen Shakespeare relates the plays to the urban scene through naming, metaphor, and allusion as much as through representation. What was heard on stage is at least as important as what was seen. Each chapter covers a range of plays by genre. Traditional generic distinctions, as we now realize, were inexact and protean, but the Folio's division into comedy, history, and tragedy provides a rough guide to what audiences expected to hear and see as they surmised the kind of play they were watching. The conclusion to each chapter relates its mode of citizen consciousness to the loose generic expectations of the period. My choice of plays is, I believe, comprehensive, much more so than is usual in a book of this sort. The tragedy chapter is something of an exception to this, for I deal solely with Roman tragedy. Again, it is citizen language, and not the direct representation of citizens on stage, that mandated my selection. *Hamlet, King Lear,* and *Macbeth* contain some urban references, but the language of these dramas fuses tragedy and sovereignty so intimately that it falls outside my study. *Romeo and Juliet* and *Othello* are rife with city vocabulary and might have been included if space and the argumentative focus on classical culture in the chapter had permitted. I could have included plays like *The Taming of the Shrew* or the romance–history hybrid *All is True* in the earlier chapters, but one can't write about everything. As it is, some would say I take on too much. Since I am challenging the critical consensus that Shakespeare is overwhelmingly concerned with aristocratic-monarchic life in mostly rural settings, I have felt it necessary to search far and wide in the canon to establish a counter-archive.

Chapter 1 deals with comedy. *The Comedy of Errors*, *Measure for Measure*, and other plays partly portray city life. Yet in the absence of full-fledged citizen comedy in Shakespeare, we also find an interweaving of urban types with metaphors of citizenship, like the "citizens" of the forest in *As You Like It* or the "burghers on the flood" in *The Merchant of Venice*. The latter play, as critics have recognized, is an example of how economic participation and exclusion helped define alien status. The chapter traces the more subtle presence of alienage in *Love's Labour's Lost* and *The Merry Wives of Windsor* as well. In many of these comedies, a rural or pastoral setting obscures controversial urban matters while setting off urban language all the more sharply. Women, largely but not totally excluded from the trades and citizen status, are keys to how comedy demarcates citizen and noncitizen identities.

Chapter 2, entitled "Civil Butchery," is divided into two sections, on the first tetralogy and *King John*, and the second tetralogy. Together, these sections offer a complete reading of all the histories through the citizen theme. I show how the earlier histories depict actual citizens and their dealings with aristocrats and the monarch. The second tetralogy partly excludes citizens, the way Richard Helgerson and others have shown, but it preserves citizen culture through metaphor and allusion in a fashion the original audience would have understood. Real and metaphorical butchery mediate the transition from chivalry to popular violence in the aristocratic conduct of the civil wars.

Chapter 3 approaches Shakespeare's Roman tragedies through the contrast between the citizen–soldier of the classical republican tradition and the citizen–freeman and city-wife of contemporary London. Soldierly virtue is featured in *Titus Andronicus* and *Julius Caesar*, but it is undermined by the military role accorded the alien Goths in the earlier play and by the plebeian mob of tradesmen in the second. As in *Antony and Cleopatra*, the patrician warrior is finally seen as inadequate to the ideals of Roman virtue as well. A substantial reading of

Coriolanus traces the complete divorce of military from economic models of citizenship: its hero denies both the birthright of the plebeians and his own patrician identity, leading an alien army against Rome itself.

The chapter, and the book, conclude with the tragicomedy *Cymbeline*, which recapitulates themes from the Roman plays and from earlier chapters. A late play, *Cymbeline* confounds the old Elizabethan distinctions between citizens and soldiers, and even citizens and strangers, within an emerging idea of the state on the Roman imperial model. It serves as a retrospective vantage point from which this study's central concerns may be assessed: how the diad of citizen and alien split political subjectivity in the period, and helped sustain the denotative, metaphorical, and allusive texture of Shakespeare's plays across the dramatic genres.

CHAPTER 1

COMEDY: CIVIL SAYINGS

Comedies by Shakespeare are usually linked to London, if at all, under the categories of "city comedy" or "citizen comedy," and more often than not they fail to meet the expectations which attend these terms. *Measure for Measure* has emerged as the chief example of a city comedy manqué. According to Jean E. Howard, as we have noted, Shakespeare shares the citizen dramatists' concern with the monitoring and punishment of wayward desire in an urban setting. But he also differs from them, as we see in this problem play, "an urban representation" in which the middling sort and its institutions are elided.[1] It is setting and "representation" that determine the extent to which a given comedy fits the citizen mold. *Measure for Measure* is set at least in a Vienna reminiscent of London. Alexander Leggatt calls *The Merry Wives of Windsor* "Shakespeare's only citizen comedy" because its theme of marriage and cuckoldry melds with the town of Windsor and its lively burghers.[2] Perhaps *The Comedy of Errors* and *The Merchant of Venice* should be included in the list of plays whose concern with marital matters, civil society, and punishment in an urban setting mark them as something like city comedy.[3]

But the citizen resonance of all these plays echoes beyond their settings and plots. In the case of *Measure for Measure*, it is not only the suburbs, the brothel, or the prison intrigues that convey a metropolitan tone; the allusive and metaphorical language the characters speak is equally important. "Nay," Constable Elbow tells the pimp and tapster Pompey Bum, "if . . . you will needs buy and sell men and women like beasts, we shall have all the world drink brown and white bastard."[4] The intermingling strains of bastard, the sweet Spanish wine, betoken the blending of different complexions and races through the bawdy houses and their issue. The joke also appears in Dekker's *The Honest Whore*, Part 1, Middleton's *A Faire Quarrell*, and other plays.[5] It relays the city experiences of buying, drinking, and mixing with others, and alerts us to anxieties about aliens of various kinds in the urban scene. Stranger merchants were among the chief customers of London's brothels.[6] Later in *Measure for Measure*, the disguised Duke Vincentio complains that "the strong statutes" of Vienna "Stand like the forfeits in a barber's shop,/As much in mock as mark" (5.1.318–5.1.320). Barbers apparently posted humorous lists of penalties for bad behavior in their shops. The reference opens a small window on a droll piece of customer relations practiced by members of the Barber–Surgeons' company, while subtly pitching company practices and city laws against each other. Jests and allusions like these form a linguistic continuum that flows alongside the plot's realization of the play's city setting. And a play need not be set in a city or town to sustain such urban language. *All's Well that Ends Well*, set mostly in rural Rossillion and the royal court, has Lavatch's joke about the answer that "is like a barber's chair that fits all buttocks."[7] Gail Kern Paster has remarked that Shakespeare "avoided contemporary London as a subject for dramatic expression"; seemingly "the provincial," he "constructed a life built around the antithesis, city and country."[8] Antithesis, how- ever, implies relation. It is necessary to look at a much wider range of plays than the near-city comedies to judge the place of the city on Shakespeare's comic stage.

  The Comedy of Errors, one of Shakespeare's earliest plays, combines city language with an explicit city setting in Ephesus, which is ruled by Duke Solinus. At the beginning of the play, Egeon of Syracuse has been arrested as an alien because of a bloody trade dispute between his city and that of the duke. Ephesians have been punished in Syracuse "for wanting guilders to redeem their lives," and so Egeon must produce a thousand marks or die at the end the day, his goods, such as they are, confiscated.[9] It is "the statute of the town," not the ulti- mately sympathetic Duke Solinus, that is responsible for his doom (1.2.6; 1.1.141–1.1.145). Commercial law regulates alienage amidst international instability; it uses the sovereign power over life and death, but its real concern is money and property, the protection of its merchants abroad and the appropriation of strangers' wealth at home when justified. The designation of "guilders" as the currency of Syracuse imparts a subtle Netherlandish cast to Egeon and the city of his nativity. *Comedy of Errors* is the only Shakespeare play in which guilders appear, and they stand out from the equally foreign but more conventional "marks" and "ducats" later on. Though fanciful and far removed from

English dealings with merchants from the Low Countries or the Spaniards who occupied them, Egeon's predicament would have been very intelligible in its outlines to an Elizabethan audience.

It is Egeon's story of shipwreck and separation from his wife and one of his sons that seems to win the duke over to his cause despite Ephesus's laws. The pregnant Emilia's obedience in following her husband to Epidamnum and their "unjust divorce" by sea and wind (1.1.104) recast Egeon's plight as the consequence of a disrupted marriage. Critics have long recognized that the comedy plays off St. Paul's discussion of marriage in the epistle to the Ephesians.[10] Wives are enjoined to be subject to their husbands as the Church is subject to Christ; husbands should love their wives as they love their own bodies (Ephesians 5: 21–33). Egeon's story prepares us for his son Ephesian Antipholus' marital difficulties with Adriana by providing a contrasting ground of domestic harmony and forcible estrangement.

Ephesians bears on the setting and themes of *The Comedy of Errors* in another way. I quote from Ephesians 2 in the Geneva Bible of 1560 (the wording of the Bishop's Bible of 1586 is almost identical):

> ye were, I say, at that time without Christ, & were aliantes from the commune welth of Israel, & were strangers from the couenants of promes, & had no hope, & were without God in the worlde.
>
> But now in Christ Iesus, ye which once were farre of, are made nere by the blood of Christ.
>
> For he is our peace, which hathe made of bothe one, & hathe broken the stoppe of the particion wall,
>
> In abrogating through his flesh the hatred, that is, the Law of commandements which standeth in ordinances . . .
>
> Now therefore ye are no more strangers & foreners: but citizens with the Saintes, and of the householde of God,
>
> And are buylt vpon the fundacion of the Apostles and Prophetes, Iesus Christ him self being the chief corner stone,
>
> In whome all the buylding coupled together, groweth vnto an holie Temple in the Lord.[11]

The symbolic temple of the community replaces the literal Temple of Diana for which pagan Ephesus was renowned (Acts 19: 27). Before their conversion, the Ephesians were aliens and strangers from the commonwealth or city of God; now they are its citizens. The language of urban belonging is particularly appropriate in ministering to the inhabitants of a burgeoning city at the crossroads of several cultures, and it is given added point when the translations use the common terms for ethnic others in late sixteenth-century London.

In addition to alien or stranger and citizen, Ephesians 2 sets out a series of relations and images: distance and nearness, an abrogated law, partition walls, the household, foundations, buildings, the temple. These elements also run through *The Comedy of Errors*—some of them are realized in the evident staging of the play itself, with its three doors or houses, its shouting over partitions, and the space that represents the Abbey at the end.[12] Alienage and citizenship provide the overarching framework for the chain of associations in both bible passage and play. Another Pauline echo resonates in the urban atmosphere of Ephesus itself, or at least in how its most lively Syracusan visitors apprehend it. In Acts of the Apostles 19, Paul arrives at Ephesus and encounters itinerant exorcists (like Doctor Pinch) and practicers of magic arts; when some exorcists misuse Jesus' name in their spells, they are overpowered by a possessed man and flee naked from his house (Acts 19: 16).

The reputation of Ephesus informs Syracusan Antipholus' description of the city in Act 1, Scene 2:

> They say this town is full of cozenage,
> As nimble jugglers that deceive the eye,
> Dark-working sorcerers that change the mind,
> Soul-killing witches that deform the body,
> Disguised cheaters, prating mountebanks,
> And many such-like liberties of sin. (1.2.97–1.2.102)

The ill fame of the biblical Ephesus expands to encompass the urban experience itself, or more particularly the stranger's encounter with a strange city. "Liberties" refers to the sorcerers and cheaters, of course, but the word was used for areas in and around London that were not part of the city fathers' jurisdiction, often the location of theaters and brothels as well as settlements of aliens.[13] Persons slide into places in the passage, and it is as if Ephesus were one large liberty and its citizens all players, a sort of inside-out city from the perspective of some in Elizabethan London.

At the beginning of the scene, a merchant warns Antipholus of Syracuse to lie about his city of origin; apparently, it is as easy to confound Syracusans and Epidamnians as it was the Flemish and French. Syracusan Antipholus gives a thousand marks to his servant Dromio for safekeeping and proposes "go lose myself,/And wander up and down to view the city" (1.2.30–1.2.31). But when he is left alone, he engages in soliloquy rather than tourism:

> I to the world am like a drop of water
> That in the ocean seeks another drop,
> Who, falling there to find his fellow forth,
> (Unseen, inquisitive) confounds himself.
> So I, to find a mother and a brother,
> In quest of them, unhappy, lose myself. (lines 35–40)

Syracusan Antipholus loses himself in introspection, not among the city streets. The urban experience reveals an unsettled identity, and this is underlined when the wrong Dromio enters without the money. "We being strangers here," Syracusan Antipholus demands, "how dar'st though trust/So great a charge from thine own custody?" (lines 60–61). As in the opening scene, it is especially important for strangers to have money to compensate for their unstable status. Instead of the thousand marks, Dromio recalls sixpence owed to a saddler—a contemporary English detail—and then offers his mistaken master, in effect, real estate instead of liquid capital: "My charge was but to fetch you from the mart/Home to your house, the Phoenix, sir, to dinner" (lines 74–75). Ephesian Antipholus' house is given a name because it is a shop with the sign of the Phoenix as well as a dwelling. The alien Antipholus is slotted into the settled commercial life of a citizen. He does not go to "Peruse the traders, gaze upon the buildings" as he intended (line 13)— he is invited home to one of the buildings. This is what convinces him he is in a town of "liberties," however, rather than sober freemen.

In Act 2, we discover that settled citizens do exercise a sort of freedom outside the home and away from their wives. "A man is master of his liberty," Luciana tells her sister Adriana, Ephesian Antipholus' spouse, but women's "headstrong liberty" is doomed to woe (2.1.7, 2.1.15). In a speech based on a partial reading of Ephesians 5 as well as Genesis, Luciana further imposes the model of mastery or sovereignty upon civic domesticity (lines 16–25). It is the wider citizen context of *The Comedy of Errors* as much as anything else in the play that will call her views into question without entirely undoing the gender hierarchy they bolster. When Adriana speaks to the wrong Antipholus out-of-doors, she lays the claims of civil reputation upon her husband while also using the language of sovereign diplomacy: "Keep then fair league and truce with thy true bed,/I live unstain'd, thou undishonoured" (2.2.145–2.2.146). The visitor replies that he is "As strange unto your town as to your talk," explaining emotional estrangement as foreignness, accurately, in his case (line 149).

Nevertheless, he soon resolves to play along and entertain the offered fallacy (line 186). Unlike his father Egeon, this Syracusan merchant undergoes alienage under sentence of assimilation rather than isolation and death.

As in Plautus's *Memaechmi*, the comedy indulges the masculine fantasy of walking into another man's house and enjoying his wife's food and company, although the alien Antipholus' attentions immediately shift to the sister. The corresponding dangers of assimilation are embodied in the kitchen wench Nel, whose other name, Luce, loosely links her with the unattached Luciana. Dromio fears her sweaty and engulfing claims upon his body and its privy marks (3.2.101, 3.2.141). Famously, he finds out countries in this watery globe, but in doing so he traces the geographical circumstances of contemporary London's most noticeable foreign and alien communities. There is Ireland and Scotland in the buttocks and the hand. France is "armed and reverted, making war against her heir" in the forehead: the reference to the French civil wars recalls one explanation for the presence of French religious exiles in the city. England itself is located around Nel's mouth or nose, but its mention is an excuse for another allusion to France via the Channel, "the salt rheum that ran between France and it." Spain plays a part in the anti-blazon along with its conquests in America or the West Indies, both associated with the nose and hot respiration. There was no Spanish community in London, but Spanish imperialism in the Low Countries was another cause of armed reversion and the exile of their inhabitants. "Where stood Belgia, the Netherlands?" asks Syracusan Antipholus. "O, sir, I did not look so low," Dromio replies (3.2.112–3.2.138). The servant's encounter with Nel convinces his master to flee from Ephesus, for "the mermaid's song" of Luciana threatens a prettier version of the same liquid dissolution (line 163; and see lines 45–52).

Anxieties about residential appropriation and urban spaces course throughout the language and staging of Act 3. Luciana upbraids Syracusan Antipholus for neglecting his wife: "Shall love in building grow so ruinous?" (3.2.4). Ephesian Antipholus is shut out of his own house and shop, the Phoenix, by Nel-Luce and Dromio of Syracuse, who yell at him and his Dromio through a wall or barrier, unseen by them (3.1). The citizen Balthasar advises him not to break the door down in broad daylight to avoid harming his reputation, or his wife's, "For slander lives upon succession,/For e'er house's where it gets possession" (3.1.104–3.1.105). Together they go off to the Tiger, an inn or brothel, and this resort to the liberty outside the home introduces the complications of the courtesan and the debt for the chain. When Ephesian Antipholus is arrested for the debt, Syracusan Dromio twice invests a lot of energy in describing the officer who holds him: the sergeant or constable is a devil clad in an everlasting garment of leather and steel, a shoulder-clapper who blocks "The passages of alleys, creeks [winding lanes] and narrow lands" (4.2.33–4.2.38), and "he that came behind you, sir, like an evil angel, and bid you forsake your liberty" (4.3.18–4.3.20). The officer's role as a policeman of borders and in-between spaces calls attention to Ephesian Antipholus' gradual descent into outlaw status. Suddenly subject to the law for want of ready cash, the Ephesian's plight resembles the alien Egeon's at the start of the play; both are seized for want of "guilders," the second occasion for the word in the canon (4.1.4). The courtesan claims Ephesian Antipholus took her "ring" in exchange for the promise of the chain. When the Syracusan denies her both the ring and the chain, she concludes that Antipholus is mad and tells Adriana that he broke into her house and stole the diamond (4.3.78–4.3.93). Adriana later exaggerates the charge before the duke:

> desp'rately he hurried through the street,
> With him his bondman, all as mad as he,
> Doing displeasure to the citizens,
> By rushing in their houses; bearing thence
> Rings, jewels, any thing his rage did like. (5.1.140–5.1.144)

House-breaking, accidental, threatened, and wholly imagined, has finally transformed Ephesian Antipholus from a citizen into an outsider.

The change is less a conversion than a reversion to an earlier state. In the final act, where both Antipholi come together with their father Egeon, we discover what we already knew without fully recognizing: Antipholus of Ephesus was not always an Ephesian. He came to the city from Corinth with the duke's uncle, the famous warrior Menaphon (5.1.365–5.1.368), and then fought for it. Now he cries for justice,

> Even for the service that long since I did thee
> When I bestrid thee in the wars, and took
> Deep scars to save thy life. (5.1.191–5.1.193)

Machiavelli's soldier–citizenry may be reflected in a passage that turns away from the mercantile backdrop of the play toward the city–state model of political subjectivity. Antipholus became a citizen of Ephesus mainly because of his military service to the sovereign.

In a speech to Adriana, the duke reveals that marriage accompanied military service in the denization of Antipholus:

> Long since thy husband serv'd me in my wars,
> And I to thee engag'd a prince's word,
> When thou didst make him master of thy bed,
> To do him all the grace and good I could. (5.1.161–5.1.164)

The conjuncture of soldier and citizen under sovereignty is closer to the classical republicanism of Machiavelli's *Principe* rather than his *Discorsi*. Luciana's understanding of marriage in terms of the husband's sovereign mastery, as we have seen, cuts against the burgher ideal of a well-balanced household and the good reputation it guarantees. The duke implies that his sovereign influence and the mastery it lent Antipholus lay behind citizen marriage all along, but this revelation does not resolve the conflict between sovereignty and citizenship in the play. Neither the duke nor Egeon, the lost husband and father, is able to unravel the "intricate impeach" at the end of the comedy (5.1.270).

It is left to the Abbess to sort things out. As a religious authority early in the scene, she disciplines Adriana's claims on her spouse in a roughly Pauline manner that also underlines how her abbey has replaced Diana's shrine as the real temple at Ephesus (5.1.68–5.1.86). When she becomes Emilia and Egeon's wife again, she relinquishes even this authority. Yet the play closes with neither the husband nor the sovereign fully restored to dominance. The Abbess blends religious and citizen language in restoring the principals to their identities in her final speech:

> The duke, my husband, and my children both,
> And you, the calendars of their nativity,
> Go to a gossips' feast, and joy with me,
> After so long grief, such nativity. (5.1.403–5.1.406)

The sponsors of a baptism gather at a gossips' feast, but the word alludes to the common sense of neighborly chatter as well. The word "nativity" is repeated in the Folio text, and I have altered the modern edition to preserve a recognizable rhetorical device. Nativity is both emphasized and quibbled upon. In the period it could refer to "Birth as determining nationality," as in the OED's definition and its first example, from a guide to drawing up legal documents:

> Instrumentes bee either of such persons as haue natural capacity by birth, which euerie leige subiect beeing borne within her Maiesties dominion hath by his natiuitie.

Or by making, as euery stranger borne hath, being by act of
Parliament naturalized, or made a Denizen.[14]

Syracusan Antipholus came to the city as a stranger, and Ephesian
Antipholus has reverted to the outlandish origins that military service
and the duke's patronage once tamed. But they have regained their
nativity as citizens of a higher order than Syracuse, Corinth, or Ephesus.
Paul's citizenship of the saints and the household of God may be
hinted at, with its mixture of civic and familial or marital terminology.
But *The Comedy of Errors* remains opaque on the sublation of subject
or citizen status by religious identity at the end.

The influence of Shakespeare's secular city of Ephesus as the dangerous meeting-ground of citizens and strangers is found throughout
the comedies. The city itself, however, often drops out of the picture.
At the end of the canon, of course, we have *Pericles*, a reprise of the
early play's Plautine devices and Pauline themes. But Ephesus is only
one setting among many in the romance plot: its sea voyages and displaced events defy urban fixity. In *Twelfth Night*, the sailor Antonio is
arrested after lending his purse to Sebastian, who is invited into a great
lady's house when she mistakes him for his disguised sister. There is
no city at all in this comedy, where the errors take place between a
ducal court and a country manor. Aside from its Induction, *The Taming
of the Shrew*, closer in time to *The Comedy of Errors*, is mostly set in
Padua, but the taming itself occurs at Petrucchio's rural estate.

Love's Labour's Lost presents a somewhat different, and somewhat
more complicated, case than these plays. It is shot through with urban
concerns despite the total absence of city settings for its apparently rustic and aristocratic action. The prominent role played by the Spaniard
Armado offers a clue to the urban texture of the comedy. The local
schoolmaster, Holofernes, gives his first impressions of Armado in
terms that suggest how an idea of the polyglot city serves as an intellectual setting for the play. The Spaniard is "too affected, too odd, as it
were, too peregrinate," or too much of a wanderer or stranger:

> I abhor such fanatical phantasimes, such insociable and point-device
> companions, such rackers of orthography, as to speak "dout" *sine* "b, "
> when he should say "doubt," "det" when he should pronounce "debt":
> d, e, b, t, not d, e, t. He clepeth a calf "cauf," half "hauf"; neighbour
> *vacatur* "nebour," neigh abbreviated "ne." This is abhominable, which
> he would call "abominable." It insinuateth me of insanie.[15]

This is a very funny and very puzzling passage. Holofernes believes
that in certain words letters like "b" and "gh," unsounded in

Shakespeare's time as in ours, are to be pronounced, according to orthography. The schoolmaster may be saying that Armado wants to rack or distort spelling by omitting letters like "b" or "gh" on the page, but it is more likely that Armado implicitly tortures orthography by enunciating words as if they were written phonetically. As Keir Elam explains, Holofernes's terms are borrowed from contemporary manuals in the lively debate over English spelling instruction and reform.[16] John Hart and William Bullokar would invent new characters in order paradoxically to simplify spelling by, among other things, removing superfluous letters; Richard Mulcaster and Peter Bales wished merely to regularize the status quo in both spelling and pronunciation.[17] Holofernes's position is unique, however: he would both spell and pronounce letters that common idiom elides, partly, one suspects, to restore plausible derivations like "debt" from Latin *debitum*, and false but credited ones like "abominable" from *ab homine*. He is a pedantic fool, but the satire registers the same uneasiness over "the tyranny of writing" that the pessimistic Saussure felt: "visual images lead to wrong pronunciation; such mistakes are really pathological. . . . Mispronunciations due to spelling will probably appear more frequently as time goes on."[18]

Holofernes's own name probably derives from Rabelais's Thubal Holofernes, who taught the young Gargantua to copy his texts in Gothic script before the invention of printing.[19] Recently, John Drakakis has very usefully related Holofernes's rant to Benedict Anderson's concept of print capitalism and its creation of national consciousness.[20] According to Anderson, print languages

> created unified fields of exchange and communication below Latin and above the spoken vernaculars. Speakers of the huge variety of Frenches, Englishes, or Spanishes, who might find it difficult or even impossible to understand one another in conversation, became capable of comprehending one another via print and paper.[21]

To read this a little differently from Drakakis: print made the national possible by preserving the local, by allowing dialect, and I would suggest accent as well, to coexist with a standardized, visual monolect. It is significant that the object of the schoolmaster's scorn is a stranger or alien. One odd thing about Armado is that he has mastered his second language—he may be verbose and silly, but he knows enough not to pronounce the l in "calf," whatever his stage accent was like. Armado's case is doubly odd in comparison with the stereotypical Spaniard of sixteenth-century English theater, who is usually so proud that he refuses to speak the audience's tongue at all.[22] Holofernes's extreme conservatism in pronunciation and spelling reflects misgivings about the potential inclusiveness of the new world of print culture. In her recent overview of print's relation to *Love's Labour's Lost*, Carla Mazzio notes that Edmund Coote's handbook *The English Schoole-Maister* (1596) offered instruction to strangers, women, and servants, all of whom may be found on the fringes of Navarre's academe.[23]

Attention to aliens is actually well-attested in English language manuals, particularly spelling manuals. In *An Orthographie*, John Hart directs his method toward "vnlearned naturall English people" and "Secondly for straungers or the rude countrie English man," an awkward redoubling that nevertheless couples strangers with foreigners, as English subjects born outside London were called by the city's residents. William Bullokar—whose scorn for silent b, l, and gh caught Elam's eye—promises in his subtitle an "easie and speedie pathway to all Straungers, to vse our language, heeretofore very hard vnto them." In the text, Bullokar observes that strangers condemn English as barbarous and without order or sensibility. He seeks to correct this false impression by concentrating on pronunciation, omitting superfluous characters, and including a chart of English sounds that are hard for aliens to pronounce.[24] On the other side of the debate, Peter Bales suggests a technique for rote learning of spelling as it is, to help English speakers, "and partlie for the benefit of Straungers," although he hedges in the final poem on his triple system of shorthand, spelling, and calligraphy: "Swift, true, and faire, together ioyne in one:/(My Countrymen) to profit you alone."[25] Bales's ambivalence may have the same source as Holofernes's exasperation with Armado. The unified, silent supra-vernacular of English print culture admitted aliens to the national culture. Moreover, passable spelling and pronunciation according to emerging urban standards may have helped some strangers or their offspring to pass for English in ways that were not welcome to all. It is true that complaints against aliens often concerned their self-seclusion from English society rather than assimilation to it, but fears about passing often accompany accusations of aloofness and divided loyalty: this is a paradox that many members of minority groups have had to face in different eras. Hart had already employed an unsettling analogy along these lines, precisely when decrying the preservation of superfluous letters in pedantic spellings that commemorate the non-English derivation of certain words:

> it is even as we would not have any straunger to be conversant, nor dwell amongst us, though he be a free Denison, . . . except (of a

certaine fond curiositie) he should weare continually some mark, to be knowen whence he is, I think, to thend we should be able to know thereby how to refuse him when some of us listed.[26]

By the end of the sixteenth century, some Londoners might have welcomed such marks on strangers, just as Holofernes would mark alien derivations in the pronunciation of words.

Frances Yates told part of the story in claiming long ago that opposition to French and Flemish foreign language teachers had found its way into both antialien feeling and *Love's Labour's Lost* in the early 1590s.[27] Rioting by London apprentices in June 1595 was partly about economic competition by strangers, mostly in the cloth trade. While it is difficult to believe that rivalry over French lessons played a role in the unrest as Yates seems to suggest, alien influence on Londoners and their language could have formed a share of the threat. Strangers learning English rather than English speakers learning French or Italian may also have been a source of worry for the dissidents. The Dutch Church Libel of May 1593 began with the address:

> Ye strangers yt doe inhabite in this lande
> Note this same writing doe it vnderstand
> Conceit it well for savegard of your lyves
> Your goods, your children, & your dearest wives.[28]

The stress on strangers understanding or noting the writing may be an ironic touch in the Dutch Church Libel. In complaining about alien merchants and unregulated artisans, the rhyme typically accuses Protestant immigrants of religious hypocrisy and cowardice in escaping persecution for profiteering in London. The surviving copy of the entire libel links it with the French Church, probably a mistake for the nearby Dutch congregation, although French, Flemish, and Dutch people were often confused, along with the Germans who had formed an earlier wavelet of European immigration. The verses also compare the ravenous aliens to Jews, as James Shapiro has pointed out.[29] The May posting is significant, since it recalls the "Ill May Day" riots against strangers of 1517.

Yates links 1593 and 1595 to *Love's Labour's Lost* by citing the conclusion of this exchange about Costard and Jaquenetta from the start of Act 3:

> *ARMADO.* Warble, child, make passionate my sense of hearing.
> *MOTH.* [*Sings.*] Concolinel.

ARMADO. Sweet air! Go, tenderness of years, take this key, give
enlargement to the swain, bring him festinately hither. I must
employ him in a letter to my love.
MOTH. Master, will you win your love with a French brawl?
ARMADO. How meanest thou? Brawling in French? (3.1.1–3.1.9)

Yates finds rioting against French speakers in Moth's French dance or
bransle.[30] Historians now doubt that rioting took place in 1593, but
unrecorded disturbances on a smaller scale could have occurred.[31] I
think the allusion to "brawling" in this sense holds. "Concolinel" may
have been heard by some in the audience as the beginning of a French
song ("Quand Colinelle").[32] Moth's reply also adds a commercial
touch whose antialien connotation has not been remarked: "No, my
complete master; but to jig off a tune. . . . with your hat penthouse-
like o'er the shop of your eyes" (3.1.10, 3.1.15–3.1.16). Armado's love
is set out in the windows of his eyes; his hat is the raised shutter that
typically sheltered tradesmen's wares. In London noncitizens were
forced by law to erect lattices in their windows as well to prevent their
goods from being seen in the street.[33] But citizen merchants displayed
their products freely, especially along Goldsmith's Row in Cheapside,
renovated in 1594 and a marvel to visitors from abroad like Thomas
Platter.[34] Boyet seems to recall this vista of aristocratic consumerism in
his description of the love-struck King's solicitation of the Princess:

> Methought all his senses were locked in his eye,
> As jewels in crystal for some prince to buy;
> Who, tendering their own worth from where they were glassed,
> Did point you to buy them along as you passed. (2.1.241–2.1.244)

Elsewhere in the play, love's merchandise is showcased lower down on
the male anatomy. Overhearing Longaville say he will tear up his poem
during the sonnet eavesdropping scene, Berowne quips "O, rhymes are
guards on wanton Cupid's hose:/Disfigure not his shop" (4.3.55–
4.3.56). Guards are embroidery on hose or barriers before a house; the
disfiguring of Cupid's shop glances at rioting against shopkeepers as well
as the way love poetry covers up, and calls attention to, wanton desires.
    Berowne's attack on Cupid at the end of 3.1 compares Rosaline to
a luxury item that is more trouble than it is worth:

> A woman that is like a German clock,
> Still a-repairing, ever out of frame
> And never going aright, being a watch,
> But being watched that it may still go right! (3.1.185–3.1.188)

In this case, female rather than male genitalia are invoked in the bawdy innuendo of the "clock" or watch that must be watched to "go" right. Clock-making had long been associated with aliens from northern Europe: Edward III, for instance, brought three Dutch craftsmen to London for the purpose.[35]

The confusion of erotic metaphors with the language of buying and selling reaches its climax when the men, having abandoned their vow to avoid women, woo the ladies in Russian disguise.[36] The commercial promise of the Muscovy Company of merchant adventurers is evoked or mocked in this scene. There was no Russian community in London, and the strangeness of the false Muscovites belongs to a more academic order of ethnicity than the French, Low Countries, and German references.[37] Nevertheless, intimations of actual immigration figure in an episode mostly taken up with courtly love-games far from the urban streets. Katherine plays a typical match in her covert identification of the masked "Long(a)ville": "sir, I long./ . . . . 'Veal', quoth the Dutchman" (5.2.244, 5.2.247). Such syllabic punning is characteristic of the empty circulation of signifiers that make and unmake masculine aristocratic identity in the court scenes. But the subsequent teasing of Longaville as a horned calf headed for the butchery of cuckoldom partly depends upon the popular link between the Dutch and gluttony. Because he pronounces English "well" as "veal," the Dutchman condemns himself through what comes out of his mouth, like Longaville. Dutch *viel* also means plenty, as it does in Dekker's *The Shoemaker's Holiday*, where Lacy disguises himself as a Dutch artisan and a Dutch sea-captain has "veale ge drunck."[38]

Marston's *The Dutch Courtesan* is a somewhat later play that features a Dutch accent, and in its citizen *milieu* we also find the explanation for another nonce reference to the Muscovite disguise. Mistress Mulligrub, a vintner's wife, advertises herself as well as his wares in the shop: "though my husband be a citizen and's cap's made of wool, yet I ha' wit and can see my good as soon as another."[39] After the lords leave, Rosaline says "Well, better wits have worn plain statute-caps" (5.2.281). Sumptuary laws apparently mandated that apprentices and citizens wear simple woolen caps on occasion.[40] Rosaline's remark flatters a large part of the public theater audience by contrasting the courtiers' aristocratic goings-on with the practical wit of the citizenry, whose civic language the scene often echoes. Holofernes's pageant of the Nine Worthies, which parallels the Muscovite masque on the demotic level of adventure plays and urban spectacle, as Meredith Skura has pointed out, is directly related to citizen culture.[41] William Carroll describes Richard Johnson's "The Nine Worthies of London" of 1592, in which representatives of the Grocers and other companies took the Worthies' places.[42] As Judas Maccabaeus, the schoolmaster is mercilessly flouted for a face as rigid as his pronunciation:

> BEROWNE. Saint George's half-cheek in a brooch.
> DUMAINE. Ay, and in a brooch of lead.
> BEROWNE. Ay, and worn in the cap of a tooth-drawer. (5.2.611–
>   5.2.613)

We do not know what the audience made of the lords' cruelty. Holofernes's exercise in a citizen mode is clearly inadequate, however, and the insults culminate in his association with the lowly tooth-drawer. Caps entail status once more, since the badge on the cap indicates the wearer's occupation; the tooth-drawer with his leaden brooch was evidently the lowest of the low, perhaps a vagrant or mountebank who aped one mark of the citizen's identity.[43] The citizen audience is invited to join in the scapegoating of its failed member, or employee. Furthermore, the schoolmaster is hooted off stage as "Monsieur Judas," a natural title from the French Boyet, perhaps, but redolent of Londoners' disdain for would-be monsieurs from across the Channel (5.2.624). Holofernes, who is seen policing the borders of correct pronunciation at the start of Act V, has become assimilated to the "peregrinate" outlandishness he attacked in Armado.

The ambiguous status of Holofernes—he is both native and strange, a school "master" and a servant—is also part of the urban atmosphere of the play. "He teaches boys the hornbook" (5.1.44), as Moth says, and the use of this word for the horn-covered ABC that served as a primer establishes his school as English in character despite the Navarrese setting of the action. "Do you not educate youth at the charge-house on the top of the mountain?" Armado asks Holofernes. The mountain is from a colloquy by Erasmus, but the phrase "charge-house" has defied explanation (5.1.75–5.1.79). I think the simplest interpretation, initially offered by Theobald, is the best—that the school is supported at someone's charge, making it an endowed school like most others.[44] There were several ways of becoming the master of an endowed school in Elizabethan England. Schools were often sponsored by various livery companies or trades, and membership in a company was the normal prerequisite for London citizenship. But Holofernes's inseparability from Nathaniel the "parish curate" (5.2.532) hints that he has been hired to run an endowed school administered by the parish.

The parish was the basic unit of local government in many parts of England, and particularly in London.[45] The vestry, a board composed of worshippers chosen from citizens living within its bounds, nominated the officials that the roughly corresponding ward appointed, such as constables.[46] Nathaniel, Holofernes, and Constable Dull, three characters constantly linked in the subplot, thus intimate the microcosm of the parish, the most familiar division of city administration to the London audience. The same would hold true for many a country village, and Shakespeare further asks us to transport this to his imaginary Navarre, which seems split between the King's court and a countryside inhabited by Jaquenetta and the "swain" Costard with little room for civic culture in between (5.1.119). Nevertheless, London lives in the language the characters speak rather than the action they present, and London constituted the most complete example of how police, education, and religion operated together on the neighborhood level. London was also the setting of the public theaters, where this cluster of local ideological apparatuses might be subjected to public scorn.

Shakespeare's probable contribution to the play *Sir Thomas More* is the *locus classicus* for the citizen–alien opposition in his canon and Tudor-Stuart drama in general. A glance at its relation to *Love's Labour's Lost* will round off my discussion of the comedy's urban context. The setting, Ill May Day itself, is ominous, but the crisis begins with an amusing complaint about the strangers' introduction of exotic vegetables into England:

> LINCOLN. . . . our infection will make the city shake, which partly comes through the eating of parsnips.
> CLOWN. True, and pumpions together.[47]

Pumpions are pumpkins—the later form of the word with its "-kin" ending suggests the curious Dutch connotation the vegetable retained for a while in English. The unhealthy, watery, and alien qualities of the pumpkin lie behind Costard's description of his role in the Worthies show: "I am, as they say, but to parfect one man in one poor man— Pompion the Great, sir" (5.2.500–5.2.501). The poor man will be reduced to an outlandish melon by the pedants' display; as Costard gets the name "Pompey" right a few lines later, it is likely the swain is making an orthographically adjusted joke that the apprentices would appreciate. When More himself steps forth to face down the rioters in the history play, they demand "the removing of the strangers, which cannot choose but much advantage the poor handicrafts of the city" (2.3.76–2.3.77). More tells the apprentices that if they succeed they will in effect have taken the King's place, "Authority quite silenc'd by your brawl" (line 84). "Brawling" is not uncommon in Shakespeare and his contemporary playwrights, but the use of the word to designate the century's archetypal antialien revolt strengthens the possibility that "French brawl" in *Love's Labour's Lost* is a pointed allusion, whether or not Shakespeare contributed to the More play.

More brings his lengthy pacification to an end by asking the rioters to imagine themselves in exile among a barbarous nation that would "Spurn you like dogs, and like as if that God/Owed not nor made not you. . . . /This is the strangers' case" (2.3.145–2.3.146, 2.3.150). In *Love's Labour's Lost* the Princess questions Armado's faith using similar, if gentler, terms:

> *PRINCESS.* Doth this man serve God?
> *BEROWNE.* Why ask you?
> *PRINCESS.* 'A speaks not like a man of God his making. (5.2.522–
> 5.2.524)

Both passages cite the common expression "He is not a man of God's making." Although the phrase is proverbial for an unusual or unfamiliar sort of man in general, its contexts in both *Sir Thomas More* and *Love's Labour's Lost* suggest that it could take on an antialien meaning at a time when linguistic, ethnic, and religious differences were often joined.[48] Armado obligingly throws in an unfortunate Spanish phrase (*"fortuna de la guerra"*) four lines later. Of course, stranger communities in London were Protestants from France or Holland, not Spaniards; most of them had been driven out of their homelands by Catholic Spain. Yet it is telling that the Dutch Church Libel informs religious refugees from the Low Countries "With Spanish gold, you all are infected," and accuses them of employing this gold to bribe the nobles to take their side.[49] In his outlandishness, Armado comes to represent every alien; all strangers, even Protestants, are assimilated to "tawny Spain" (1.1.171) and its infectious influence.

The deliberate confusion of Protestant émigrés with other strangers of more pronounced ethnic and religious difference from the English has also been perceived in *The Merchant of Venice*. This play returns us to the overt city setting of *The Comedy of Errors*. It is in Belmont, however, a courtly land repeatedly associated with sovereign rather than urban power, that we run through the gamut of European ethnicity early in *The Merchant of Venice*. In Act 1, Scene 2, Nerissa quizzes Portia on the "four strangers" who have most recently contemplated the trial of the caskets; there are in fact six strangers in the list, the Neapolitan, the County Palatine (south German or perhaps

Polish), the French lord, Falconbridge of England, the Scottish lord, and the Duke of Saxony's nephew. Familiar regional stereotypes are duly attached: pride in horsemanship to Naples, eclectic clothing to the Englishman abroad, drunkenness to the (second) German. When asked her opinion of the Frenchman, Monsieur Le Bon, Portia retorts with a familiar phrase: "God made him, and therefore let him pass for a man."[50] Le Bon is a braggart, a fencer, and "every man in no man" (57)—a French kinsman of the Spanish Armado. Like the aristocratic setting of *Love's Labour's Lost*, Belmont sublates urban anxieties over religious and other differences through courtly competition.

Venice, however, is the major setting of the play, and the frequent parallels between Belmont and Venice frame and emphasize the urban coloring of the Belmont plot and its language. For example, Morocco succeeds the European visitors and undergoes the trial, choosing the gold casket and suffering "labor lost" (2.7.74). Misliked for his complexion (79), he must leave Belmont having promised never to marry. Launcelot, it is later revealed, has endangered the "commonwealth" by impregnating "the Moor" in Venice, a less answerable act than Lorenzo's marriage to the converted Jessica (3.5.34–3.5.36). Launcelot's out-of-wedlock affair casts a retrospective light upon Morocco's foiled attempt at marital miscegenation in Belmont. Both reflect fears about the small but remarkable African presence in London that culminated in Elizabeth's expulsion orders, documents that had as much to do with the politics of citizenship and alienage in the 1590s as with developing notions about race.[51]

In another, more distant, echo of Belmont in a Venetian scene, Le Bon is recalled when Salerio recounts an encounter with a countryman of his in Venice:

> I reason'd with a Frenchman yesterday,
> Who told me, in the narrow seas that part
> The French and English, there miscarried
> A vessel of our country richly fraught. (2.8.27–2.8.30)

London citizens might have noticed several points in this brief passage, which brought the play suddenly closer to its original audience. The narrowness of the English Channel promises quick passage for émigrés or invaders, but it is also dangerous for shipping, whether the vessels carry aliens or the goods with which they compete against English merchants. Since three of Antonio's argosies mysteriously return by Act 5, however, it is possible that Salerio's Frenchman is as unreliable as Portia's. Venice was paralleled with London and England in general in contemporary literature; it was also the model for a citizen-run state that had partly subsumed sovereign power and wisdom.[52] The survey of European nobles in Belmont takes place in a sovereign or courtly context, but it sets up the opposition between strangers and inhabitants that rules the Venetian scenes. It does so by emphasizing the international rivalries that partly lie behind the depiction of Morocco and, especially, Shylock as well.

Long ago it was suggested that Shylock is a stand-in, not for Jews, a notoriously small population in late-sixteenth-century England, but for London's French, Flemish, and Dutch aliens. Andrew Tretiak maintained that censorship forbade the depiction of violent and vengeful European strangers on stage during riotous times. Shylock's biblical language intimated the Old Testament severity attributed to Protestant émigré communities, however, and their social and particularly religious exclusiveness is echoed in his declaration "I will not eat with you, drink with you, nor pray with you" (1.3.32–1.3.34).[53] James Shapiro has recently argued a subtle and persuasive version of this case. The Master of the Revels, he notes, acting as censor, had demanded that the term *Lombard* replace *stranger* and *Frenchman* in the manuscript of *Sir Thomas More*. Few Lombards still resided in London: "there was no problem redirecting hostility against a largely fictive minority population that was an easy target and peripheral to the real object of anti-alien sentiment." Jews played the same role from the start in *The Merchant of Venice*.[54] Shapiro also points out that aliens are explicitly compared with Jews in the Dutch Church Libel, a parallel to which I shall return later. It must be said that Shylock also displays many specifically "Jewish" qualities drawn from the armory of European anti-Semitic stereotypes. Conversely, London's aliens were overwhelmingly accused of illegal manufactures and sales, and only secondarily and rather vaguely of usury; Shylock is depicted solely as a moneylender, not as a master of a workshop or as a vendor. He remains separate from others in a way that evokes but outdoes the exclusiveness of French or Dutch aliens. Portia has no Jewish suitors: might Shylock have traveled to Belmont before Bassanio and immediately penetrated the conceit of the lead casket?

Shylock's status remains undecidable, an example, perhaps, of an indeterminacy in alienage that shadows the indeterminacy of citizenship. Yet his separateness demands, even if it finally exceeds, historicist efforts to place him in early modern London. Such a reading of the play, however partial, casts light on a number of key passages. The citizen *milieu* of the play is clear from the start. Salerio tells the melancholy Antonio:

> Your mind is tossing on the ocean,
> There where your argosies with portly sail
> Like signiors and rich burghers on the flood,
> Or as it were the pageants of the sea,
> Do overpeer the petty traffickers
> That curs'y to them (do them reverence)
> As they fly by them with their woven wings. (1.1.8–1.1.14)

Maritime trade superposes the city upon the sea; the citizen Antonio's ships are like burghers themselves, peering down upon the lesser merchants who curtsy to them on the rocking waves. They are also compared to the pageant-wagons that figured in civic celebrations like those of the Lord Mayor. Their "woven wings" look forward to the first crisis of the action, however, the cross-dressed Jessica's absconding from her father's house during the preparations for one such public masque: "I . . . knew the tailor that made the wings she flew withal," Salerio will later claim (3.1.24–3.1.25).

Jessica is present at Belmont to confirm that Shylock will go hard on Antonio when Salerio announces his pursuit of the bond for the pound of flesh. "He plies the duke at morning and at night," Salerio explains, "And doth impeach the freedom of the state/If they deny him justice" (3.2.276–3.2.278). In the trial scene, Shylock himself tells the duke: "If you deny it, let the danger light/Upon your charter and your city's freedom!" (4.1.38–4.1.39). His terms are by now familiar to us: the "freedom" of the (city-)state is the citizenship shared by its freemen, and its "charter" is the document granting this freedom. *Charter* also recalls the charters of the livery companies who in practice determined access to the freedom for most citizens for economic reasons. Yet charters were granted by royal authority, and Venice was famously a republic. Shakespeare's "duke" is simultaneously a sovereign who hovers over a city government composed of merchant citizens, and a Venetian *Doge*, elected for life but non-sovereign, a first among equals, and hence easily threatened along with them by a stranger with a claim on a higher, unidentified political power. In both cases, Venice's freedom is somehow chartered, like that of an English town: despite the classical—or at any rate civic—republican setting of Venice, Shakespeare has difficulty conceiving of citizenship apart from sovereignty and subjecthood.

Antonio brings out the commercial element in Shylock's case in a passage that comes between the versions quoted above:

> The duke cannot deny the course of law:
> For the commodity that strangers have

With us in Venice, if it be denied,
Will much impeach the justice of the state,
Since that the trade and profit of the city
Consisteth of all nations. (3.3.26–3.3.31)

The grammatical crux in this sentence demands that we combine "the course of law" with the strangers' "commodity" or profit—to deny one is to deny the other in miniature or in principle, and to do so will hurt Venice's reputation as a hub of international trade and finance where all are equal under the law. William Thomas's *History of Italy* (1549) contains an oft-cited account of Venice's toleration toward aliens, and it also notes the profit that accrues to the city from taxation and duties on Jewish usury.[55] In Antonio's view, it is the "justice" and the "profit" of the city that are both at stake, not its "freedom." But, just as justice and profit are linked through the Aristotelian approach to justice as the division of goods within society, so is citizenship implicated because it is an economic category.[56] Additionally, the economics of citizenship and alienage in Venice depends on a separate but supposedly equal distribution of privilege and gain. The seemingly disinterested Balthazar asks, "Which is the merchant here? and which the Jew?" as Portia enters the scene of the trial (4.1.170).

Shakespeare's ideally impartial Venice serves as an extreme caricature of the situation in England. In 1559, Elizabeth had issued a proclamation on the keeping of the peace between English and strangers that promised equal protection to both under her laws. Edward Coke, however, summarized a trend in recent legal thought in 1609 when arguing in the *post-nati* matter that aliens have comparable economic rights to subjects under the law only as long as they are friends or allied in war; once they become enemy aliens they lose this protection.[57] The *coup de grace* that the disguised Portia delivers upon Shylock may reflect this line of thought. According to the strict laws of Venice, a stranger's goods will be confiscated and his life placed at the duke's mercy,

If it be proved against an alien,
That by direct, or indirect attempts
He seek the life of any citizen. (4.1.345–4.1.347)

By willing danger to the life of Antonio, a citizen—and the terminology suddenly firms up and becomes oddly "modern" here—the alien Shylock has become an enemy and is subject to economic and capital penalties. In her initial verdict, Portia-Balthazar had just preserved the letter of commercial law in Venice by allowing Shylock to take his pound of flesh from Antonio, but only flesh and not blood, and only an exact pound—practical impossibilities. She began by arguing that Shylock should show mercy toward his debtor, rather than insist on the letter of an equal law that might also condemn him. Mercy

> becomes
> The throned monarch better than his crown.
> His sceptre shows the force of temporal power,
> The attribute to awe and majesty,
> Wherein doth sit the dread and fear of kings:
> But mercy is above this sceptred sway,
> It is enthroned in the hearts of kings,
> It is an attribute to God himself. (4.1.184–4.1.191)

Mercy is a royal quality, borrowed from above; once more the ultimate reference is to a sphere of sovereign authority outside the civic world of Venice, here made over into a divine sphere as well. The duke finally assumes this mantle when Shylock is subjugated to his "mercy" as an enemy alien in Portia's final judgment. The paradox of Shylock's situation is exquisite: only by not demanding his due as a protected alien can he remain a protected alien, for only by upholding sovereign mercy and not pressing his economic rights can he avoid being judged an enemy. Conversely, citizenship itself derives from sovereign protection somehow, since it is chartered by an authority external to the play. Both citizens and aliens must internalize an occult sovereignty, however, and simply do what should come naturally: "there is no power in Venice/ Can alter a decree established" (4.1.214–4.1.215). Sovereignty remains an absent center that still grounds citizen and alien status in *The Merchant of Venice*: citizenship is limited on the one hand by economic exclusion, and on the other it is bound by the general economy of sovereign mercy and violence. It remains pre-modern after all, but in a way that Enlightenment ideals of citizenship may not have escaped from yet.

Alien and citizen, merchant and Jew: these oppositions in the comedy conceal other, less clear-cut tensions in late sixteenth-century London. Aliens, citizens, and merchants were all in play there, and the Dutch Church Libel discloses that Jews were dealt a symbolic hand, too. The libeler tells the strangers:

> Your Machiavellian Marchant spoyles the state,
>   Your vsery doth leave vs all for deade
> Your Artifex, & craftesman works our fate,
>   And like the Jewes, you eate us vp as bread.[58]

As Shapiro suggests, the final line may hint at the Host-desecration and ritual cannibalism attributed to Jews by many Christians.[59] But more significantly, it is a quotation from the book of Psalms, from the fourth verse in the related Psalms 14 and 53: "Have all the workers of iniquity no knowledge? who eat up my people as they eat bread." The specific association of the iniquitous with the Jews may come from the citation of Psalms 14 and 54 in Romans 3:10. These are also the psalms that begin: "The fool hath said in his heart, there is no God." The libel implicitly accuses Protestant émigrés of becoming the spiritual Jews of stereotype, hypocrites who fled religious warfare and who now deny God's punishing power by exploiting English Protestants. Biblical knowledge, including perhaps the layering of a New Testament reading over Old Testament texts, serves as the admonitory *lingua franca* between native and alien Christian communities.

Also of interest in the passage is the division of labor between merchant and "Artifex" in the offending stranger community. As the rest of the libel makes clear, alien craftsmen produce cheap and ornate goods, and alien merchants then peddle these wares, undercutting English workers and retailers alike. Usury is tacked onto the charge against the stranger merchants. The aliens may have worked this way, but if they did, they were partly copying the structure of London guilds. Furthermore, many livery companies were preoccupied by conflict rather than cooperation between their artisanal and merchant members. In some cases, craftsmen accused the merchants, who usually ruled the companies, of managing wholesale prices, export restrictions, and use of alien labor against them. Merchants were also accused of usury.[60] By depicting stranger artificers and merchants working hand in glove to exploit the English in turn, the libeler both holds up a demonic model of unity to London readers, and attempts to consolidate native craftsmen and merchants against this common enemy. I find in its reflection of guild structure a strong indication that the Dutch Church Libel, for all its surface crudity, was produced by company members.

Occasional rifts between artisans and merchants in London companies were modulated by the continual charity expected of company leaders, especially various forms of poor relief.[61] Charity, of course, seems to be the leading "lesson" of *The Merchant of Venice*, a counterpoint to the slippery charge of usury that relates equally to alien merchants, English merchants in companies, and the medieval inheritance of anti-Semitism. Shylock refuses to have a doctor by "for charity" when Antonio's flesh is cut because it is not in the bond (4.1.257). Antonio, on the other hand, is "the fool that lent out money gratis" (3.3.2), thus lowering the interest rate to Shylock's disadvantage (1.3.39–1.3.40). The "Christian curs'y" of no-interest loans answers the "curs'y" of the petty traffickers in Salerio's nautical metaphor of Antonio's initial prosperity (3.1.44; 1.1.13). Despairing of any leniency from Shylock, Antonio says: "I oft deliver'd from his for-feitures/Many that have at times made moan to me" (3.3.22–3.3.23). A royal merchant, he has upheld the merciful exchange of social cour-tesy and economic obligation between elites and subalterns in his community. In Shakespeare's London, wealthy company members, usually merchants, often advanced money to young men interest free, and also contributed by bequest to permanent company funds that offered more or less free loans.[62] As usury was common among Christians despite its often hypocritical condemnation, interest-free lending stood out as one mechanism by which merchants kept the peace with their artisan brothers.

In exonerating Antonio by scapegoating Shylock and all that he represents symbolically and locally, *The Merchant of Venice* partakes in, and perhaps exposes, the peacekeeping mechanisms of London guilds and English urban society in general. Riot, as we have seen, was a con-stant fear. Ian Archer has demonstrated that there were no actual "anti-alien riots" of the Ill May Day variety in the 1590s: instead, numerous libels and other presentations threatening violence against aliens were part of a negotiating strategy between the poor, in and out of companies, and the elites.[63] The tensions of spring 1593 that pro-duced the Dutch Church Libel and the rioting at Tower Hill two years later were directed at native abuses as well as the supposed alien threat. Although the authorities were troubled by antialien sentiment because of its powder keg reputation after 1517, verbal and occasion-ally physical attacks on strangers were finally acceptable fronts for a violence that really surged toward company leaders, justices of the peace, and nobles supposedly bribed with Spanish, Dutch, or French gold. It is not surprising that the public theater was one setting for these negotiations.

The theater's role, a critical one in several senses, is particu-larly apparent in the case of *The Merry Wives of Windsor*, the only Shakespearean comedy set wholly in England. "Riot" figures in this play's opening episode, but in a different sense than *More*'s antialien crowd-scene or *Love's Labour's Lost*'s "brawl." Justice Shallow, a guest at Windsor's Garter Inn, has evidently pursued Sir John Falstaff all the way from Gloucester and *2 Henry IV* because, as he charges, "you have beaten my men, killed my deer, and broke open my lodge."[64] Disturbances of the peace involving three or more people certainly constitute riot in the technical sense, although the magnitude of Shallow's anger at the affront is ridiculous. "I will make a Star Chamber matter of it," he says, intending to bring the offense directly to the attention of the monarch's Privy Council rather than following Gloucestershire or circuit court channels. The Council did accept cases of riot, especially when the nobility or sedition was involved. Shallow is addressing Hugh Evans, a Welshman who has become a Windsor parson. As Rosemary Kegl points out, Evans attempts the mediating role the community expected local officials to assume when small-scale matters threatened to come to court, especially courts outside local jurisdiction.[65] He is hampered by his stage-Welsh status and its linguistic limitations, or excesses. For instance, when Shallow insists "The Council shall hear it; it is a riot," Parson Evans either mistakes the purview of Star Chamber or assumes that a Church council falsely superseding his own local influence is meant: "It is not meet the Council hear a riot: there is no fear of Got in a riot" (1.1.32, 1.1.33–1.1.34). In the encounter with Falstaff and his followers, Evans is mocked by Sir John for urging "good worts" instead of "words" in his bid at mediation, and he himself scorns the verbal peculiarities of both Pistol and Bardolph, provoking the former (1.1.112, 1.1.135–1.1.136, 1.1.159).

The governing irony of the scene, of course, is that Shallow, a Justice of the Peace, has set about disturbing the peace of Windsor ("if I were young again, the sword should end it," 1.1.37–1.1.38). Despite his good intentions and partial success, Evans is wordily hapless as a peacemaker and easily drawn into brawls himself, as the near-duel with Caius soon shows. Shallow and Evans each represent authorities that are much larger than Windsor—the judicial system, with its ties to the court through Star Chamber, and the Church. This is fitting, however, for they are both outsiders, or foreigners, to the community. Evans is Welsh, and so outside "England" itself let alone its home counties, although he is a subject of the Crown. Shallow is an esquire "In the county of Gloucester, Justice of Peace and Coram . . . and Custalorum" (1.1.5–1.1.7), corruptions of his Latin titles as a quorum justice and keeper of the rolls for his county, additional offices that emphasize the local judiciary's responsibility to the state. According to Slender, Shallow is "a gentleman born" and so fit to challenge Falstaff. He "writes himself 'Armigero' in any bill, warrant, quittance, or obligation— 'Armigero' " (1.1.9–1.1.11). He is qualified to bear a coat of arms, in other words, but his armigerousness is bound up with the writerly enactment of legal authority on behalf of the Crown more than birth or place. Shallow's recourse to the Privy Council jeopardizes local autonomy and its ad hoc methods of maintaining the peace: for example,

Evan's plan to marry off Ann Page to Slender, or the enlistment of Page, Parson Evans, and the Host of the Garter as "umpires" in Slender's accusation of theft against Pistol, Nym, and Bardolph (1.1.125–1.1.128).

At this point, it is necessary to acknowledge the substantial differences between the initial episode of the play in the Folio of 1623 (F), the text on which all modern editions are based, and the First Quarto of 1602 (Q), traditionally assumed to be a "bad" or memorially reconstructed quarto from which many key readings have nevertheless been salvaged by textual editors. In Q, Shallow enters angry at Falstaff and threatens to make a Star Chamber matter of the dispute, but his main purpose is evidently a visit to Page, who is present from the start of the scene. Shallow proposes the match between Ann and Slender; he has not arrived in pursuit of Falstaff.[66] In F, Evans suggests the marriage project to redirect Shallow's anger at Falstaff and make peace. The phrase "In the county of Gloucester" is found only in F. In Q, Page, Evans, and the Host are supposed to mediate between Shallow and Falstaff over the poaching offense, which must then have taken place locally; this is the "matter" that is "pud to arbitarments," not the picking of Slender's purse (A3 verso). It is unclear in Q whether or not the ponderous JP is a complete outsider to the community, while in F he is an interloper whose power is a displaced and abstract extension of the royal authority that the Garter ceremony represents in a benign form off-stage.[67] According to Leah S. Marcus, "The folio version of *Merry Wives* is a comedy of small-town and rural life, steeped in rustic customs and topography but also imbued with the 'high' presence of the royal court; the quarto version is 'lower,' closer to the pattern of city or 'citizen' comedy."[68] It has long been recognized that the text of Q might be based on a lost comedy of citizen life set in London or, more probably, a simplified or simply different version of the play in which the Windsor setting, though mentioned in the title and the Fairies scene at the end, has otherwise been rendered less distinct.[69] Marcus provides a comprehensive survey of instances where Q substitutes either urban or topographically vague allusions for F's rural and small-town references. Instead of carrying Falstaff to Windsor's Dotchet (or Datchet) Mead in Act 3, Scene 3, for example, Mrs. Ford's men take him to the "Launderers" in Q.[70] Marcus adds, or emphasizes, a new element by including the presence of the court in the Folio version. Folio *Merry Wives* has become the preferred copy-text for the play because it encapsulates the ideological compromise represented by the notion of "Merry England," an alliance of the royal court with the rural countryside and its humble inhabitants. The phrase may be a

Victorian one, but as Marcus argues the rapprochement it betokens goes back to the Stuart monarchy. A sub-urban if not suburban location, Windsor marks the fictional spot where court and country join to squeeze out the city and its citizens. Marcus follows Peter Erickson in discounting much earlier critical interest in the Order of the Garter and its courtly politics as an explanatory matrix for the entire play, and she does so by defending Q's respectability as a relatively uncorrupted text and a source of alternate meaning.[71]

Like *Love's Labour's Lost*, Folio *Merry Wives* and the modern conflated texts derived from it exclude the city as setting. If Q is the earlier version, the process of revision enacted this exclusion on the level of the rewritten and printed text; if, as seems probable, the Folio version came first, then Q represents a return of the urban repressed through the *mise-en-scene* itself. While these bibliographic allegories of reading are attractive, the analogy with *Love's Labour's Lost* also recalls the importance of archive and language as well as content and setting. Just as it would be wrong to state, as Marcus does not, that the underdog Q is a politically or formally "better" text than F because it suggests an urban and middle-class setting, it is also hasty to conclude that F is less concerned with citizenship and the attendant anxieties of alienage than Q. Folio *Merry Wives* may squeeze out London and its people on the scenic level, but on the level of language it actually possesses more in the way of urban allusions than the Quarto does.

To return to the opening scene with the Folio as our copy-text is to recall that Shallow would resort to the Privy Council sitting as Star Chamber because he accuses Falstaff of "riot," a term absent in Q. Star Chamber heard many cases of riot and London officials turned to it to police criminal and seditious public disturbances throughout the period when civic measures failed.[72] Falstaff got into a scuffle over hunting somewhere in Gloucestershire, it would seem, but the word "riot" retains an urban connotation in F anyway. Fenton, who "kept company with the wild Prince and Poins," is barred by Page from courting his daughter because of "My riots past, my wild societies" (3.2.66–3.2.67, 3.4.8). Ann's suitor, like his heir-apparent patron, is both a courtly and metropolitan figure here; as Marcus points out, Fenton is an amorous local boy in Q, and he is not linked to the wild Prince Harry of urban legend.[73] Hunting is the governing metaphor for Diana's foresters and their purse-taking in *1 Henry IV*, although Falstaff also employs the language of youthful social rebellion in robbing the "caterpillars" of their wealth.[74] Sir John, like F's Fenton, carries urban riot with him to the country, as do his three followers, to Slender's detriment.

When Slender accuses Nym of the theft, the corporal threatens reprisals "if you run the nuthook's humour on me" (1.1.151–1.1.152). *Nuthook*, an implement for dragging nut-tree branches within reach, was thieves' cant for a constable or arresting officer; Doll uses the term in *2 Henry IV* when the constables hand her over.[75] Pistol has just labeled Evans a "mountain foreigner" (1.1.145). To a London audience, the word connotes an unfree inhabitant born outside the city, and Pistol adds "mountain" to underline Evans's Welsh origins as well. Given the joke about the charge-house on the mountain in *Love's Labour's Lost*, it is tempting to see a glancing blow at the parson's duties as a schoolmaster, vividly depicted in 4.1. Constable, parish priest (or "the priest o' th' town," 2.1.140), and schoolmaster: as with Dull, Nathaniel, and Holofernes, the triplet of low-level local officialdom is intimated in Evans's social role and his efforts to make peace between the country-folk and city-schemers who have converged on Windsor. Falstaff later says that "the knave constable" almost placed him in the stocks as the witch of Brainford (4.5.114). The parish vocabulary was hardly peculiar to London. But the incursion of the tavern world of the second historical tetralogy, with its pick-purses, humors, and nuthooks, lends the Windsor setting an urban atmosphere from the first scene onward. Moreover, all these examples are found only in the Folio version.

Slender is an unstable character who combines rural and urban attributes. In both Q and F, he asks Ann about barking dogs and bears in the town in the absurd attempt at courtship that follows the opening wrangles of Act 1, Scene 1 (lines 263–264; Q, A4 recto). In F, however, he brags in greater detail: "I love the sport well, but I shall as soon quarrel at it as any man in England. . . . I have seen Sackerson loose twenty times, and have taken him by the chain" (1.1.266–1.1.267, 1.1.270–1.1.272). Sackerson the bear was a star of the Paris Garden, a bear-baiting pit close by the Globe Theater.[76] Has Slender merely visited London, Bartholomew Cokes-like, or has he resided there, a participant in metropolitan "riot" like Fenton? Other very specific London references attach themselves to Falstaff, the prime scapegoat for urban–rural mixing and the anxieties it provokes. In both Q and F, Falstaff imaginatively prowls through the city and its corporeal, indeed olfactory, topography as he woos Mrs. Ford. "I cannot cog," he claims, "like a many of these lisping hawthorn-buds that come like women in men's apparel, and smell like Bucklersbury in simple time." Falstaff recalls women dressed as men and men who behave like women all at once, and places them in Cheapside's Bucklersbury Street where members of the Grocers' Company and other herb-sellers had their fragrant shops. Doesn't he love Mrs. Page? "Thou mightst as well say I love to walk by the Counter-gate, which is as hateful to me as the reek of a lime-kill," or kiln, Falstaff replies (3.3.63–3.3.73; cf Q, D4 verso). The previous association of untoward women and smell reappears in the assimilation of poor Mrs. Page to both the common city nuisance of lime-making, the source of mortar for building, and the depths of the debtors' prison in Southwark.

Falstaff's imaginative geography of London bridges both texts and brings out the latent urban character of F's language, or its "red-lattice phrases," as he calls Pistol's tavern-window shaded speech (2.2.25–2.2.26). It is only in Q, however, that the city emerges as an implicit physical setting as well as a linguistic presence, right alongside the Windsor references. The town and its forest dominate the final scene, yet it is here as well that Evans instructs the "fairie" Pead (or Bead, without the stage-Welsh "p"):

> go you & see where Brokers sleep,
> And Foxe-eyed Seriants with their mase,
> Goe laie the Proctors in the street,
> And pinch the lowsie Seriants face. (G2 verso)

In F the Fairies are sent off to bless the Castle and its Garter ceremony (5.5.56–5.5.74). Brokers, proctors, and serjeants are all titles found in the mercantile and legal professions of London. The Q speech counterbalances Evans's injunction to the first Fairy, who is sent to bother lazy servants in country houses.

Another scene in Q where the city seems literally just beyond the audience's line of sight is set in Doctor Caius's dwelling. Mrs. Quickly hides Slender's man Simple in "the Counting-house" rather than F's "closet"; Caius then retrieves "my simples in a boxe in de Counting-house" and discovers the servant (B3 verso; cf. F, 1.4.35, 1.4.58). The unwitting pun on "simple(s)" takes us back to Bucklersbury Street in simple-time and its herb-sellers, as well as Slender's obscure urban prehistory as Simple's master and a would-be romancer. In Q, Caius may be closer to an herbalist or apothecary himself than a physician, and his counting-house is a conventional stage space in a mercantile dwelling, an apt location for blending medicine with commerce.

Caius's later command that his servant look "ore de stall" to see if Evans is coming in the missed-duel scene may mean that he is waiting in or around a shop with a stall, but I think a barnyard setting is just as likely (D1 verso). In any case, it is significant that potential urban references cluster around Caius because "the French doctor" (1.4.98) is an alien—whether herb-seller or surgeon, haunter of city streets or Whitehall, he would be a familiar figure to early modern Londoners. C. J. Sisson may have been wrong in identifying him with the prominent court physician Peter Chamberlain of France, but this and other examples of European medical men of all classes resident in London attest to Caius's general pedigree.[77] There is also John Caius, who reestablished Gonville and Caius College, Cambridge as a seat of medical learning. An Englishman, Caius was nevertheless a notorious recusant, and he had a close if vexed professional relationship with the Belgian anatomist Vesalius. The title of Caius's only surviving English work, *A Book Against the Sweating Sickness* (1552), is apposite to Falstaff's plight in and out of the buck basket.[78]

The foreignness and extravagance of medicine during the later sixteenth century may be indicated in the Host's puzzling epithets for Shakespeare's Doctor Caius: "Thou art a Castalian-king-Urinal: Hector of Greece, my boy!" (2.3.31–2.3.32). A *urinal* was a glass for "casting" or examining urine, and *Castalian* suggests Castilian or Spanish, perhaps with reference to *King* Philip of Spain, whose oppression of the Netherlands sent many francophone Walloons to England. There were more Walloons than exiles from France in the French Church in London.[79] Hector was from Troy, not Greece, but if "grease" is meant, then the scatological greasiness of *Love's Labour's Lost* (4.1.136) may be relevant. The Spaniard Armado plays Hector, and he writes of "physic" and fluids in his letter to the King (1.1.226–1.1.237). Hector Nunez and Roderigo Lopez, who were both Iberian and Jewish, were the most prominent physicians at Elizabeth's court. Don or "Dun" Armado from "tawny Spain" stands for both non-English alienness and non-European blackness (4.3.195, 1.1.171). In *Merry Wives*, the Host calls Caius "my Ethiopian"; the F reading "my Francisco" for Q's "my francoyes" or *françois* in the next sentence encapsulates the fusing of French and Spanish qualities under cover of the doctor's expanding otherness.[80] Caius is the chief alien encroacher in his play, just as Armado is in *Love's Labour's Lost*, and both figures are defined largely by irregular speech. Caius, however, is much closer to the kind of stranger one might actually have encountered outside the theater, despite his less sympathetic, painfully broad characterization.

The urinal is king and castalian in both Q and F. References to aliens in the context of citizen life are especially abundant in the Folio text. For the remainder of my reading of *The Merry Wives of Windsor*, I refer to a conflated edition based on F, noting divergences and common phrases between the texts if they pertain to citizen culture. When Falstaff sends Bardolph to the Host to become a tapster, he does so to reduce the expense accrued by his hangers-on and helpers. He dismisses Pistol and Nym as well, when they refuse to carry a letter each to Mistresses Page and Ford. "French thrift, you rogues," he says, for his retinue will now consist only of "myself and skirted page," who is sent off with both the missives (1.3.80). Mrs. Quickly does complain of her numerous tasks in Caius's service during the next scene (1.4.89–1.4.92). There is little external evidence that the French or other strangers were known for small households, although Caius's stinginess and irascibility toward servants bears comparison with that of Shylock, who parts with Launcelot, locks his doors, and mutters "Fast bind, fast find.—/A proverb never stale in thrifty mind" (*Merchant* 2.5.54). Thrifty minds would certainly have suited the impecunious and closed immigrant communities of London, whose inner workings remained mysterious to their English neighbors. Another common complaint of the London Companies, however, concerned the great number of short-term apprenticeships alien artisans offered to their own people.[81] Stranger households were too large in the public mind, not too small. In 1523, Parliament prevented them from employing more than two journeymen, but strangers circumvented the enforcement of such measures throughout the century, at least according to the citizens. The weavers petitioned the French Church itself in 1595 on a number of matters, including workshops that "keep more looms and servants than any freemen dare do."[82] Falstaff's "French thrift" may reflect the required limitations on French, Walloon, and other households, just as "French brawl" could mean rioting against, not by, francophone aliens. Or, it might be an ironic invitation to catcalls from an audience of apprentices and their citizen masters.

Falstaff, that thorough scion of Merry England, is nevertheless associated with the strange and exotic in a number of other places, too. In 1.3 he calls Mrs. Page "a region in Guiana," and says that she and Mrs. Ford "shall be my East and West Indies, and I will trade to them both" (lines 65, 67–68). A braggart soldier like Armado, Falstaff recalls Philip of Spain and his mercantilist empire with this witticism. Closed trading brings his ambitions close to home, however, to Spain's competitors. Mrs. Page soliloquizes over her letter: "What an unweighed behaviour hath this Flemish drunkard picked—with the devil's name—out of my conversation, that he dares in this manner assay me?" (2.1.22–2.1.25). Many goldsmiths in London were Dutch or Flemish, and "assay" is a technical term of their art: the implicit "gold" Falstaff seeks in his West Indies, unweighed even though Mrs. Page's behavior has not been light, is being further tested.[83] Flemings, like the Dutch, the Germans, and the Danes, were supposed to be heavy drinkers and eaters. Falstaff, who mentions sack in the letter, fits the bill. Critics have placed Falstaff between court and tavern worlds, as well as masculine and feminine bodily dispositions.[84] His gluttony, avarice, and urban connections station him between England and Europe just as surely, or unsurely, in *Merry Wives*. Mrs. Ford truculently caps the buck basket arrangements with the vow: "we'll use this unwholesome humidity, this gross watery pumpion" (3.3.35–3.3.36). As in the riot scene of *Sir Thomas More* and Costard's jape about impersonating "Pompion the Great" in *Love's Labour's Lost*, the pumpkin comically imparts an unhealthy, swollen, and damp air to the proceedings, invoking the watery landscape of the Low Countries as well as Falstaff's dropsical bulk. These are the only appearances of the vegetable in Shakespeare.

Describing his sojourn in the basket, Falstaff also refers to food, cooking, and water:

> stopped in like a strong distillation with stinking clothes that fretted in their own grease—think of that—a man of my kidney—think of that—that am as subject to heat as butter . . . And at the height of this bath, when I was more than half stewed in grease, like a Dutch dish, to be thrown into the Thames and cooled, glowing hot, in that surge, like a horse-shoe. (3.5.103–3.5.112)

Falstaff goes from knightly and English kidney to a Dutch dish; the domestic becomes foreign when everyday tasks like cookery, laundry, bathing, and smithery are blended chaotically together as boundaries disappear. Dutch cooking was reputed to be fat and buttery, like the Falstaff of *1 Henry IV*, who is "As fat as butter" (2.4.504; see also 2.4.117–2.4.120). The worst thing the knight can say of Ford—to his face, in disguise as Brook—is "Hang him, mechanical salt-butter rogue!" (2.2.267). Salt-butter was an inferior product imported from Flanders, where they kept the best butter for themselves; rude mechanical townsmen like Ford could afford it. A few lines later, Ford transfers the play's dairy complex to Mrs. Ford:

> I will rather trust a Fleming with my butter, Parson Hugh the Welshman with my cheese, an Irishman with my aqua-vitae bottle, or a thief to walk my ambling gelding, than my wife with herself. (lines 290–294)

In Q, the Fleming and butter are omitted, leaving Hugh Evans and cheese (one of many Welsh cheese jokes), the Irishman and whiskey, and the horse thief, who anticipates the "German" subplot at the

Garter Inn. Mrs. Ford is another pleasurable possession who can't be trusted, only this time commodity and abuser are joined in one. Here we have an instance of the other as a "thief of enjoyment," in the phrase's ordinary language if not its full psychoanalytic sense.[85] The ethnic neighbor enjoys his food, or rather our moderate version of his food, to excess. We have gelded our horse and taught it to amble, but the thief will free it, returning the beast to criminality rather than nature. The breakdown of bodily boundaries is also at stake. The woman should not be trusted with the urban interloper because she cannot be left to herself: femininity is already other, already enjoys itself and thus threatens our enjoyment of it. This is Ford's citizen perspective. Falstaff's suffering is different, for his true punishment may be that he experiences the impossible from the citizen point of view—he is both alien and autochthonous at once, female as well as male, base and aristocratic. As in *Love's Labour's Lost*, anxieties about the other's enjoyment extend to a medium of the play itself, that is, language. Evans replies to Falstaff's repeated jibes about cheese in his stage-Welsh accent: "Seese is not good to give putter: your belly is all butter." The food metaphor governs here, too: having "fretted" in women's clothes like a Dutch dish, Falstaff complains that he stands taunted "of one that makes fritters of English" (5.5.141, 5.5.144). Evans, Caius, and Mrs. Quickly all slice, dice, and fry the English language.

Habitation as well as diet endangers citizen enjoyment in the play. The Fords and Pages are comfortable neighbors who pass back and forth between their houses, but almost everyone else is displaced in some sense. Caius's dwelling is ringed about by Quickly's worry and its master's aversion to visitors (1.4). We never see Evans's parsonage. Shallow and perhaps Slender, from Gloucester in the Folio, stay at the Garter Inn (2.3). Falstaff and his original train do as well, at a cost of ten pounds a week (1.2.8). Fenton drifts in and out, "haunting" Page's house, and enlisting the aid of "good mine host" at the Garter (3.4.67, 4.6). The Inn is less a place than placelessness itself, so much so that Falstaff accepts Brook's sudden appearance there, and the audience is not surprised to hear about "the German" and company in 4.3. Ford enters as Brook to bribe Falstaff to tempt his wife, portraying the stranger's love for Mrs. Ford with a trope. It is "Like a fair house built on another man's ground, so that I have lost my edifice by mistaking the place where I erected it" (2.2.209–2.2.211). Sexual punning aside, the figure recalls the fantasies of housing and possession in *The Comedy of Errors*. In addition, it expresses the bourgeois splicing of adultery, theft, and real estate that Patricia Parker has examined in *Merry Wives* itself.[86]

The image also has a complex antialien background. It is unlikely, as once was thought, that the lines refer directly to the Theater, built on leased ground and eventually disassembled after the lease expired in 1597 to build the Globe in 1599 across the Thames. Buildings erected on others' property were common enough to be proverbial in the period. The proverb took on new life, however, in a city where aliens needed housing and unscrupulous builders took advantage of both strangers and unwitting landlords. In 1587, for example, a land-lord sued to recover rent when he discovered tenements had been built on the Tower bulwark near St. Katherine's precinct.[87] Tower Ward and St. Katherine's were two places where Dutch church con-gregants had settled; they were typical of the hitherto neglected spots within the city and, as more often, outside its bounds where strangers lived.[88] Complaints about builders subdividing properties to squeeze in more aliens were a regular part of the citizen litany.[89] In Q *Merry Wives*, the passage reads "like a faire house set vpon Another mans foundation" rather than "ground," and it omits the dispirited explana-tory clause (C4 verso). A royal proclamation of 1602 summarized two decades' worth of frustration with London's growth, command-ing an end to divided buildings and mandating that a new house could only be constructed "upon the foundation of a former dwelling."[90] The Quarto's language has an even clearer pertinence to contemporary housing disputes than the Folio's, so this is one case where the urban setting latent in Q also affects its vocabulary. Since it was permissible, and soon obligatory, to build on an existing foundation in order to limit the density of housing, Q's Brook may also be suggesting that Mrs. Ford, the "faire house" in this reading, is almost his already. Since he is Ford, she is indeed: two houses do occupy the same space because Brook's is a fiction erected in the Garter Inn.

The Host, with his fantastical epithets like "Kaiser" and "Cavaliero," carries the placeless spirit of the Garter with him through town and field. He calls Page, Ford, and Shallow "Anheers" when he leads them off to watch the would-be duelists. This could be another Dutch reference, derived or corrupted from *myn-heers*, meaning "gentlemen" (2.1.209 note), but it may also be a rendering of *anier*, French for "muledriver."[91] In any case, it works as a multilingual nonce-term. Caius would strike Evans as dead as a "herring" (2.3.11), but the Host makes peace between these symmetrically outlandish neighbors, "Gallia and Gaul, French and Welsh, soul-curer and body-curer" (3.1.89–3.1.90). It is soon after this that they apparently resolve to disguise themselves as Germans, as if to up the foreign ante while bringing in their revenge.

We first hear of "the German" and "the gentlemen" and their request for three horses to meet a duke who is coming to court in 4.3. Q refers only to "three gentlemen" and "Duke the Stanger[*sic*]" at this point (F2 verso). Later, Bardolph reports the horses stolen by the "cozeners," who rode off like three Doctor Faustuses or German devils. "Germans are honest men," the Host insists (4.5.62–4.5.66). Evans comes in to warn him about "three cozen-Germans" who have tricked local inn-keepers out of horses and money, and Caius completes the jest by telling him that no "Duke de Jarmanie" is expected at court (lines 70–77, 81–84). The Quarto's Caius, however, claims that "a Germaine Duke" has come to court and cozened the hosts of Brentford and Reading, and Evans calls the thieves "three sorts of cosen garmombles" (F4 verso). This word may combine the obscure insult "geremumble" with "German" or "Garmain," and there is an outside chance it also refers chiastically to the former Count Mompelgard, whose attainment of the Garter as Duke of Wurtemberg in 1597 has been used to date the play in a still-controversial manner.[92]

Arguing for 1598 and the public theater as the home of the play, Barbara Freedman has shown that two other well-known incidents involving foreign noblemen may lie also behind the cousin-Germans, and that popular suspicion of German duplicity in trading relations was a factor as well. Emperor Rudolph expelled the Merchant–Adventurers in 1597, and Elizabeth told the Mayor and Sheriffs of London to expel the Hanse merchants from the Steelyard the following year.[93] Commercial dealings were probably a consideration in entertaining Mompelgard and giving in to his Garter ambitions in the first place.[94] German-ness in *Merry Wives* seems part of a different order than French and Dutch ethnicity—the aristocratic brotherhood, or cousin-hood, of the Garter ceremony. But the two orders of strangeness interpenetrate in the play just as they did in court and city politics. Q's phrase "Duke the St[r]anger" renders alien and noble status convertible even though it seems to be an attempt at a noble title. The Host's faith in the honesty of Germans would be as likely to raise a laugh from an urban audience as a court assembly; square dealing as much as aristocratic honor were at stake, more so for the unfortunate proprietor of the Garter Inn, a business that relied in part upon strangers just like many others did. When Evans and Caius, aided perhaps by Nym or Pistol, execute their jest at his expense, they take advantage of his dependence on the court by turning themselves into gentlemen Germans off to meet a duke, reflecting the mix of middle- and upper-class interests that the English perceived in the German towns and sometimes sought to emulate.

Among the immediately preceding allusions to citizen culture and its perceptions of aliens, only "French thrift," "Dutch dish," "fair house," and the Germans appear in Q as well as F. In linguistic terms, Folio *Merry Wives* is more reflective of citizen concerns than the Quarto, not less, despite Q's occasional hints at an urban setting. This does not preclude a court audience for either version, no more than the language of *Love's Labour's Lost* determines the audience for that overtly aristocratic comedy. Wherever the locations of the earliest performances of both plays might have been, their language conveyed an urban sensibility that was intelligible to high and low. In moving from venue to setting, we see that Windsor in *Merry Wives* already provided a mix of court and town life in the fictional world on stage: the court traveled between London and Windsor, became part of town life when it was in Windsor, and its Garter Feast could be held in either London or Windsor, depending on the queen's presence.

The final scenes of the Folio provide another Windsor allusion that links London to the town in a less expected manner. Fenton plans to steal Ann Page out from under both Caius and Slender during the Herne's Oak episode. Slender will take a disguised boy to Eton, while Mrs. Page,

> firm for Doctor Caius, hath appointed
> That he shall likewise shuffle her away,
> While other sports are tasking of their minds,
> And at the dean'ry, where a priest attends,
> Straight marry her. (4.6.27–4.6.31)

Mrs. Page tells Caius to "take her by the hand, away with her to the deanery," and confidently announces that "she is now with the Doctor at the deanery, and there married" when Slender's deception is revealed (5.3.2; 5.5.201–5.5.202). But Caius has been fobbed off with a boy as well, and Fenton gets the girl in the play's final blending of aristocratic and middle-class interests. The word "deanery" appears nowhere else in Shakespeare, and its repetition has suggested another example of local color to editors: the deanery of St. George's Chapel at Windsor Castle may be meant.[95] It is also significant that the deanery is linked with Caius, the French doctor. In 1550, the Dutch and French communities in London had been granted the church of Austin Friars. The French immediately requested a separate place of worship, and the Privy Council allowed them to rent the nearby hospital of St. Anthony, leaving the friary church to the Dutch. These were the Dutch and French churches mentioned in the reports of the Dutch

Church Libel. The landlord of the French church at St. Anthony's was the Dean and Chapter of Windsor.[96] In *The Merry Wives of Windsor*, the deanery is emphasized as the site of Caius's ultimate disgrace: instead of marrying an English woman, "I ha' married *un garçon*, a boy; *un paysan*, by gar; a boy" (5.5.203–5.5.205). Intermarriage is trumped by a same-sex union construed in part as class humiliation. The deanery is another indefinite location that links Windsor with London and one of its stranger communities. The loss of St. Anthony's to the French implicates Windsor in the ethnic politics of London real estate. The comic undoing of miscegenation at the Windsor deanery curtails Mrs. Page's newfound power over her family, but it also blocks an ambitious Frenchman's plan to build his house on another man's land.

Early modern pastoral puts the complex into the simple, or the city into a simplified idea of the country.[97] In *The Merry Wives of Windsor*, the jarring presence of a Frenchman and his alien accent in a country town parodies this movement, but his comeuppance rectifies the pastoral balance in the end. The action moves to France itself in *As You Like It*, a more recognizably pastoral exercise. The well-worn convention of aristocratic rustication and disguise literalizes the complication of the simple in pastoral. The disguises in *As You Like It* retain an urban as well as a courtly cast, despite the possible echoes of rural masquerade and political protest in Rosalind's cross-dressed figure and Celia's umber-darkened face.[98] As in Thomas Lodge's *Rosalynde* (1590), the play's principal source, Shakespeare's heroine chooses the name *Ganymede* for her new self. In doing so, she chooses a common term for a man's boy lover; the contemporary word "catamite" was also derived from the Greek name. As a slang term, "Ganymede" was a recognizable court and city usage, despite the pastoralism of its classical origin in the tale of the shepherd youth snatched by Jove.[99] In *Merry Wives*, Caius evidently fears that a Ganymede has been thrust upon him in the rural chapel. Celia takes a new name as well, saying she will call herself by "Something that hath a reference to my state. / No longer Celia, but Aliena."[100] As with Ganymede, the pseudonym is borrowed from *Rosalynde*. Lodge's character was originally named Alinda, however, and so the change from Celia to Aliena in the play is more marked. Shakespeare adds the umber with which she resolves to besmirch her face; as Celia declines from the class and gender standards of the light-complexioned court lady, she also recalls tawny aliens on the stage, such as Armado and perhaps Caius. The complexities of urban alienage, as well as Celia's alienation from her status as Duke Frederick's daughter, lie behind the name she adopts in Shakespeare's version.

An air of alienage also hangs about Orlando in the forest. He represents the insertion of the city into the country. In verses read aloud by Celia-Aliena, he exclaims:

> Why should this desert be,
> For it is unpeopled? No.
> Tongues I'll hang on every tree,
> That shall civil sayings show. (3.2.122–3.2.125)

As Samuel Johnson maintained, "civil" is opposed to the solitary or natural state of life here.[101] The poems Orlando tacks onto trees convert them into subjects, populating and urbanizing the wilderness. Yet their sayings are commonplace and trite, "citizen" rather than courtly. "Have you not been acquainted with goldsmiths' wives, and conned them out of rings?" Jaques asks (3.2.266–3.2.268). A city comedy of adultery, he suggests, is the hidden source of Orlando's amorous language. Rosalind does not know what to make of the tree-hanged verses or their author, either. She wants to consume the news of his identity. "So you may put a man in your belly," Celia jokes. "Is he of God's making?" Rosalind replies (3.2.201–3.2.202). Once more, the familiar proverb betokens anxiety over the origins of someone who uses language in a strange manner. It appears later in the play, submerged in Rosalind-Ganymede's debate with Jaques, who now appears in the guise of a traveler. "Look you lisp," she chides, "disable all the benefits of your own country; be out of love with your nativity, and almost chide God for making you that countenance you are" (4.1.31–4.1.35). "Nativity" is used in the sense of birth as a determinant of nationality, just like it is at the end of *The Comedy of Errors*. Orlando wanders in while Ganymede-Rosalind rails at "Monsieur Traveller." It is Jaques, the play's scapegoat, who symbolically relieves Orlando of the suspicion of alienage.

As You Like It blends civility and rusticity in other ways. Duke Senior lives in the forest of Arden "like the old Robin Hood of England" (1.1.116). As in *Love's Labour's Lost*, the country scenes in the play connote Englishness, although a detailed urban setting is not sketched in for either the court or Oliver's nearby house and lands. Instead, the forest itself is made over in the city's image through the speech of some of its inhabitants. The exiled duke, who begins Act 2, Scene 1 by placing the country far above the court, nevertheless continues with his regrets about the hunting of deer: "poor dappled fools," they are the "native burghers of this desert city," killed in their own confines (2.1.22–2.1.25). In a "Poem in Commendation of the Solitarie Life" published with *Scillaes Metamorphosis* in 1590, Lodge refers to "the citizens of Forest," and in *Rosalynde* itself he describes trees as "citizens of Wood."[102] Orlando converts trees into wooden citizens by giving them tongues through his verses. In Thomas Nashe's *Pierce Penilesse* (1592), the knight's allegory tells of a fair deer poisoned by the evil bear: "when . . . all the nimble Cittizens of the Wood betooke them to their Laire, this youthfull Lorde of the Lawnds, all fainte and malcontent . . . strayed aside from the rest of his fellowship, and betooke him all carelesly to the corrupted fountaine."[103] Following Lodge and Nashe, Ganymede and Aliena visit a woodland pastoral setting and find as much urbanity as they bring with them.

The melancholy Jaques shares the duke's moral style and its central metaphor. A lord reports Jaques's address to a stricken deer, who has been "Left and abandon'd of his velvet friend":

> Anon a careless herd,
> Full of the pasture, jumps along by him
> And never stays to greet him. "Ay," quoth Jaques,
> "Sweep on you fat and greasy citizens,
> 'Tis just the fashion. Wherefore do you look
> Upon that poor and broken bankrupt there?"
> Thus most invectively he pierceth through
> The body of country, city, court. (2.1.50, 2.1.52–2.1.59)

Jaques's rhetorical vision superposes an urban vista upon the forest: the unfortunate deer, earlier called a "hairy fool" (2.1.40), becomes a bankrupt citizen abandoned by his "fat and greasy" fellows and his velvet-coated or court-affecting friend, according to the current fashion of city ways. As the lord puts it, Jaques is like a swordsman who runs through the triple-bodied *socium* of traditional satire, sandwiching the city between the court and the country as he skewers all three. In much of *As You Like It*, as in some of the other comedies discussed in this book so far, the city is a kind of excluded middle between the other two terms, but in this passage its place is firmly and memorably fixed.

The metaphorical subtext of *As You Like It* sustains a subtle and comical connection between deer, citizens, and fools, a reflection perhaps of the country, city, and court triad. Duke Senior speculates that Jaques has been "transform'd into a beast," because he has proved so elusive (2.7.1). When we finally see them together, Jaques describes his encounter with Touchstone in the forest and his resolution to become a fool himself:

> I must have liberty
> Withal, as large a charter as the wind,

> To blow on whom I please, for so fools have;
> And they that are most galled with my folly,
> They most must laugh. And why sir must they so?
> The why is plain as way to parish church. (2.7.47–2.7.52)

Fool-ship is implicitly bound to citizenship in this speech. The fool's liberty echoes the freedom of the burgher; folly must be given a charter by the duke, just as cities and their guilds were chartered by the Crown. The "why" of the fool's comic authority is as plain as the way to parish church, not only because of the visibility of the local steeple, but because the parish served as the central venue for foolish citizens and their ways. Jaques's view remains an aristocratic one: he can only understand the freedom of the city by likening it to the license of the court jester. Both are spaces, or counter-spaces, allowed by sovereign power, spaces for criticism that are nevertheless comically self-confounding. As a fool on the citizen model, then, he will criticize other citizen-fools, turning satire upon itself—but only by attacking types, not individuals, of course. "What woman in the city do I name," he asks, "When that I say the city-woman bears/The cost of princes on unworthy shoulders?" (2.7.74–2.7.76). As so often, the satire of citizenship begins with the figure of the citizen's wife, extravagant and, as the verb "bear" possibly bears out, concupiscent. Jaques's later jibe at Orlando about rings and goldsmiths' wives is of the same genre.[104]

The mention of the city-woman hints at another aspect of the deer–citizens–fools complex: when they are cuckolded, foolish citizens become horned beasts. Once again, the city becomes the country and the country the city; the joke underlies the sentimentality of Jaques's bankrupt and abandoned stag in the forest. Examples from elsewhere in Shakespeare and his contemporaries are too numerous to list, but one especially comes to mind. Mrs. Page points to the horns of Falstaff's Herne disguise and says, "Do not these fair yokes/Become the forest better than the town?" (*Merry Wives* 5.5.108–5.5.109). The deer-slaying scene in *As You Like It* drives the association home, with all of its uncanny mixture of pagan resonance and urban humor. Jaques demands that he who killed the deer sport its horns as a Roman "branch of victory," and asks for a song, which runs:

> Take thou no scorn to wear the horn,
> It was a crest ere thou was born.
>   Thy father's father wore it,
>   And thy father bore it. (4.2.5, 4.2.14–4.2.17)

Touchstone, rather than the anonymous deer-slaying lord, becomes the main scapegoat for the anxiety of adultery in the play, just as

Jaques takes on the anxiety of alienage. In Act 5, Jaques compares the stage, destined to fill with couples, to Noah's Ark, and when Touchstone enters with Audrey, he announces: "Here comes a pair of very strange beasts, which in all tongues are called fools" (5.4.36–5.4.38). When he departs a few moments later he famously gives their marriage two months (5.4.191).

Jaques's pessimism seems justified because of Touchstone's earlier ruminations upon his first attempt at marriage, which he overheard. Waiting for Sir Oliver Martext in the forest, the fool had told Audrey:

> here we have no temple but the wood, no assembly but horn-beasts. But what though? Courage! As horns are odious, they are necessary. . . . Poor men alone? No, No. The noblest deer hath them as huge as the rascal. Is the single man therefore blessed? No. As a walled town is more worthier than a village, so is the forehead of a married man more honourable than the bare brow of a bachelor. (3.3.43–3.3.46, 3.3.50–3.3.55)

The fooling is particularly rich in this overlooked passage, and it foreshadows both Ganymede-Rosalind's trial of Orlando in Act 4 and Hymen's puzzling role at the conclusion of the comedy. The assembly of horn-beasts and the noblest deer recall the citizen-deer of Duke Senior and Jaques. The urban community has been transposed to the forest again, but this time to the parish church or temple itself and the private rite of marriage. Private is really public, however, for the cuckold's horns, like the deer's, are the common burden of males rich and poor. And this is good, partly for its leveling effect—Touchstone's urban view is quite different from Jaques's aristocratic attempt to enter the mode of citizen satire.

The commonalty of horns is also good for a mysterious reason: married cuckolds are more honorable than bachelors just as walled towns are worthier than country villages. Shakespeare may be thinking of defensive structures known as "horn-work" (3.3.55 note). The equation of the single life to the rural scene and marriage to the town sets up the closing movement of the play, in which the main characters no sooner pair off than they prepare to leave Arden. Sylvius and Phoebe are an exception, it is true, but this reminds us of how the pastoral setting itself has blocked love until now. The walled town is the locus of love fulfilled in marriage, but also of cuckoldry, and perhaps we are to recall this as Orlando and Rosalind, and Oliver and Celia, leave the forest with Touchstone and Audrey. But why are horns necessary as well as odious? The honor of married life conceals dishonor while buttressing an unspoken compact among men. In Act 5, Hymen's entrance and the song that attends it suggests an oddly practical reason as well:

> Wedding is great Juno's crown,
> O blessed bond of board and bed.
> 'Tis Hymen peoples every town;
> High wedlock then be honoured.
> Honour, high honour and renown
> To Hymen, god of every town. (5.4.140–5.4.145)

Marriage generates population: Orlando had earlier claimed that his poems of unrequited love peopled the forest by giving tongues to trees, but it is in town that the real work takes place. Honor is invoked again, thrice, but with Touchstone's praise of the horns in mind, the audience might surmise that cuckoldry is at least as responsible for peopling towns under the aegis of marriage as high wedlock itself.

The policing of sexuality across the shifting bounds of marriage returns us to *Measure for Measure*, the Jacobean comedy that may now seem less alone as the chief "urban" play in Shakespeare's canon. Lucio complains of the precise Angelo in terms Touchstone and the praisers of hymen would understand: "this ungenitured agent will unpeople the province with continency" (3.2.167–3.2.169). His comrades in the bawdy house of Act 1, Scene 2, with their talk of venereal disease, contribute to the well-known association of soldiers with sex and the spread of alien contagion among the population of city and suburb, the flip-side to needed procreation. The First Gentleman contrasts his "English kersey" cloth with Lucio's "pilled" or bald French velvet, a syphilis patch; Lucio acknowledges the French crown he owes to Mrs. Overdone, the bawd (1.2.32–1.2.33, 1.2.48). He has already accused the second cavalier of willingly saying grace in any language, or in any religion, as their friend adds (1.2.22–1.2.23). It is no wonder that Constable Elbow fears that Overdone's tavern will supply white and brown bastard (3.2.3).

In spite of the urban ambience of the tavern-brothel scenes, Jean E. Howard has pointed out the virtual absence of citizens and especially artisans as characters in *Measure for Measure*. The contrast with the city comedy of Marston, Dekker, and others is marked. Indeed, Shakespeare's Vienna is bereft of the mechanicals, if not quite the salt-butter rogues, that we find in the ancient Athens of *A Midsummer Night's Dream*. As Howard observes, "Vienna seems to have no legitimate tradesmen and no civic culture separable from the person of the duke," a manifestly sovereign, if not absolutist, figure. All this prepares us for a reconsideration of the history plays in chapter 2, where the divergence from the citizen-history of a drama like Heywood's *Edward IV* seems equally stark.[105]

Nevertheless, *Measure for Measure* remains tied to London by its "proclamation," which echoes the proclamation of September 16, 1603 mandating the destruction of suburban "houses" to discourage the plague and the dissolute persons who supposedly spread it.[106] Claudio's arrest somehow "agrees" with the proclamation (1.2.73). Pompey Bum delivers the bad news to Mrs. Overdone:

> *Mis. O[verdone]*. What proclamation, man?
> *Pom[pey]*. All houses in the suburbs of Vienna must be plucked down.
> *Mis. O[verdone]*. And what shall become of those in the city?
> *Pom[pey]*. They shall stand for seed: they had gone down too, but that a wise burgher put in for them. (1.2.87–1.2.92)

In standing for seed, the city brothels undergo yet another exchange of urban for rural space. The wise burgher who effects the transformation, clearly biding his time, reminds us that many brothels outside and within the city limits were owned by citizens like Richard Watwood, a member of the Grocer's Company. Philip Henslowe, longstanding rival to Shakespeare's acting company, was both a dyer and a brothel-keeper as well as a theatrical impresario and exponent of citizen drama. He was just embarking upon his conversion to distinguished court and city office-holder when *Measure for Measure* was first performed—but the point is that his mixed career was fairly typical, and Pompey's jibe need not be directed at him or any other enterprising freeman in particular.[107] Angelo uses the language of urban spaces in bitterly condemning himself for accosting the intended nun Isabella. "Having waste ground enough," he asks, "Shall we desire to raze the sanctuary/ And pitch our evils there?" (2.2.170–2.2.172). If "evils" means privies, as some evidence suggests, then Angelo is likening himself to people who encroach on present or former ecclesiastical property with lavatories or the middens they produce. "Thieves for their robbery have authority," he says in the same soliloquy, "When judges steal themselves" (2.2.176–2.2.177). Brothels—called "houses of resort" or of "profession" in the play (1.2.93; 4.3.2–4.3.3)—are implicitly compared to privies or "houses of office."[108] In general, Angelo is like those wise citizens who condemn prostitutes while keeping bawdy houses themselves.[109]

The year 1603 also saw a further strengthening of the office of Provost Marshal by London's Court of Aldermen. Marshals had been assigned to direct constables in the searching out of vice in the 1590s, a measure that probably indicates a lack of faith in the lower officials. The duties of the Provost Marshal and his assistants included escorting vagabonds to prison as well as overseeing constables.[110] The Provost in *Measure for Measure* explicitly performs the first of these functions, if not the second, parading Claudio through the streets of Vienna at Angelo's command (1.2.108–1.2.111). He is sympathetic to his prisoner's plight, and ultimately bows to the authority of the Duke's signet in agreeing to the supposed Friar's elaborate plan to fake Claudio's execution (4.2.186–4.2.194). The Duke pretends to dismiss the Provost, and then rewards him with a higher place for his "care and secrecy" at the end (5.1.459, 5.1.527–5.1.528). Just as the Aldermen's commissioning of the Provost Marshal occurred under pressure from the Privy Council, so Shakespeare's Provost holds a city office that is commandeered by royal authority.[111]

Elbow contrasts with the Provost as an inept royal officer at the local level. He calls himself "the poor Duke's constable," an example of his verbal misplacings, but finally an accurate clue to his position (2.1.46–2.1.47). In *Much Ado About Nothing*, Dogberry and the watch are likewise "the poor Duke's officers." Constables "present the Prince's own person," and may arrest him if they meet him in the night.[112] By mid-Tudor times, constables were mediating figures, paradoxically chosen at the local level but representative of royal authority. Escalus asks if there are not other men in Elbow's ward who can serve as constable, and is told that when his neighbors are chosen, they pay Elbow to serve in their place; the deputy then asks for the names of six or seven men, "the most sufficient of your parish" (2.1.262–2.1.270). Escalus's assumptions about jurisdiction correspond to the situation in London, where constables were chosen by parish vestries but remained officers of the ward, the secular unit of government. There is less evidence that candidates were reluctant to serve and often bought their way out, although this was the Privy Council's fear.[113]

In *Love's Labour's Lost*, Constable Dull is tied to the parish, but in *Much Ado About Nothing* and *Measure for Measure*, the constable's implication in the sovereign side of his awkwardly split mandate is emphasized. The hasty Leonato, governor of Messina, who is as good as "any man in the city," is about as responsible as his bumbling constable for delaying the revelations that exonerate Hero (3.5.25). Don Pedro, the prince Dogberry claims to present, also takes the blame (5.1.270–5.1.272). If citizenship remains bound up with sovereignty, sovereignty is also dragged downward by the mechanisms of citizen government. In the late comedy, Escalus is made to sound a lot like

Elbow in his unwitting *double entendres* about handling Isabella darkly by the final scene (5.1.271–5.1.278), just as Angelo knowingly compares himself to a justice who steals.

Citizen life is in fact degraded throughout *Measure for Measure*. There may be no tradesmen proper in the play, but the improper trades of pimp and hangman adopt an artisanal identity. Mrs. Overdone is "custom-shrunk," Escalus asks if Pompey's "trade" is lawful, and Isabella accuses her desperate brother of trading in sin (11.2.77; 2.1.223; 3.1.148). The hangman Abhorson insists that he practices a "mystery" and compares it abstrusely to being a tailor, since he claims the clothes of the executed. He takes on Pompey as a sort of apprentice and offers him instruction in "my trade" (4.2.41–4.2.44, 4.2.52). The ex-bawd compares his past and present occupations amid a catalog of city types (4.3.1–4.3.20). The hangman, however, is a direct arm of the governing authority, though a proverbially disreputable and abject one. In threatening Claudio's life, Angelo partakes of both abhorrent trades. As Isabella exclaims,

> O, 'tis the cunning livery of hell
> The damnedst body to invest and cover
> In precise guards! (3.1.94–3.1.96)

"Livery" might refer to a servant's uniform, making Angelo a minor devil, but given the commercial language that is associated with procuring in the play it could also call up the livery companies and their liverymen. Angelo's earlier application of the term to Isabella works best in this sense:

> Be that you are,
> That is, a woman: if you be more, you're none.
> If you be one—as you are well express'd
> By all external warrants—show it now,
> By putting on the destin'd livery. (2.4.133–2.4.137)

Maturing within the company of women, Isabella must now assume the livery—an expensive obligation as well as a privilege, and one often resisted by company members.[114] The unreformed Angelo speaks like a wise burgher again, putting in for a kind of prostitution in language that signifies both civic status and subservience to aristocratic power. His sayings are civil and uncivil at once.

Despite the degradation of citizens and their language in *Measure for Measure*, citizenship remains a constant point of reference in the play, as it does throughout Shakespearean comedy. I would like to consider how comedy as a dramatic genre binds together the very different plays discussed, briefly taking *A Midsummer Night's Dream*, a familiar and in some sense typical comedy, as my concluding example. Descending from Greek new comedy *via* its Roman practitioners, the romantic comedy of Shakespeare's time makes love and marriage the chief means by which identity is formed. In other words, comedy is about identity formation or subjectivation; romantic complications are the medium though which different modes of subjectivation are worked through on stage. Love-plots were very important to audiences, but it was their emotional charge and entertainment value that drew spectators into the theater of identity. Citizen identity had its role in this shadowy playhouse, as we see in the blend of marital and civic confusions in *The Comedy of Errors* and *The Merry Wives of Windsor*. The citizen–subject increasingly served as an ambivalent model for aristocratic subjectivation as well. Economic language and apprehension about strangers and their effect on population invade symbolic preserves like Navarre's learned court or the forest of Arden and its pastoral games, and they almost reach *The Merchant of Venice*'s Belmont itself. Sex and reproduction were the other side of love, after all, and immorality, disease, and illegitimate procreation were particularly associated with the city, as *Measure for Measure* finally exposes.

A Midsummer Night's Dream, with its half-classical, half-medieval setting in Athens and the surrounding forest, is an early work that seems largely innocent of such matters. But contention over a birth lies at the heart of its Fairy subplot. The child that Oberon demands of Titania in the forest is the son of a votress of her order, an Indian woman whose belly swelled like the sails of trading ships just as she herself fetched "merchandise" for her mistress's amusement (2.1.123–2.1.134). Procreation, commerce, and the outlandish, are brought together in this image of women as producers and consumers. The argument ruins the seasonal cycle and the universal fertility it brings. Tellingly, existing marriages like the Fairy couple's interest Shakespeare at least as much as the courtship trials of his juvenile leads. Mature marriage raises the issue of reproduction, or the lack of it, rather than romance. *The Comedy of Errors* and *Merry Wives* deal with troubles of the marriage bed, and the city or town wife figures largely in them, although not as an object of contempt as with Jaques and other satirists. We will meet the citizen's wife again in later chapters. In *A Midsummer Night's Dream*, we have both married and soon-to-be married couples: Theseus and Hippolyta, already a little at odds like husband and wife, are at a mid-point between Oberon and Titania, old hands at wedded life, and the squabbling young people, whose courtships are for awhile entirely blocked. Oberon's concluding blessing ensures that the mortals' rightful "issue" will be free of blemish and disease (5.1.389–5.1.400). His spell may be a remnant of the play's original occasion in some aristocratic wedding celebration. But the emphasis on marriage, childbirth, and legitimacy also pertains to the non-courtly audiences before whom the play was "sundry times publickely acted."[115]

The mechanicals of *A Midsummer Night's Dream*, "Hard-handed men that work in Athens," bring a note of contemporary town life in England to the marriage celebrations.[116] Peter Quince refers to "our company" (1.2.1), a phrase that melds their impromptu acting troop with craft-guild membership. Of course, in the sixteenth century, the mechanicals would have been members of different companies, to press the allusion further. Their names reflect their occupations: for instance, Bottom is a weaver, from the spindle for winding yarn, Starveling is a tailor, proverbially thin, and Snug is a joiner.[117] It may be significant that Oberon's "brawls" with Titania have caused the seasons to confuse their "wonted liveries," so that the world "now knows not which is which" (2.1.87, 2.1.111–2.1.114). The Fairies inhabit the woods beyond the city, and they are also linked with more foreign locations still, especially the India of medieval romance and early modern commerce. Beset by Oberon's love-juice, Titania will soon translate Bottom from the somewhat muddled world of his Athenian neighbors to the eternal summer of her bower, despite the ass's head Puck gives him. It is Puck who calls the neighbors "A crew of patches, rude mechanicals,/ That work for bread upon Athenian stalls" (3.2.9–3.2.10). This is a simple but memorable line, stocked with metonymic import. The stalls or shops of Athens look forward to the shop-window similes in *Love's Labour's Lost*, and to the stalls, casements, and bulks that figure citizen street-life in the history plays and Roman tragedies. The forest, on the other hand, betokens the world outside the city that challenges the identity-formation of its urban and courtly inhabitants alike. It is theater that puts the city into the country and then brings moonlight into a city chamber, with comic results.

A Midsummer Night's Dream, then, is a paradigm for the way rural settings in many comedies encode urban anxieties about identity, class, gender, and reproduction. London citizenship lies behind the verbal scrim of all the plays discussed in this book. Furthermore, citizenship here implies a form of political subjectivity for those who enjoy it, one based on economic ways of imagining social life. These include a jealous guardedness about the means of production, reproduction, and consumption, a loyal but often fearful relation to the half-visible sovereign power that still controls exchange, and abhorrence, to employ Holofernes's word, of aliens who threaten commercial competition, rivalry for royal protection, and, increasingly, ethnic difference. The corporative sense of citizenship requires exclusion, then. What is most striking about the comedies considered above, even the ones with non-city settings, is the anxiety about strangers that courses through them. Because he is an alien merchant, Egeon must proffer money or be killed by sunset; Armado is a dangerous rival for the monarch's attentions; the city's economic freedom depends on upholding Shylock's murderous bond; Falstaff rues being turned into a buttery Dutch dish. As the rhetorical performance that produces the last example shows, the exclusionary subjectivity of London citizenship is most fully realized in language, particularly the language of food, the body, and everyday life in general. Everyday life is the traditional purview of comedy and its civil sayings, but in the following chapters we shall see that language on the material level serves as the defining medium of citizenship throughout Shakespeare's drama.

CHAPTER 2

HISTORY: CIVIL BUTCHERY

According to Richard Helgerson, as we have seen, "Shakespeare's history plays are concerned above all with the consolidation and maintenance of royal power." Citizens did not interest Shakespeare much, except as the contrasting ground against which his monarchs and aristocrats defined themselves. We must turn, as Helgerson does in an unrivaled survey, to the Henslowe history plays to distinguish the victims of sovereignty among the urban middling sort. On the whole, Helgerson is right insofar as we stick to what he terms "image" or "representation" in the theater.[1] But if we return to the language of Shakespeare's history plays, we uncover an underworld of citizen speech that brings the plays closer to many in their original London audiences than the hieratic stage action at first suggests. Furthermore, citizens and citizen-types do appear in the histories, however circum-scribed or caricatured their roles seem in comparison with the suffering creations of the Henslowe authors. There is a shift between the first and second tetralogies from London settings to London language, although even in the "Henriad" Eastcheap remains a key location and reference-point. Understanding citizen and alien in Shakespeare's historical language will significantly alter, even if it does not overturn, the prevailing sense that his serious English dramas serve the interests, themselves conflicting, of court and Crown. In what follows, I offer a complete rereading of urban language and representation in all of Shakespeare's history plays. The present chapter is divided in two parts: part I deals with the first tetralogy, and includes a digression on *King John*; part II takes up the second tetralogy.

Let me add a note on my approach to textual matters in the first tetralogy. I accept recent editorial opinion that Shakespeare's hand was the determining one throughout its first three plays, although extensive collaboration, particularly involving Thomas Nashe in my view, generated these complex histories.[2] For all their many variations, I assume the First Quarto and First Folio texts of *Richard III* were written by Shakespeare. The following readings are based on modern editions that take the Folio versions of all four plays as their copy-texts. Consequently, I refer to the *Henry VI* plays by parts, like the Folio does; when necessary, I designate the first editions of parts 2 and 3 by short titles as *The Contention* and *The True Tragedy*.[3] I begin my analyses with the second part of *Henry VI* because it was probably the first play of the series to be written, followed shortly by the third part, which was clearly composed as a sequel sometime before 1591. The play known as the first part of *Henry VI* was written and performed between part 3 and *Richard III*.[4] For my purposes, it provides a retrospective survey of London's role as setting or geographical benchmark of the earlier plays that deal with later stages in the overall historical narrative. Neither the first nor second tetralogies may have been written as self-contained "cycles" or "chronicle histories," of course. It is telling, however, that the chronological composition and relative uniformity of the second tetralogy accompany the move away from London settings—even one as colorful as Eastcheap—to London language and metaphor in the later grouping of history plays. Shakespeare developed an abstract sense of the city's persistent presence in the words and actions of his aristocratic characters that matches London's phantom propinquity in the comedies.

I: THE FIRST TETRALOGY AND
KING JOHN

King Henry VI, Part 2 begins with the presentation of Margaret of Anjou to Henry by the scheming Marquess of Suffolk, who has persuaded the young king to marry her and make her queen of England. The fall of the Duke of Gloucester, Protector of the realm under Henry, is the central event in the first three acts of the play. In the opening scene, Gloucester decries Suffolk and bridles at the exchange of Anjou and Maine for the dowerless bride. The Cardinal resents his display: "What though the common people favour him,/Calling him 'Humphrey, the good Duke of Gloucester'/ . . . He will be found a dangerous Protector."[5] Gloucester's territorial patriotism, founded as it is on the sacrificial victories of English soldiers in his brother Henry V's French wars, has endeared him to the people. Yet there is another side to his reputation, which his enemies at court attempt to exploit.

The Cardinal accuses Gloucester of over-taxing the commons and the clergy. He also tells Buckingham and queen Margaret that Gloucester has subjected prisoners to cruel and unusual punishments, and that he has sold offices and towns in France (1.3.129–1.3.130, 1.3.133–1.3.138). Somerset claims that "Thy sumptuous buildings and thy wife's attire/ Have cost a mass of public treasury" (lines 131–132). Gloucester's wife, Eleanor Cobham, accompanies him, and the queen punctuates these accusations by finding an excuse to box her on the ear (line 139 SD).

Eleanor is made the scapegoat for the troubling aspects of her husband's legacy in official history and popular memory. She eggs him on to seize the crown for himself, and employs a witch, a conjurer, and a priest to raise spirits and foresee future obstacles (1.4).[6] The Cardinal and Suffolk have suborned John Hume to entrap her and besmirch Gloucester (1.2.91–1.2.99). But Eleanor lends herself to a ruse that plays upon the somewhat incoherent set of popular associations upon which her character is constructed. The conjuration scene links her to the world of village witchcraft. Somerset's jibe about her clothes recalls the satirical figure of the townsman's or citizen's wife, whose extravagant tastes drive her husband to overextend himself.[7] Queen Margaret has already sown this association in the minds of the audience:

> Not all these lords do vex me half so much
> As that proud dame, the Lord Protector's wife.
> She sweeps it through the court with troops of ladies,
> More like an empress than Duke Humphrey's wife.
> Strangers in court do take her for the Queen.
> She bears a duke's revenues on her back
> And in her heart she scorns our poverty. (1.3.76–1.3.82)

A protector's wife might well aspire to become an empress, but for a London audience in particular, the speech patterns here recall the sort of accusations city wives tossed at one another. The queen caps her rant by calling Eleanor a "base-born callet" (line 84).

Margaret is worried that strangers, in the modern sense of foreigners, think of Eleanor as queen of England because of her rich clothing. Anxiety about the alien gaze and its often ignorant potential for leveling social distinctions is characteristic of the shifting urban scene immediately outside the court as well. It is Margaret who is the stranger, of course, and Eleanor tellingly calls her "proud Frenchwoman" when she receives that clip on the ear, like a London wife rebuffing an alien neighbor.[8] "Could I come near your beauty with my nails," she says, "I'd set my ten commandments in your face" (1.3.141–1.3.143). The billingsgate continues as she turns to Margaret's put-upon husband:

> Good King, look to't in time:
> She'll pamper thee, and dandle thee like a baby.
> Though in this place most master wear no breeches,
> She shall not strike Dame Eleanor unrevenged. (lines 145–148)

The chief ("most") master of the house is a woman who dominates her weak consort, reversing the roles of husband and wife, as well as ruler and subject. Eleanor's criticism is pointed and sophisticated, but she makes it in markedly demotic speech. Like the historical Duchess of Gloucester, before being sent to prison Eleanor is sentenced to a public shaming in the streets just as prostitutes were (2.4.17–2.4.36).[9] Gloucester's wife embodies the negative side of the good Duke Humphrey's popular reputation, ideally leaving him free of blame in the eyes of the audience, if not of the Parliament on stage that eventually effects his demotion.

The Eleanor scenes are interwoven with an episode that bears directly upon livery company structure and thus citizen subjectivity in London. A group of petitioners approach Suffolk and the queen. Among them is Peter, apprentice to an armorer, who accuses his master, Horner, of "saying that the Duke of York was rightful heir to the crown . . . , and that the King was an usurer" (1.3.26–1.3.27, 1.3.31). He means "usurper," as Margaret realizes, but the apparent mistake effects more than the comic undermining of a nonaristocratic character. Henry VI was in debt to city moneylenders and sustained their usury, although he did not lend money himself (line 31 note). The city has infiltrated the court, and court ways penetrate the city in turn when Gloucester later decrees that Peter must meet Horner in a chivalric trial-by-combat (lines 208–210). God's justice decides treason cases, and God will determine whether Peter's master really implicated York in his disloyal declaration. Horner denies the charge, but Peter is adamant: "By these ten bones, my lords, he did speak them to me in the garret one night as we were scouring my Lord of York's armour" (lines 191–193). The armorers' workplace in this instance was a garret or watchtower, not a shop, which already places them within the chivalric purviews of the court. Peter's "ten bones" or fingers recall Eleanor's "ten commandments" a few lines earlier; these characters share a popular manner of speech. The Peter and Eleanor scenes both involve role-reversals, apprentice over master and wife over husband. Women play a remote part in the master–apprentice conflict as well: Horner's name suggests that he has cuckolded other men with their wives, which may render him less sympathetic. Queen Margaret presides over the petition and combat scenes, coming purposely to see the trial, which is presented as a comic or mock-heroic spectacle (2.3.52–2.3.53).

In a typical aristocratic outburst, York calls Peter "Base dunghill villain and mechanical," but Horner evokes social hierarchy and its well-known resentments *within* the livery company world to discredit Peter further: "My accuser is my prentice, and when I did correct him for his fault the other day, he did vow upon his knees he would be even with me" (1.3.194, 1.3.199–1.3.201). Peter's charge of treasonous speech proves accurate, but Horner's account of his apprentice's motive in making it may be correct as well, especially since he has a witness (line 201). Nevertheless, Peter's words have immediate consequences: Gloucester decrees that Somerset be made regent in France instead of York, whose name is now clouded with suspicion (lines 206–207). A labor dispute thus taints court politics; conversely, the dispute is brought to court and forcibly played out in a travesty of chivalric combat. Although a mock-epic encounter that demeans citizen culture is the result, mixing popular and aristocratic modes of violence also threatens the identity of the nobility. An anxiety about the debasement of aristocratic violence runs throughout the rest of the first tetralogy—indeed, characters in the Shakespeare canon in general view single combat with irony-tinged nostalgia at best, and Peter's defeat of Horner may be the origin of this motif.

As Ronald Knowles has shown, the combatants emerge with sand-filled combat flails, a lower-class weapon that departs from the sources' implication of arms and armor.[10] The fearful Peter continues to speak as if the armorer's professional experience with the nobility's weapons gives him the advantage:

> Here, Robin, an if I die, I give thee my apron; and Will, thou shalt have my hammer; and here, Tom, take all the money that I have. O Lord bless me, I pray God, for I am never able to deal with my master, he hath learnt so much fence already. (2.3.76–2.3.80)

He is speaking to a retinue of his fellows, one of whom tells him to "Fight for the credit of the prentices" (lines 72–73). The episode sends up the heroic citizen tradition of such plays as *The Four Prentices of London*, but it glances at the potential for social disorder in citizen claims to chivalry as well. The apron, which appears again during

Jack Cade's rebellion in *2 Henry VI* and in several Roman tragedies, is a humble but insistent emblem of craft identity.[11] Signs of civil unrest attend both master and man, despite the burlesque tone of the scene. Defeated, the drunken Horner confesses treason as he dies; York admonishes Peter to thank God and the liquor his master consumed, but first he commands: "Take away his weapon" (line 97).

Cade's rebellion in Act 4 is the main occurrence of civil disturbance in the play. For all his concern with public order, the Duke of York is presented as the rebellion's secret instigator. "I have seduced a headstrong Kentishman," he confides to the audience, "To make commotion, as full well he can,/Under the title of John Mortimer," cousin to Richard II's supposed heir (3.1.355, 3.1.357–3.1.358). York discovered his false Mortimer while campaigning in Ireland, where Cade savagely engaged the kerns and also took on their appearance to spy upon them (lines 359–369). His wildness in battle identifies him with the Irish enemy he fought and successfully infiltrated; some historians and members of Henry VI's government assumed that the historical Cade was Irish, or Anglo-Irish.[12] The immediate cause of the rebellion, somewhat occluded in the play, was the court's threatened reprisals in Kent after Suffolk's murder off its coast. The rebels claimed "that Kent should be destroied with a roiall power, & made a wild forrest," an image that recalls the Irish campaigns.[13] In *2 Henry VI* itself, the figure of Cade is enough to create a parallel between Kent, on England's watery border to the southeast, and Ireland, beyond the sea to its northwest. At the symbolic center is London, and the dominant imaginary movement of the play is toward the center, as disruptive forces, accompanied by milling crowds, converge on the city. In a parallel episode, the deceiver Simpcox, traveling with his wife from the far north and attended by a rout who proclaims his falsely miraculous release from blindness, is a small-scale example of the play's centripetal force. The royal court, stationed at St. Alban's shrine, is this impostor's goal. Cade and his army converge on London itself even when the king and his court flee the city and leave him to deal with the Lord Mayor (4.4). "By this," his setter-on reasons, "I shall perceive the commons' mind" (line 373). York means the common people of the realm, but it is the commons of London whose mind is principally at stake in the world of the play.

At his first appearance, Jack Cade rouses his followers by promising that "All the realm shall be in common, and in Cheapside shall my palfrey go to grass" (4.2.63–4.2.64). Cheapside was the location of Goldsmith's Row, and it was also the route along which criminals like Eleanor Cobham were paraded.[14] In a reversal of pastoral, the country will be put into the city when London's principal street for shopping and the display of power is converted to pasture. A similar logic lies behind Cade's rejoinder to Dick the Butcher's well-known proposal to first "kill all the lawyers," again, in London: it is indeed a lamentable thing that the skin of a lamb should be made into parchment to undo a man (lines 71–75). The city has already absorbed the country so as to exploit it, and butchers like Dick, who process animals and their hides, occupy one point of exchange between rural and urban economies. As a Stratford glover's son, Shakespeare would have understood the situation from both sides. The rebels want to take over the national movement of goods from country to city, reversing or at any rate evening-out the relations of exchange. Cade's utopian proposals, such as "There shall be in England seven half-penny loaves sold for a penny" (lines 60–61), would also have appealed to the London commons of the 1590s, many of whom had rioted over the price of grain and other staples.

After his forces kill the Stafford brothers, Cade declares: "the bodies shall be dragged at my horse heels till I do come to London, where we will have the Mayor's sword borne before us. . . . Come, let's march towards London" (4.3.11–4.3.13, 4.3.16–4.3.17). *The Contention* lacks the reference to the mayor's sword, and adds "for tomorrow I meane to sit in the Kings seate at Westminster."[15] In the Folio text, Cade's goal is clearly civic authority and its symbols, not the royal court. Having entered the city, he sits on the milestone that marks the center of England's system of high roads:

> Now is Mortimer lord of this city. And here, sitting upon London Stone, I charge and command that, at the city's cost, the Pissing Conduit run nothing but claret wine this first year of our reign.   (4.6.1–4.6.4)

Pissing Conduit was a humbler example of the masonry structures with taps or pipes from which most Londoners obtained their water. The speech appears in *The Contention*, but without the phrase "at the city's cost." Cade next calls for the burning of London Bridge (line 14). The scenes of the rebels in London are preoccupied with boundaries, limits, and points of intersection, and London Bridge proves the major landmark, in the play as in the historical record. Upon achieving the judicial murders of Lord Saye and his son-in-law Crowmer, Cade commands that their heads, stuck on pikes, be made to kiss at every corner; they become the new "commodities" raised upon "bills" at Cheapside, which has become a killing-field rather than a village commons (7.7.118–7.7.128).

Historically, Cade paraded the heads back to Southwark and its inns, his original headquarters; a contingent of loyal citizens barricaded the still-intact London Bridge and stopped his men from reentering the city.[16] In the play Cade is still calling "Kill and knock down!" in Fish Street, north of the Thames, when Buckingham arrives to offer the royal pardon that robs him of his wavering followers (4.8.1–4.8.2). Topographical confusion is palpable in Cade's despairing address to them:

> And you, base peasants, do ye believe him? Will you needs be hanged with your pardons about your necks? Hath my sword therefore broke through London gates, that you should leave me at the White Hart in Southwark? I thought ye would never have given o'er these arms till you had recovered your ancient freedom; but you are all recreants and dastards and delight to live in slavery to the nobility.   (lines 21–28)

The fudging of the city's boundaries in the drama is meant to suggest that many Londoners had joined the provincials by this point. Cade uses the language of citizenship to appeal to both groups: will city-dwellers as well as country folk remain peasants beneath the aristocracy, or reclaim the "freedom" that evokes a generalized, almost modern sense of national citizenship as well as a mixing of burgess status with the ancient constitution of the country?

Cade's own abuses as Lord Mortimer doom his appeal. From the start, the citizen vocabulary of the rebellion was undermined by Cade's claim—at York's prompting—of a royal bloodline for its leader. He promises that when he is king "all shall eat and drink on my score, and I will apparel them all in one livery, that they may agree like brothers and worship me their lord" (4.2.68–4.2.70). A number of explanations have been offered for the livery reference: the costumes of historical rebels, the disguises of Whitsun mummery, the grey cloth of More's *Utopia*, and more plausibly an imitation of the liveried retainers of great magnates.[17] For the London audience, however, Cade is also offering a democratization of the civic identity embodied on public occasions by the upper echelons of the livery companies with their ceremonial robes. Every man will share in the brotherhood of a single company and the citizenship that accompanies it—as long as they revere him as their lord and master. The historical Cade did succeed with a number of common citizens and civic leaders in London until he became too violent and disordered for their taste.[18] In *2 Henry VI*, it seems that only the "rascal people" join him and "The citizens fly and forsake their houses" (4.4.49–4.4.50). A group of citizens requests military aid from Lord Scales in the Tower on behalf of the mayor; they are loyal, but they are implicitly sent to remind the Crown of its continued responsibilities after Henry ignominiously flees London (4.5.2–4.5.5). By the time the royal pardon is proposed, the distinction among citizens, common city-folk, and foreigners from Kent has become blurred.

The terminology of trades and shops is a subset of the citizen language in the play. It also bridges the village and metropolitan worlds, reminding Londoners that their civic identity shares a common set of tools with the countryside and is dependent on rural raw materials. As two rebels await the first entrance of their leader, they complain "Virtue is not regarded in handicraftsmen," for "The nobility think scorn to go in leather aprons" (4.2.9–4.2.11). Cade leads the rebels because he wears an apron himself: he is a cloth-worker, a "shearman," and thus a member of a craft particularly associated with social protest (line 124). As the first rebel says, "Jack Cade the clothier means to dress the commonwealth, and turn it, and set a new nap upon it" (lines 4–5). A series of metaphors for change and violence drawn from the trades begins with this image of reversal and making anew. A tanner will use their enemies' skin for dog's leather, a weaver's arrival means their thread is spun, and with Dick the Butcher "sin is struck down like an ox, and iniquity's throat cut like a calf" (lines 20–26). Dick, as we have seen, is a memorable character in himself. Completely loyal to Cade's regime of violence, he nevertheless offers frequent asides that deflate his master along with other authority figures. He links the name *Cade* with a "cade" or barrel of herrings, for instance, and doubts his leader's claim not to fear fire because he has already been branded for stealing sheep (lines 30, 58).

> CADE. My father was a Mortimer—
> BUTCHER. [*aside*] He was an honest man, and a good bricklayer.
>
> (lines 35–37)

The buried quibble on *Mortimer* and "mortar" undermines both Cade's effrontery and an aristocratic family name that will be bandied about to much confusion throughout both tetralogies. Dick has a Falstaffian aptitude for staking the middle ground and turning a phrase. The play doesn't let the spectators forget that he is a butcher as well, and once he reminds us himself (4.7.49).

Dick's prominence in the rebellion scenes has drawn the attention of critics like Caroline Spurgeon who have noticed that butchery is a major image in parts 2 and 3 of *Henry VI*. The butcher's trade, with animals at one end, fancy leather goods at the other, and food in between mediates between country and city. Knowles argues that it also links elite forms of aggression with popular ones through image and metaphor, which is why it is virtually absent from the earlier, more noble landscape of *1 Henry VI*.[19] I modulate this verdict in my treatment of part 1, later. The debasement of aristocratic warfare in *2 Henry VI* is seen in the Staffords' unexpected and ignoble deaths, and in Cade's praise of Dick after the battle:

> They fell before thee like sheep and oxen, and thou behaved'st thyself as if thou hadst been in thine own slaughterhouse.

Cade will reward him with a monopoly to kill livestock and produce meat during Lent, which he will lengthen to increase the profit (4.3.3–4.3.7).[20] Both military truculence and royal munificence in victory are travestied by translation to the scale of things that tradesmen value. Another allusion to butchery occurs during Cade's capture and death in Alexander Iden's garden, back in Kent. Starving and deserted by all his followers, including Dick, the rebel defies Iden with a high-flown speech to his sword:

> Steel, if thou turn the edge or cut not out the burly-boned clown in chines of beef ere thou sleep in thy sheath, I beseech God on my knees thou mayst be turned to hobnails. (4.10.55–4.10.58)

In his sordid desperation, Cade would reduce fighting to the butchering and cannibalizing of his brawny opponent. The threatened conversion of his sword to hobnails recalls the armorer's craft as well as biblical ploughshares, and the phrase "on my knees" harkens back to the apprentice Peter's oath to get even with his master. An armorer fights with his apprentice in Act 2, and a rebel threatens to butcher a true man near the end of Act 4. The encounter between Cade and Iden is another mock-epic single combat, for all Iden's somewhat exaggerated virtue. The crafts of armorer and butcher provide two asymmetrical but analogous sets of images for an unsettling mixture of aristocratic with citizen forms of violence.

The Duke of Gloucester's fate in Act 3 occasions the central instances of metaphorical butchery in the history. King Henry initiates the image: when Suffolk arraigns Gloucester for treason in Parliament, the hapless king compares him to a butcher who seizes a calf "And binds the wretch and beats it when it strains,/Bearing it to the bloody slaughterhouse" (3.1.210–3.1.213). Gloucester's secret murder by a pair of Suffolk's assassins proves Henry's fears true. Warwick accuses him before the king by continuing the royal simile:

> Who finds the heifer dead and bleeding fresh
> And sees fast by a butcher with an axe,
> But will suspect 'twas he that made the slaughter? (3.2.188–3.2.190)

"Are you the butcher, Suffolk?" the queen asks her favorite in feigned surprise. "Where's your knife?" (line 195). Suffolk says he wears a sword instead of the butcher's proverbial knife, overlaying the popular language with a knightly challenge that already seems mock-heroic. Warwick accepts, but the combat is overtaken by the commons, who storm the chamber and secure the banishment that leads to Suffolk's murder at sea. From the fourteenth century through Henry VI's reign, London-dwelling aristocrats complained about butchery and the smell of offal in the streets, and there were several attempts to ban the killing of animals within the city walls. The Butchers' Company Ordinances of 1607 continued to reflect these disputes.[21] Henry's evocation of the cruel butcher, and Warwick's picture of the butcher caught just after an illegitimate slaughter, show how butchery remained in especially sharp counterpoint to aristocracy within the early modern city.

Covert slaughter is already disgraceful. Aristocratic butchery breaks out in the open in the final battle scenes, in which the Yorkists take up where Jack Cade and his crew left off, in civil war. York's son Richard, the future Richard III, kills Somerset, who has replaced Suffolk in Queen Margaret's affections. There is little to link Richard with butchery at this stage except his historical reputation, and the recollection in his name of Dick the Butcher in the preceding episodes. But Somerset's defeat at his hands is declassed in several ways. "So, lie thou there," Richard apostrophizes his dead enemy,

> For underneath an alehouse' paltry sign,
> The Castle in Saint Albans, Somerset
> Hath made the wizard famous in his death. (5.2.66–5.2.69)

A spirit raised by the conjurer Bolingbroke for Eleanor Cobham had warned that Somerset should avoid castles (1.4.35). Instead of a chivalric citadel, a commercial sign bearing a castle's image serves as Somerset's scutcheon. The incident reminds us of Eleanor's demotic persona and its village magic at the climax of the play, and also of her great rival the queen. "Erect his statue and worship it,/And make my image but an alehouse sign," she jealously demanded of Henry as he mourned Gloucester's slaughter (3.2.80–3.2.81). Richard's slaying of Somerset may recall the initial episode that combines aristocratic and popular forms: by one reckoning, it is likely that the actor who played Peter also played the young Richard of *2 Henry VI*.[22] Somerset, it will be remembered, was made regent of France in place of York because Peter's accusation against the armorer indirectly implicated the duke. The ignoble skirmish between a master and his apprentice resurfaces yet again at the end of the play to bedevil both Lancaster and York. "Sound drum and trumpets, and to London all," Warwick cries in the final lines, recapitulating the dominant movement of the action from margin to urban center (5.3.32).

The story resumes in London as *King Henry VI, Part 3* opens, confirming our sense that these plays were written in sequence. Aristocratic butchery continues in this history and it is given added point by London settings and references throughout. As Henry confronts York and his forces at Westminster in the first scene, he complains that "the city favours them," and refuses to fight then and there: "Far be the thought of this from Henry's heart,/To make a shambles of the Parliament-House."[23] Shambles are butchers' stalls or slaughter-houses; several districts in London where meat was sold were known as "the shambles," the principal one being St. Nicholas Shambles, not far from St. Paul's.[24] Much later, in a phantasmagoric episode during a north-country battle, Henry overhears a father who has unknowingly killed his son in the fighting:

> What stratagems, how fell, how butcherly,
> Erroneous, mutinous, and unnatural,
> This deadly quarrel daily doth beget! (2.5.89–2.5.91)

A son who has similarly killed his father explains "From London by the king was I pressed forth" (2.5.64); most of Warwick's Yorkist army is from London, too (2.1.111–2.1.112). The cresting importance of "common soldiers" and "the common sort" in the Wars of the Roses is traced throughout *3 Henry VI* (1.1.9; 5.6.87). However jarring the symmetry of the father–son scene and its heightened rhetoric of recognition and lament seem to modern taste, it probably brought the costs of civil war home to the original London audience as well as the contrite king on stage.

Henry's follower Clifford, known historically as "the butcher," is not as reticent as his king. Driven to revenge his father's death at the hands of York, Clifford has resolved to kill and cut up the other side's children.[25] In *3 Henry VI*, he slays both Rutland, York's youngest son and a mere boy in the play though not in history, and York himself, with Queen Margaret's help. The words *slaughter-man* and *slaughtered* appear in both scenes (1.3.169; 1.4.57). "Are you there, butcher?" Richard demands when he hears Clifford's voice as the armies confront each other. " 'Twas you that killed young Rutland, was it not?" (2.2.95, 2.2.98). After the final battle at Tewkesbury, of course, it is "misshapen Dick," as the boy prince calls him, who takes on Clifford's role of child-killer (5.5.35). The prince is stabbed by the three brothers, Edward, Richard ("Sprawl'st thou? Take that"), and Clarence; his mother the queen, finally defeated, calls them "Butchers and villains! Bloody cannibals!" (lines 39, 60). Desiring death, she asks "Where is that devil's butcher, Richard?" (line 77).[26] But "Dick" has already left for London, "to make a bloody supper in the Tower" where Henry is imprisoned (line 85). As in Cade's bearding of Iden, metaphorical cannibalism accompanies the human slaughter. Henry ends the series of metaphors as he began them with his uncle Gloucester's capture in *2 Henry VI*. "So first the harmless sheep doth yield his fleece," he says as Richard approaches him, "And next his throat unto the butcher's knife" (5.6.8–5.6.9). When Richard compares Henry to Daedalus and the dead prince to Icarus, the king allegorizes the myth to make his son's murderer the sea that "did swallow up his life" (line 25).

The sea image goes back to an earlier, joyous one that celebrated Henry's ostensible safety at the center of his realm:

> My sovereign, with the loving citizens,
> Like to his island girt in with the ocean,
> Or modest Dian circled with her nymphs,
> Shall rest in London till we come to him. (4.8.19–4.8.22)

The formerly traitorous Warwick is speaking. In an ironic *coup de theatre*, almost immediately Edward, York's pretender and the next king, invades the stage and captures Henry with the words: "You are the fount that makes small brooks to flow:/Now stops thy spring, my sea shall suck them dry" (lines 54–55). The Yorkists are the ocean that surrounds the Lancastrian monarch, and the citizens of London, far from being loyal, desert him. According to Edward Hall, a principal source, when Edward came to London to take the king, "the communaltie . . . ranne in hepes out of the citie, to mete him, and saluted hym as their kyng and sovereygne lord."[27] Warwick's allusion to Diana had already struck a discordant note—not only does the urban context render Henry feminine, it also reaches outside the stage-play world to remind Queen Elizabeth's court of its dependence on the city and its suburbs by the Thames.

King Henry VI, Part 1, probably produced after parts 2 and 3, returns the audience to an earlier, heroic time, mostly through the figure of Sir John Talbot. Much of the action takes place beyond the seas in France, where Talbot and his men fight for their monarch's right. Talbot represents aristocratic violence in its most honorable form, not in his person so much—the Countess of Auvergne calls him a "shrimp"—but in his authority over his soldiers.[28] Thomas Nashe, who probably had a large hand in *1 Henry VI*, cited the success of the players' Talbot in his defense of the public theater in *Pierce Penilesse*:

> How would it have joyed brave *Talbot* (the terror of the French) to thinke that after he had lyne two hundred yeares in his Tombe, hee should triumphe againe on the Stage, and have his bones newe embalmed with the teares of ten thousand spectators at least. . . . I will defend it against any Collian, or clubfisted Usurer of them all, there is no immortalitie can be given a man on earth like unto Playes. What talke I to them of immortalitie, that are the onely underminers of Honour, and doe envie any man that is not sprung up by base Brokerie like themselves? They care not if all the auncient houses were rooted out, so that, like the Burgomasters of the Low-countries, they might share the government amongst them as States, and be quartermaisters of our Monarchie.[29]

This passage is invariably cited in discussions of both the history play and antitheatricality during the 1590s. Less remarked upon is the statement's internal dynamic, which is also present in *1 Henry VI*: even as citizens and other urban inhabitants are enlisted in the charismatic recreation of a glorious national past, the financial and political leaders of the city—who were often aligned with critics of the theater—are stigmatized as greedy cowards.

Nashe's defense of plays as reliquaries of aristocratic honor in an age of base brokery might appear weak to those who had seen *The Contention* and *The True Tragedy*, for there is plenty of corruption in these histories. "They say 'A crafty knave does need no broker,' " Hume brags as he entraps Eleanor and Gloucester in *2 Henry VI*, "Yet am I Suffolk and the Cardinal's broker" (1.2.100–1.2.101). Suffolk, Cardinal Winchester, and even Warwick seem little better than quartermasters to the Crown at times. *1 Henry VI* itself is free neither of noble skullduggery nor the language of butchery, at once violent and tradesmanlike, that accompanies it in the other plays. The dying Mortimer tells the future York, heir to his royal claim, that he should not wish harm to himself, for "Thou dost then wrong me, as that slaughterer doth/Which giveth many wounds when one will kill" (2.5.109–2.5.110). Once again the butcher is linked with cruel excess, as someone who overdoes his task. Joan la Pucelle persuades the Duke of Burgundy, originally an ally of England, to support the French: "See then, thou fight'st against thy countrymen/And join'st with them will be thy slaughter-men" (3.3.74–3.3.75). Despite Talbot's chivalric nobility, the English forces already appear as little more than butchers to their Gallic counterparts. There is a grim irony in the over-confident Alençon's early estimation of his starving opponents: "They want their porridge and their fat bull-beeves" (1.2.9); the French will eventually serve that turn on the spit.

The Duke of Burgundy, historically as in the tetralogies, was the ruler of the Flemish. His role plays upon the antialien sentiments of the contemporary London audience. "Done like a Frenchman," Joan says of him when he crosses over, "Turn and turn again" (3.4.85). As a sort of clown, she jests upon the popular confusion of French and Flemings as well as upon her own side. In the early acts of the play, the Walloons—also confused with Flemings proper—are allied to English through Burgundy (2.1.10). Foreshadowing acts of treachery occur almost immediately, at Orleans:

> Here had the conquest fully been sealed up,
> If Sir John [Falstaffe] had not played the coward.
> He being in the vanguard, placed behind
> With purpose to relieve and follow them,
> Cowardly fled, not having struck one stroke.
> Hence grew the general wrack and massacre.
> Enclosed were they with their enemies.
> A base [Wallon], to win the Dolphin's grace,
> Thrust Talbot with a spear into the back.
> (1.1.130–1.1.138; text altered)

The words I have bracketed restore readings from the Folio, the only early text of the play. Although anachronistic, "Wallon" or Walloon reflects both the fictional situation in the play and the resentments of 1590s Londoners. Modern editors are right to prefer Fastolfe to Falstaff for reasons of clarity, but a reminder of the fat knight of the *Henry IV* plays and *The Merry Wives of Windsor* is useful, as well. Although thoroughly English, "Falstaffe" is associated with alien treachery both here and in the Burgundy plot. He is the one who brings news of Burgundy's defection to the English court at Paris, and he is promptly baffled by Talbot for his own desertion (4.1). The odd

Flemishness that adheres patchily to the later Falstaff in *Merry Wives* may have its source in these scenes (we catch brief glimpses of it again in the second tetralogy).

Anxiety about aliens in the city and Southwark also lies buried within the historical record.[30] Act 1, Scene 3, in which Gloucester arrives to survey the Tower of London only to find Woodville barring his way at the behest of Winchester, bishop and cardinal, portrays a serious crisis that took place throughout 1425. The Protector faced down the Chancellor, and the authorities of the city of London, Southwark, where the bishop of Winchester had his palace, and the church were also at stake. In the play, Gloucester and his blue-coated men swarm the Tower; the Cardinal himself appears with his followers, and only the arrival of the Lord Mayor prevents a pitched battle. Historically, Winchester seized control of the Tower of London in February 1425 as an assertion of power: he gained control over important prisoners as well as a garrison, and he may have planned to transport the four-year-old king to London and lodge him there. But the Cardinal's immediate aim was to secure a base in the city from which his soldiers could police its increasingly unruly inhabitants, who were threatening public order in Southwark as well.[31]

Substantial threats against alien merchants were a rallying-cry in the unrest, and many strangers lived in the liberty of Southwark and were protected by Winchester. Bills against Flemings were stuck up on both sides of the river, including the gates of the bishop's palace. According to Holinshed, a probable source for the play, the Cardinal later claimed he occupied the tower primarily for this reason, "strangers being under the defense, in so much that in doubt thereof, strangers in great number left the land."[32] Winchester had several citizens arrested for treason and was later accused of exempting the Flemings from lodging with citizen hosts; a violent demonstration followed in April. In October, the Cardinal mustered his forces and blocked his end of London Bridge to prevent attack by an army of Londoners massed north of the Thames.[33] For all this, *1 Henry VI* makes no mention of antialien violence and places these words in the Cardinal's mouth as he addresses the Mayor:

> Here's Gloucester, a foe to citizens,
> One that still motions war and never peace,
> O'ercharging your free purses with large fines. (1.3.62–1.3.64)

The purses are "free" because they stand for the citizens' burgess freedom as well as their generosity, taxed by Gloucester's French wars.

Yet it was Winchester who was a foe to citizens; Gloucester was their champion in 1425.[34]

Why is antialien sentiment absent from the Tower episode and its aftermath? Winchester's comments do gesture toward recognition of citizen grievances, and it is possible that an earlier version took in the wider historical canvas, including the aliens. Agitation against strangers on stage angered royal authority in the early 1590s, as the censorship of *Sir Thomas More* shows. But there is another answer. *1 Henry VI* treats popular struggle as if it was nothing more than a means for magnates to compete with one another. Having absorbed popular violence, aristocratic brutality had already been depicted as subdued to it throughout parts 2 and 3, where butchery is given free reign. The occluding of ethnic strife by elite rivalry in part 1 is another example of the dialectical relation between popular and aristocratic violence in the first tetralogy.

In the Parliament scene, the Mayor enters once again to beg for an end to the fighting that besets his city. "Pity the city of London, pity us," he cries, "Our windows are broke down in every street,/And we, for fear, compelled to shut our shops" (3.1.77, 3.1.84–3.1.85). In the person of its chief representative, the citizens appear preoccupied with commerce and totally dependent on the king's protection. Earlier, after Gloucester and Winchester retreat from the tower, the Mayor reveals what is supposed to be a distinctly citizen view of the crisis:

> See the coast cleared, and then we will depart.
> Good God, these nobles should such stomachs bear!
> I myself fight not once in forty year. (1.3.87–1.3.89)

The cowardly mayor, astonished at his betters' high blood, calls to mind the brokers and usurers who fail to appreciate what Talbot represents to Thomas Nashe. Nashe compared such anti-theatrical citizens with Flemish burgomasters; it is ironic that fear of social unrest over Flemish and other aliens lay behind their preference for peace during the reigns of Henry VI and Elizabeth I. Shakespeare and the other authors of *1 Henry VI* made sure that citizens and the common sort did not trample on the field of honor the way they do in parts 2 and 3. At the same time, the speaking part given to the Lord Mayor anticipates the major political crises of Shakespeare's *Richard III*.

In the final play of the first tetralogy, the citizens and their civic leaders play a conspicuous if equivocal role. When Prince Edward arrives in the city after Edward IV's death, he is greeted with the phrase: "Welcome, sweet Prince, to London, to your chamber."[35]

The Lord Mayor is there to welcome him, but these words are spoken by the Duke of Buckingham, Richard's right-hand man and the aristocrat who manages relations between Crown and city for much of the play. Stow, similarly echoing a common phrase, calls London "the hart of the Realme, the Kinges chamber, and princes seate."[36] Ideally, the king's chamber is the principal city "directly subject, and yielding immediate revenue to the king" (OED I.6). Yet neither part of the definition was completely accurate: London was chartered by the Crown with certain freedoms in 1319, and royal taxation of the city was seldom "immediate." In 1616, Henry Wright claimed that cities were rarely the starting-points of rebellion because their citizen-subjects were more exposed to surveillance and shame. In particular, "the said Citie of *London*, being the *Chamber* of the Prince, wherin euer he presumeth that hee may be most safe, the Citizens euen out of their loue and loyalty to their Prince, haue euer thought foule scorne that themselues should be found untrue."[37] Indeed, Edward is menaced by Richard and Buckingham, not by the citizens. Yet *Richard III* questions whether London is merely the chamber of the king or a relatively independent site of competing interests that nevertheless lends itself to royal management and control.

Several citizens discuss the changing times in a brief scene that seems to suggest a confused and easily led London:

> 1 *Cit[izen]*. Good morrow, neighbour: whither away so fast?
> 2 *Cit[izen]*. I promise you, I scarcely know myself. Hear you the news
>   abroad?
> 1 *Cit[izen]*. Yes, that the King is dead.
> 2 *Cit[izen]*. Ill news, by'rlady; seldom comes the better. I fear,
>   I fear,'twill prove a giddy world. (2.3.1–2.3.5)

Men's hearts are full of fear, the Second Citizen later says (line 38); he claims half-jokingly not to know where he is going. His apprehensions about a giddy world are echoed by a Third Citizen, who recalls—perhaps ironically—how well the land was governed by councilors under Henry VI. Things will be worse under a new child-ruler because of "emulation" or rivalry within the royal household: "O, full of danger is the Duke of Gloucester,/And the Queen's sons and brothers, haught and proud" (lines 26–27). Despite their fear and disarray, the neighbors' conversation reveals a surprisingly accurate knowledge about the basic situation at court, principally that Richard, Duke of Gloucester, is dangerous. They also try to interpret what they know, along a spectrum that runs from optimism (the First Citizen), through caution (the Second), to resignation (the Third). By the end of the short scene, the Third Citizen asks the Second "Whither away?" and is told "Marry, we were sent for to the Justices" (line 46). So was I, replies his questioner. It is a mystery what the Justices, probably the Justices of Assize, want from the citizens, but they are the direct representatives of royal authority. Citizen subjectivity may be so unstable on stage that the Second Citizen, who at first hardly knew his destination, now not only knows it but knows that the first neighbor (hence "we") has been summoned as well. But it is also possible that this moderate voice knows more than he lets on all along.

Richard respects citizen opinion and citizen power. After they have Lord Chamberlain Hastings beheaded for refusing to back Richard's succession plans, Richard and Buckingham summon the Lord Mayor to justify the execution. Buckingham apologizes for calling him after the fact:

> we would have had you heard
> The traitor speak, and timorously confess
> The manner and the purpose of his treasons,
> That you might well have signified the same
> Unto the citizens, who haply may
> Misconstrue us in him and wail his death. (3.5.55–3.5.60)

Richard and Buckingham feel they must manipulate the citizens' powers of interpretation. Following his source for the scene, Thomas More's history of Richard III in Hall's *Union*, Shakespeare has the pair dress up in old, "rotten" armor, as if afraid of sudden attack, to receive the mayor (SD line 1). When Richard asks Buckingham if he can change color and speak fearfully, the duke brags "Tut, I can counterfeit the deep tragedian" (lines 1–5). In a confirmation of late sixteenth-century suspicions about theater's power to bamboozle the citizenry, they apparently succeed in convincing the mayor that Hastings was plotting against their lives. The parallel to stage practice is comically heightened when Hastings's head is carried on just as Buckingham begins his explanation, for the severed head is the chief prop of the first tetralogy.

After all this, the Lord Mayor promises to acquaint the citizens with the noblemen's "just proceedings," but Richard remains wary: "Go after, cousin Buckingham:/The Mayor towards Guildhall hies him in all post" (3.5.65, 3.5.71–3.5.72). He scripts the speech his ally is to deliver to the assembled citizens, turning the Guildhall, the building in which the commercial and political identities of the city meet, into a theater. The theme shifts from Hastings to the late king. Buckingham will suggest that Edward IV's children were illegitimate and that he was a bastard himself. He will remind the citizens that Edward's lust "stretch'd unto their servants, daughters, wives" (lines 74, 80–81, 85–91). And in an anecdote borrowed from More, Buckingham is to tell them

> how Edward put to death a citizen
> Only for saying he would make his son
> Heir to the Crown—meaning indeed his house,
> Which by the sign thereof was termed so. (lines 75–78)

These charges all play upon masculine anxieties about legitimacy and inheritance, a preoccupation shared by royal dynasties and tradesmen's households. The sign of the Crown is a shifting signifier that moves between these worlds, to the suspicious dismay of a monarch who did not cherish what they had in common. Even though Richard's claim endangers the principle of primogeniture on the dynastic level, Buckingham will implicitly assure the citizens that he will leave them, their women, and their estates alone.

Despite his arrogant theatricality, Buckingham fails to move the Guildhall audience. "The citizens are mum, say not a word," he reports:

> But like dumb statues or breathing stones
> Star'd each on other, and look'd deadly pale.
> Which when I saw, I reprehended them,
> And ask'd the Mayor what meant this wilful silence.
> His answer was, the people were not us'd
> To be spoke to but by the Recorder. (3.7.3, 3.7.25–3.7.30)

The citizens' silent resistance does not preclude interpretation, as their speaking looks to one another prove. Their demeanor expresses the general fear that the three neighbors spoke about in 2.3. The recorder was originally the legal official who "recorded" or remembered the acts of the city and orally reported them back upon request.[38] Here, he is asked to repeat Buckingham's speech, but he does so in quotation marks in effect, distancing himself from the duke's intentions. Finally, "some ten voices" belonging to Buckingham's followers in the back of the room cry "God save King Richard," and this becomes the rationale for the mayor and a delegation of aldermen to petition Richard to ascend the throne (lines 31–44). Together, Buckingham and the compliant mayor successfully manipulate the popular "voice," using the recorder's customary role to excuse the citizens' recalci-trance and Buckingham's clients to mimic their acquiescence. Yet the detail in which Buckingham recounts citizen resistance, and Richard's astonished responses to his tale, show how anxious they are about the Guildhall's reaction.

In the remainder of this well-known scene, the Lord Mayor and his brethren arrive in person, but Buckingham serves as their spokesman or recorder. Richard feigns fear at the "troops of citizens" who approach him; has he committed some disgraceful offense in "the City's eye"? (3.7.84, 3.7.109–3.7.110). Decrying the illegitimate branch of the York family to which the realm has been consigned, Buckingham pleads with Richard to accept the crown: "your citizens entreat you" (line 200). It is at their moment of greatest political weakness that the power of the citizenry is asserted to its greatest extent. Speaking for them, Buckingham threatens Richard:

> Your brother's son shall never reign our king,
> But we will plant some other in the throne
> To the disgrace and downfall of your House;
> And with this resolution here we leave you.
> Come, citizens; zounds, I'll entreat no more. (lines 214–218)

Richard, who is not made of stones, not only accepts, but uses the citizens' supposed enforcement of his will to dismiss in advance any "scandal," "reproach," or "blots" upon his rule (lines 222–233).

Seen from another angle, it is what citizens might say about him, not what he will do, that Richard seeks to excuse in these lines. His concern here is of a piece with the prominence the play gives to citizen interpretation throughout these central scenes. After drawing up Hastings's indictment, for instance, it is the Scrivener who calls our attention to the way the Lord Chamberlain has been framed. But the Scrivener also asks: "Who is so gross/That cannot see this palpable device?/Yet who's so bold but says he sees it not?" (3.6.10–3.6.12). Even though citizens are given the power to interpret, their power is circumscribed by fear, and by their leaders' hypocrisy. Why give the freemen of London a role in the play at all, then? Shakespeare's depiction of them closely follows his source in Hall's version of Thomas More—but Shakespeare often picks and chooses from his sources, and he need not have emphasized the London material. A more likely answer lies in the way *Richard III* completes the pattern of increasing city influence that parts 2 and 3 of *Henry VI* developed. Finally, the citizens' equivocal power was dramatically effective in its immediate context: it reached out to the London audience of the 1590s, involving them in the historical action and perhaps arousing thoughts about their role in a coming accession crisis.[39] Neither properly subversive nor fully contained, citizen power, bound up as it is with language and interpretation, is simply undecidable in its extent and effects in *Richard III*, as in many of the history plays.

In this respect, *Richard III* contrasts with *King John*, possibly written around the same time but set much earlier than the tetralogies. *John* merits a brief excursus. Cardinal Pandulph assures the French king that John's intention to murder the boy Arthur will turn his people against him, causing them to interpret innocent meteorological events as signs of his downfall.[40] According to Huberd, the effort of such interpretation renders the London citizens ridiculous and threatening at the same time:

> I saw a smith stand with his hammer, thus,
> The whilst his iron did on the anvil cool,
> With open mouth swallowing a tailor's news. (4.2.193–4.2.195)

The tailor has put his slippers on the wrong feet, so anxious is he to spread the dangerous news of Arthur's supposed death and the French invasion. In a remarkable scene earlier in the action, the town of Argiers and its citizen spokesman politely defy the rulers of both England and France: it owes allegiance to the King of England, but it is unclear who that monarch is, John or Arthur. A totally inconclusive battle realizes the *aporia* in comic if bloody form. "King'd of our fear," the Citizen says, Argiers is at once omnipotent and cravenly powerless (2.1.371).[41] Undecidability and fear work in the citizens' favor in this play, at least until the Bastard suggests that the kings join forces and settle the matter by utterly destroying the city (2.1.373–2.1.396). The town resumes its subject status, but only after a dynastic marriage plan suggested by the Citizen. "That daughter there of Spain, the Lady Blanche,/Is near to England" (line 423), and Argiers should be given with her to the Dauphin. *King John* depicts a town that momentarily resists sovereign power and then cleverly arranges its own accommodation to it, seizing the patriarchal prerogative over a convenient woman in order to do so.

The presence of a woman's name in *Richard III* relates to citizen power in a different manner in the text of that play. Elizabeth or "Jane" Shore, as she was popularly known, never appears on stage. Nevertheless, she is mentioned six times.[42] Daughter of either a mercer or a goldsmith, and wife to William Shore, mercer, Jane Shore was

Edward's mistress: along with her husband, she is given a prominent role as a character in Thomas Heywood's *Edward IV*, and her own lament in *The Mirror for Magistrates*. In *Richard III*, her name is coupled with that of Edward's queen Elizabeth, her rival. Clarence says no one is safe "But the Queen's kindred, and night-walking heralds/ That trudge betwixt the King and Mistress Shore" (1.1.72–1.1.73). The way to remain in favor with Edward, Richard replies, is

> To be her men, and wear her livery.
> The jealous o'er-worn widow and herself,
> Since that our brother dubb'd them gentlewomen,
> Are mighty gossips in our monarchy. (lines 80–83)

The widow is Queen Elizabeth. As with Jack Cade's promise of a single livery, Shore's "livery" refers to the uniforms worn by servants in aristocratic households, but secondarily it recalls the liveries of London's companies. To Edward's brothers, it represents class degeneration, not citizen equality.

After Edward's death, the Lord Chamberlain Hastings takes up with "Mistress Shore," as a sarcastic quip by Richard attests (3.1.185). The reappearance of her name signifies the stubborn presence of citizen influence in the plot, feminized and weak but persistent. Yet it also serves Richard as the pretext for Hastings's downfall. In the council scene after Edward's demise, Richard suddenly bemoans his bodily deformity:

> And this is Edward's wife, that monstrous witch,
> Consorted with that harlot, strumpet Shore,
> That by their witchcraft thus have marked me. (3.4.70–3.4.72)

It is Hastings's hesitation to implicate his lover in sorcery that supposedly provokes Richard to his prearranged execution. Hastings is later accused of intended murder. "I never look'd for better at his hand," Buckingham tells the Lord Mayor in the rotten armor scene, "After he once fell in with Mistress Shore" (3.5.49–3.5.50). In another instance of how citizen power is subject to manipulation, Richard's factotum uses the name of a citizen's wife to remind the mayor that the citizenry or their leaders might be implicated in the plot as well.

In his Guildhall oration, Buckingham speaks of Edward's "enforcement of the city wives" (3.7.8). The most famous city wife was not forced, but consented to her sovereign lover, and later to Hastings.

The will of a woman is fudged just as the citizens' political will is, largely to dampen down the threat, or opportunity, posed by both. Mistress Shore stands for the exclusion of social history, civic life, and women's experience from the play in the eyes of modern criticism, all good things from our point of view.[43] In the sixteenth century, she was a tragic figure. But she also represented the negative side of citizen power to many among Shakespeare's contemporaries: the backstairs gossip, feminine wiles, and commercial influence some in the audience feared were all too present in the wings of political history.

Jean E. Howard and Phyllis Rackin argue that Richard assimilates the transgressive qualities of women from earlier history plays like Joan la Pucelle and Eleanor Cobham, who use witchcraft and strong language to advance themselves.[44] He also assumes the seductive role of Jane Shore, and with it the appurtenances of citizen culture. In words borrowed from *Measure for Measure*, Richard puts on the destined livery after all, but for his own purposes (2.4.137). His rise is often described in commercial language. Conniving at marrying Lady Anne at the outset, he realizes that he is getting ahead of himself: "But yet I run before my horse to market" (1.1.160). Once in the marketplace of power, Richard is encouraged by Buckingham to grab it directly, not as a "lowly factor for another's gain" (2.7.133). The old queen, Margaret, turns the metaphor against him:

> Richard yet lives, hell's black intelligencer,
> Only reserv'd their factor to buy souls
> And send them thither. (4.4.71–4.4.73)

A factor is an agent, often a provincial one, who deals in goods for a merchant or tradesman. Margaret combines commerce with intrigue and witchcraft in her curse. Later in the scene, Richard himself uses the language of usury in bargaining with Elizabeth to give him her daughter in incestuous marriage:

> The liquid drops of tears that you have shed
> Shall come again, transform'd to orient pearl,
> Advantaging their loan with interest. (4.4.321–4.4.323)

He will bury the two princes, Elizabeth's children, in their sister's womb, "that nest of spicery," where they will breed new copies of themselves (lines 423–425). Richard makes a demonic bid to control the female power of reproduction in the language of finance and mercantile prosperity.

Richard, of course, has long since seized the power of death, if not of life. The imagery of butchery and slaughter resurfaces throughout *Richard III*.[45] The murder of princes in the Tower, "this ruthless piece of butchery" (4.3.5), is the central example. Elizabeth knows Richard is responsible:

> No doubt the murd'rous knife was dull and blunt
> Till it was whetted on thy stone-hard heart
> To revel in the entrails of my lambs. (4.4.227–4.4.229)

Instead of a dead metaphor of slaughter, we are given specific images of entrails and a man sharpening a blade on a whetstone, his heart; butchers were never without their knives. In the final speech of the history, Richmond's words recall the symmetrical battlefield tableau in *3 Henry VI*: "The father rashly slaughtered his own son;/The son, compell'd, been butcher to the sire" (5.5.25–5.5.26). With the coming of the Tudors, however, "Now civil wounds are stopp'd; peace lives again" (line 40).

II: THE SECOND TETRALOGY

It is partly to forestall "civil wounds plough'd up with neighbours' sword" that an earlier king abruptly halts the single combat between Henry Bolingbroke, Duke of Herford, and Thomas Mowbray in Act 1 of *Richard II*.[46] Shakespeare places the assassination of Woodstock, yet another, earlier Duke of Gloucester, at the lost origin of the civil wars before the action of the second tetralogy properly begins. Bolingbroke throws down his gage and accuses his enemy of multiple treasons as well as Woodstock's death; as in Peter the apprentice's charge against the armorer, divine justice is supposed to decide the victor in a case of treason (1.1.69, 1.1.203). The "chivalrous design" of the fight is emphasized from the outset, and the abortive combat scene is fraught with trumpets, fussing over the "lists" or barriers, and elaborate rituals of leave-taking (1.1.81; 1.3.46–1.3.99, 1.3.117). Trumpets, lists, and good-byes, albeit drunken and fearful ones, succinctly punctuate the brief combat scene in *2 Henry VI* as well (2.3.54–2.3.100). Cruelly funny though it is, this trial was at least allowed to go forward. In *Richard II*, chivalry and divinity are completely frustrated, first by Richard's irony and then by his ceremonial truncheon, which stops the contest before it begins (1.1.109–1.1.110, 1.1.152–1.1.159; 1.3.118). The king interrupts the trial by combat to prevent Mowbray's role in the murder of Woodstock from coming to light, Mowbray having been set on in some mysterious way by Richard himself. According to the time line of the civil wars, the near-encounter of Bolingbroke and Mowbray should have been the primal scene of chivalric combat. But it is already belated within the Shakespearean canon of history plays, since the farcical meeting of apprentice and master came before it in the order of composition.

Initially, it seems as if Bolingbroke's role is to purge aristocratic violence of the demotic associations it acquired in the first tetralogy. Some of these associations are also at work early in *Richard II*. Conferring with Woodstock's wife, Gaunt bemoans "the butchers of his life" (line 3), and he despairingly identifies the chief killer as Richard himself (lines 37–39). The Duchess of Gloucester admonishes him:

> In suff'ring thus thy brother to be slaughter'd,
> Thou showest the naked pathway to thy life,
> Teaching stern murder how to butcher thee. (lines 30–32)

The king, it is implied, has striven to eliminate dynastic competition by the lowest means. Gaunt is his last surviving uncle, and his son, Bolingbroke, a potential rival for the crown. "O, sit my husband's wrongs on Herford's spear," the Duchess prays, "That it may enter butcher Mowbray's breast!" (1.2.47–1.2.48). She uses Bolingbroke's title and his opponent's family name, although Mowbray was Duke of Norfolk. Trial-by-combat between a nobleman and the figurative "butcher Mowbray" will right the social balance, express the divine will, and revenge her husband. But the encounter is called off in the next scene, and doubts about single combat haunt the rest of the play.

By Act 4, Scene 1, Bolingbroke has all but replaced Richard on the throne. Bagot accuses Aumerle of participation in Woodstock's murder, and when Aumerle throws down his gage, probably a glove, first one, then another, and then a third lord throw down theirs to accept the challenge. Surrey then casts down his gage to challenge one of the lords in support of Aumerle. The bombastic rhetoric and sheer repetition threaten to make the scene a travesty, and Bolingbroke, or Henry IV, proves little better at controlling the scramble for honor than Richard was. He promises to assign them all days of trial, but we never see their combats (4.1.106). Aristocratic competition is apparently subsumed in the chivalric tilts at Oxford that celebrate the coronation of the new monarch (5.2.52). When Henry IV asks after his unthrifty son Henry, Harry Percy says he recently told the prince about the "triumphs":

> His answer was, he would unto the stews
> And from the common'st creature pluck a glove,

And wear it as a favour; and with that
He would unhorse the lustiest challenger. (5.3.16–5.3.19)

The passage is a fleeting one that describes an off-stage exchange, yet it is important because it encapsulates Prince Hal's strategy for the remainder of the second tetralogy. In taking his gage from a prostitute in the London stews, he appropriates in a burlesque mode the faltering aristocratic rituals that Richard and his father try to manage. He citifies them, or reveals how they have already been invaded by city modes of violence and desire in the history world.

I will return to the prince later. In Act 1, Scene 3, single combat among aristocrats in its most exalted form is still supposed to be a vehicle of divine judgment. Richard and his council replace God's will with exile: Bolingbroke is sent away for ten years, later reduced to six, and Norfolk forever (1.3.139–1.3.153). "The language I have learnt these forty years," Mowbray protests, "My native English, now I must forgo." His tongue, a useless instrument, will be jailed within his mouth: "What is thy sentence then but speechless death,/Which robs my tongue from breathing native breath?" (lines 159–173). With all the other burdens of permanent exile, Mowbray's emphasis on language is unexpected. Perhaps he tenders a labored hint at Richard's anxiety that he might tell what he knows about Woodstock's murder. But his complaint also casts the loss of aristocratic selfhood as the assumption of alien status in another country. To imagine yourself as a stranger is to imagine yourself unable to speak the common tongue. Bolingbroke is also condemned to "tread the stranger paths of banishment" for a while (line 143). At the scene's conclusion, he declares:

Where'er I wander boast of this I can,
Though banish'd, yet a true-born Englishman. (lines 308–309)

Bolingbroke cleverly makes his very exile an opportunity to proclaim his Englishness. His enforced alienage beyond the Channel is cast in national, not citizen or strictly urban, terms. But the phrase "true-born Englishman" is also of a piece with the London common council's 1572 policy that "no citizen of this city . . . shall take as apprentice any person whose father is not the child of an Englishman born."[47] The common council's measure marked the point where a limited idea of urban citizenship began to merge with a developing, modern ideology of national belonging. Far from cleansing aristocratic identity of popular colorings, Bolingbroke similarly blends city and nation.

His language and behavior before he ascends the throne sound with a popular, and at times specifically urban, resonance.

This is particularly true in the Quarto edition of the play, where a long exchange between Bolingbroke and Gaunt, absent from the Folio, begins with the son's refusal to accept his exile with patience:

> Must I not serve a long apprenticehood
> To foreign passages, and in the end,
> Having my freedom, boast of nothing else
> But that I was a journeyman to grief? (1.3.271–1.3.274)

The terms of this study have prepared us to read Bolingbroke's metaphor. Commentators have missed the significance of "my freedom," glossing it simply as release from apprenticeship upon the completion of its indentures.[48] In likening his exile to an apprenticeship, Bolingbroke also depicts his eventual return as accession to the burgess freedom or citizenship that accompanied the end of the apprentice's service. It is a striking metaphor for a great nobleman to use, for the loss and partial recovery of aristocratic identity is mapped onto the stages of urban identity. Bolingbroke will attain the freedom, so to speak, but he will have to earn it in foreign passages. The six years of his exile are close to the mandated seven-year period of most indentures, although hardly a "long" apprenticeship. Attaining the freedom, he will only be able to claim that he "was" a journeyman, not an apprentice. Editors have struggled to justify the past tense, but the explanation may be simple. Sometimes apprentices completed their service and became journeymen or wage-laborers without shops *before* they became citizens (furthermore, this might seem a prolonged state of apprenticehood indeed).[49] Or the "end" Bolingbroke envisions may be the end of his life or career: looking back, he will recall both his minority and his journeyman-like status as a repealed but suspect courtier.

Some journeymen never became masters and householders in their companies, as Bolingbroke implies his metaphorical case will turn out. Most did, but there is evidence that the journeyman years were full of "grief" for many because of low wages and competition for labor. Idle journeymen joined with apprentices in riot and social protest during the late sixteenth century. Bolingbroke appeals to the frustrating experiences most men in the contemporary public theater audience had shared.[50] The end of apprenticeship was a key rite of manhood in early modern London. Outfitted with tools, enrolled in the freemen's register, and finally permitted to marry, the former apprentice had attained adulthood, but a number of years might pass before the jour-neyman could afford to set up shop and take a wife.[51] Bolingbroke invents a compelling figure for the transitional state to which banishment and the blockage of his implicit claim to the throne have restricted him. He confides his fears to his father, but with an eye to the rhetoric he might practice on the London freemen of his day, with whom many in Shakespeare's audience would sympathize. His final words in the scene confirm this impression: now he says he will always "boast" of being a true-born Englishman, not just a grieving journeyman.

In the next scene, Richard ridicules Bolingbroke for "his courtship to the common people" as he takes his leave of London:

> Wooing poor craftsmen with the craft of smiles
> . . . .
> Off goes his bonnet to an oyster-wench;
> A brace of draymen bid God speed him well,
> And had the tribute of his supple knee,
> With "Thanks, my countrymen, my loving friends."
> (1.4.28, 1.4.31–1.4.34)

It is not only craftsmen but itinerant women hawkers and draymen or carters who receive Bolingbroke's flattery. They are "countrymen," not citizens, subsumed in a wider national category of belonging. Freemen in the audience might worry about Bolingbroke's strategy, finding it too inclusive. In the play-world, he maintains the support of the rich "commons," respecting their purses where Richard emptied them (2.2.88, 2.2.128–2.2.130). His noble supporters speak of the faltering Richard in city terms, later echoed by Richard himself: "The king's grown bankrout like a broken man" (2.1.257; 4.1.267). By disinheriting Bolingbroke upon Gaunt's death, Richard undermines the institution of primogeniture that grounds both aristocratic and citizen wealth. He threatens his own legitimacy, as York tells him: "Take Herford's rights away, and take from time/His charters, and his customary rights" (2.1.195–2.1.196). Livery companies and the cities that sustained them were chartered, along with other entities that maintained a limited independence from the Crown. In *Richard II*, aristocratic and even royal rights are chartered, too, by "time," which governs succession, or by a higher power that charters time in turn. As in *The Merchant of Venice*, where the city's charter seemingly depends on Shylock's claim, Shakespeare blends civic and sovereign concepts of right, subjecting royal authority to citizen language while maintaining an ideal of sovereignty on the metaphysical level.[52]

If Richard menaces the legitimacy of kingship by tampering with inheritance, then Bolingbroke endangers the very definition of sovereignty itself. First as pretender, and then as Henry IV, he makes his authority partly dependent on popularity and the manipulation of his reputation. York describes his ceremonial entry into London:

> You would have thought the very windows spake,
> So many greedy looks of young and old
> Through casements darted their desiring eyes
> Upon his visage; and that all the walls
> With painted imagery had said at once
> "Jesu preserve thee! Welcome, Bolingbroke!"
> Whilst he, from one side to the other turning,
> Bare-headed, lower than his proud steed's neck,
> Bespake them thus, "I thank you, countrymen." (5.2.12–5.2.20)

Bolingbroke's obsequious behavior toward his "countrymen" is remarkable in a would-be king: even Richard III's charades do not go so far. The vivid second-hand account of citizens crowding the casements to get a look at their hero will appear again in *Henry V* and *Coriolanus*. As so often in Shakespeare, the casements connote shop windows as well as domestic ones. The London setting gives added point to York's analogy to "a theatre" in the succeeding lines, since the city was famous for its amphitheater playhouses in Shakespeare's day. The deposed Richard comes behind in procession like a prattling player who rates contempt by following the well-graced Bolingbroke on the public stage (lines 23–28).

An earlier comparison reminds us of the ill fame that hung about the theaters' neighborhoods. Queen Isabel calls Richard in defeat "a most beauteous inn," and asks: "Why should hard-favour'd grief be lodg'd in thee,/When triumph is become an alehouse guest?" (5.1.13–5.1.15). Bolingbroke is the alehouse, the lowest form of hostelry. His eldest son will render Isabel's metaphor literal in *King Henry IV, Part 1*, making his progress through the guts of the alehouse world. Searching after the prince, King Henry directs:

> Inquire at London, 'mongst the taverns there,
> For there, they say, he daily doth frequent
> With unrestrained loose companions,
> Even such, they say, as stand in narrow lanes
> And beat our watch and rob our passengers. (5.3.5–5.3.9)

The painted walls of London's streets have become dark lanes where Henry's son consorts with men who rob the people his father had so recently entertained. Prince Hal must relegitimize sovereignty despite, or rather through, the alehouse and the border between countrymen and freemen it straddles.

In *1 Henry IV*, the prince meets Poins for supper in Eastcheap after the double robbery, evidently at "the olde tauerne" there mentioned in *The Famous Victories of Henry the Fifth*, a source play. Although stage tradition calls it the Boar's Head, a historical hostelry in the area, the tavern is unnamed by Shakespeare.[53] The name *Eastcheap* summoned up a street and neighborhood in London with definite associations for the contemporary audience. As Dover Wilson demonstrated long ago, Eastcheap was a butchers' market. It was full of cookshops and other eating and drinking places, and thus a fitting resort for Sir John Falstaff.[54] There were several other "flesh markets" in London, including St. Nicholas Shambles, Leadenhall, and Newgate Market, as well as Smithfield where livestock was sold. Bartholomew Fair and its pork pies made an annual appearance there.[55] Some of these names appear in the *Henry IV* plays. Gadshill, for instance, piously calls his confederates "St. Nicholas' clerks," a well-attested slang expression for highwaymen, and the air of the shambles may hang about this allusion (2.1.60).[56] The Church of St. Nicholas Shambles was the religious center of the Butchers' Company. Eastcheap itself certainly meant butchers and their wares to sixteenth-century Londoners. The Boar's Head, whose very name connotes pork butchery, was the area's principal resort for food and drink, hence its traditional identification as the play's tavern. The Boar's Head was also the customary gathering place for butchers, after company members' funerals, for instance.[57] When Mrs. Quickly calls Falstaff to account for his marriage promise in *King Henry IV, Part 2*, she claims as witness "goodwife Keech the butcher's wife," her gossip, who had dropped by the tavern to borrow some vinegar.[58] Shakespeare's tavern is as much a part of its neighborhood as the Boar's Head was.

The connection between Eastcheap and the butchers' trade throws the counterpoint of common and aristocratic life in the Henriad into sharp relief. Eastcheap also provides a literal setting and a set of metaphorical reference-points for the aristocracy's co-optation of popular violence in both tetralogies. By *1 Henry IV*, the merest gesture toward the slaughter that has passed and is to come is all that is needed. The king ordains the supposed end of the fighting at the start of the play. England will cease cannibalizing herself, and no more "daub her lips with her own children's blood." Those opposed fronts, that

> Did lately meet in the intestine shock
> And furious close of civil butchery,

Shall now, in mutual well-beseeming ranks,
March all one way, and be no more oppos'd
Against acquaintance, kindred, and allies.
The edge of war, like an ill-sheathed knife,
No more shall cut his master.   (1.1.6, 1.1.12–1.1.18)

In the late sixteenth century, *civil* primarily denoted "Of or belonging to citizens"; *intestine* meant "Internal with regard to a country or people," but in the late 1590s *intestines* and *intestinal* were taking on their modern anatomical meanings.[59] The word *intestine* lends physicality to the idea of "civil" butchery, an inward-turning but also self-eviscerating violence. The improperly sheathed knife remains the proverbial tool of the butcher. Its master, if we continue to read the metaphor back into its origin, is a master butcher; the knife is a sort of rebellious apprentice, like Peter, who strikes down his master the armorer in *2 Henry VI*.

The play's second outright reference to butchery occurs 29 lines later, in Westmoreland's account of Glendower's victory. "The noble Mortimer," we are told,

Was by the rude hands of that Welshman taken,
A thousand of his people butchered,
Upon whose dead corpse there was such misuse,
Such beastly shameless transformation,
By those Welshwomen done.   (1.1.38, 1.1.41–1.1.45)

Witches were supposed to mangle bodies. History, or Henry's staging of how and when history is reported, brings about the externalization of civil into uncivil butchery beyond the borders of the kingdom, if not quite in the manner Henry had just proposed. The English are on the receiving end; furthermore, Mortimer joins with Glendower, marrying the Welsh leader's daughter. Although he is part of the rebel alliance of north and extreme west, Hotspur chafes at the Welsh connection, complaining that Glendower speaks "such a deal of skimble-skamble stuff/As puts me from my faith" (3.1.148–3.1.149). Shakespeare apparently invents a phrase to describe the Welshman's mixture of prophecy and personal bluster, but "skamble," as *scamble*, is a form of the word *shamble*, and in the plural it means a butcher's market or place of slaughter.[60] There is a reminiscence, then, of the news about Welsh butchery that opens the action. Mortimer's conquest by Glendower's daughter, her father's supernatural talk, and the near-magical music also recall the hint of witchcraft in the play's initial reference to the Welsh.

If butchery is driven outside of London, indeed, outside of England at the start of the *Henry IV* plays, it leaves a residue at the heart of the metropolis in the considerable person of Falstaff. The cowardly Sir John is repeatedly equated with meat and fat, the butcher's products, rather than the bloody craft itself.[61] An early exception to this pattern occurs in the Gad's Hill robbery scene, in which Falstaff goes on the attack against unarmed Canterbury pilgrims and "traders riding to London with fat purses" (1.2.123). He calls them "bacon-fed knaves," "fat chuffs," and, simply, "bacons"; "they hate us youth," he cries, incongruously clumping himself with the hungry apprentices (2.2.81–2.2.82, 2.2.85). But even here, Falstaff remains "ye fat guts" to the prince, and once the tables are turned, he "lards the lean earth" in his efforts to escape (lines 31, 104). Hal also calls him "that damned brawn," or pig, and then "Ribs" and "Tallow." He is an "obscene greasy tallow-catch," a pan for dripping pork fat, or perhaps a tallow "keech" or roll of fat (2.4.107–2.4.109, 2.4.223). In *2 Henry IV* the butcher's wife is named Keech; it was part of the butcher's trade to collect and roll up tallow for candles.[62] In that play, Falstaff is also called "Harry Monmouth's brawn" by their enemies, and he terms himself "a sow that hath overwhelmed all her litter but one" in comparison to his tiny page (1.1.19; 1.2.10–1.2.11). "Doth the old boar feed in the old frank?" Hal asks, in a possible reference to the Boar's Head Tavern as Falstaff's customary feeding-pen (2.2.138–2.2.139). To Doll Tearsheet Falstaff is a "little tidy Bartholomew boar-pig," a reference to the fair held in Smithfield and its chief comestible (2.4.227). Earlier Bardolph goes to the livestock market at Smithfield to buy Falstaff a horse, and Quickly tells the officers to seek him there at Pie Corner (1.2.50; 2.1.25). He calls himself "A wassail candle, . . . all tallow," not wax, and the prince dubs him, in a particularly vile turn, "You whoreson candle-mine" (1.2.157; 2.4.267). The Epilogue to *2 Henry IV* promises more of Sir John, "If you be not too much cloyed with fat meat" (lines 26–27).

My excuse for this list of carnal allusions is not one of the usual reasons—there is no need to prove once again that Falstaff personifies the body and its needs, or that he gives shape to visions, either utopian or dystopian, of the social significance of food. It is animal food that Falstaff embodies, and it is the sheer detail of his identification with it, the different names for it and its by-products, and the geography of its production that fascinate. A different study might consider the ecology of Falstaff's relation to meat. Here I would note, first, its varied evocation of the butcher's trade, and second, its ironic relation to the language of aristocratic and popular violence across the history plays and their landscape. A braggart but not a fighter, Falstaff is the optimistic, or opportunistic, product of civil butchery. His figurative bulk obscures the literal heap of bodies that warfare generates, as his wit partly does when he leads in his poor soldiers. They are "food for powder," gunpowder, that is, but also a food that recalls powdered beef, or meat salted for future consumption (*1 Henry IV*, 4.2.65; OED "Powdered," 2 a–b).

Bovine references balance the plays' fondness for pork. In the midst of much else, Hal calls Falstaff "that roasted Manningtree ox with the pudding in his belly," and a few lines later his butt replies, "if to be fat be to be hated, then Pharaoh's lean kine are to be loved" (2.4.446–2.4.447, 2.4.466–2.4.468). Manningtree in Essex was known for morality plays acted by guild members, accompanied perhaps by sanctioned, if somewhat immoderate, feasting (lines 446–447 note); Falstaff moralizes on the dream of dearth in Genesis 41 to defend himself as an allowed sign of God's plenty. Reconciled, he is the prince's "sweet beef" or ox when he receives his military commission (3.3.176). In *2 Henry IV*, Poins asks Bardolph about "the martelmas your master": St. Martin's feast day on November 11 was the date for slaughtering cattle and powdering the meat for winter, and a "martelmas" beef the tough and withered, but still bulky, result.[63] There are plenty of references to livestock. Doll is akin to Falstaff "as the parish heifers are to the town bull" (2.2.148–2.2.150). Justice Shallow inquires the price of "a good yoke of bullocks at Stamford fair," and one of the Gloucestershire muster is named "Peter Bullcalf o'th'green" (3.2.38, 3.2.168). Ruminating on his exploitation of the wealthy Justice Shallow, Falstaff recalls how as a student in London Shallow might have fit inside an eel-skin, but "now he has land and beefs" (3.2.320–3.2.322). Ominously, when Prince John tricks the rebels they dismiss their soldiers, and "Like youthful steers unyok'd they take their courses/East, west, north, south." Not satisfied with executing their noble leaders, John commands: "pursue the scatter'd stray" (4.2.103–4.2.104, 4.2.120). Falstaff delivers one of them to death in the next scene.

It will be noticed that these are mostly rural references rather than allusions to the practices of city butchery or the customs of the London Butchers' Company. Manningtree, Stamford, the town bull on the village green—all conjure up a geography far beyond the urban chorography of Eastcheap, Newgate, and Smithfield with its Pie Corner and boar-pigs. In *1 Henry IV* and then in *2 Henry IV*, we begin with city sites and move to country ones. In each play, we also begin with pork and are presented with beef as our second course.

Fowl and pigs, white meat, provided the portable urban flesh; bulls and cows were also brought into London, along with sheep, but only in Manningtree could you enjoy a freshly roasted ox stuffed with sausages. An emerging English national identity, as distinct from London citizenship's mobile urban character, remained strongly associated with beef, as it would through Hogarth, John Bull, and beyond.[64] Just as the butcher's craft bridged country production and city consumption, so Sir John Falstaff traverses rural and urban spaces, uniting them even as he exposes the often disreputable things they have in common. "Well, I cannot last forever," as he modestly grumbles, "but it was alway yet the trick of our English nation, if they have a good thing, to make it too common" (1.2.214–1.2.216). Falstaff's person not only joins lower-class, citizen, and aristocratic positions, it also superposes the city upon the country and vice-versa, like *The Merry Wives of Windsor* does. In part 1 and then again in part 2 of *Henry IV*, Falstaff swerves away from the metropolis toward the center of the nation. He unites (may I be allowed this culinary sally?) the white and the red, but in a parodic, carnivalesque, and ultimately self-cannibalizing manner that sits uneasily alongside the Tudor myth.

Even as Falstaff sets his sights on the English countryside, urban references, still mixed in with foodstuffs, drag the character back to the city and its ethnic anxieties. After the half-alien Dutch dish of *Merry Wives*, we might expect the Henriad's Falstaff to come across as symbolically strange or foreign. There is much less of this in the histories than the comedy. Falstaff is indeed associated with butter in *1 Henry IV*: he is the compound of Titan, the sun, and a dish of butter, he is as fat as butter, and his thieving has made him run to butter, or corpulence (2.4.117–2.4.120, 2.4.504; 4.2.60–4.2.61). In part 2, Quickly sighs "what the goodyear! [perhaps from the current Dutch, *wat goedtjaar*] one must bear" with Falstaff, but Doll complains, "Can a weak empty vessel bear such a huge full hogshead? There's a whole merchant's venture of Bordeaux stuff in him," meaning wine or cloth (2.4.57–2.4.58 and note, 2.4.61–2.4.63). Falstaff happily advises Quickly to replace tapestries, pawned for his sake, with "the German hunting, in waterwork." He refers to pre-fabricated walls with cheap murals or painted cloths already on them, imported from Flanders or Holland (2.1.143 note). This is a poor return for the fine linen shirts from Holland she bought him in part 1 (3.3.69). Gadshill boasts that his fellow-thieves are "nobility and tranquility, burgomasters and great onyers" who prey on the commonwealth (*1 Henry IV*, 2.1.74–2.1.75). *Onyers* ("Oneyres" in the early Quartos, "Oneyers" in F) might be an error for *myn-heers*, as in a similar place in *Merry Wives*. *Burgomasters* certainly betokens the Dutch, and its coupling with *nobility* deliberately confounds the distinction between heroic aristocrats and fainthearted citizen leaders found in Nashe and the *Henry VI* plays.

Prince Hal is implicated here along with Falstaff, and in fact his father will later tell him he has lost his seat in Council "And art almost an alien to the hearts/Of all the court and princes of my blood" (3.2.34–3.2.35). In *2 Henry IV*, Warwick assures Henry that

> The Prince but studies his companions
> Like a strange tongue, wherein, to gain the language,
> 'Tis needful that the most immodest word
> Be look'd upon and learnt.

Hal will cast off his outlandish friends like "gross terms" (4.4.68–4.4.73). Falstaff complains of the notoriety his fatness lends him in a similar way: "I have a whole school of tongues in this belly of mine, and not a tongue of them all speaks any other word but my name. . . . My womb, my womb, my womb undoes me" (4.3.18–4.3.20, 4.3.22–4.3.23). City anxieties about Londoners' acquiring foreign languages from aliens in schools, which as we saw in chapter 1 of this book lies behind many of the linguistic jibes in *Love's Labour's Lost*, informs these passages in *2 Henry IV* as well. It also casts a different light on Hal's strategy of "recording" lower-class city idiolects in general, like those of the apprentice vintners or drawers in part 1.[65] Hal has developed the particularly urban skill of learning and managing alien languages, in all senses of these words, in order to bargain with their speakers without becoming subdued to their interests. Such a skill suggests another side to his fond, linguistically adept inventory of Poins's possessions, principally his linen. Amid his frequent exercise at the tennis-courts, "the rest of thy low countries have made a shift to eat up thy holland" (2.2.21–2.2.22). Poins has had to turn his good shirts into underwear because the pressures of his nether regions demand it, just as the Netherlands have absorbed Dutch wealth. The intimacy—probably sexual—implied by the joke belies Hal's intention to cast his own dirty linen aside and Poins along with it, when the time comes.

Poins's diminished shirts recall the "half shirt" shared by the men in Falstaff's ragged company in *1 Henry IV* (4.2.43). In misusing his royal commission to conscript soldiers, he says,

> I press me none but good householders, yeomen's sons, inquire me out contracted bachelors, such as had been asked twice on the banns, such

a commodity of warm slaves as had as lief hear the devil as a drum.
(lines 14–18)

These moneyed men buy out their service, leaving Falstaff to impress
the indigent and keep some three hundred pounds for himself. The
key terms in this familiar passage are city terms. *Householders* were
London freemen and company members who owned their own houses
or workshops; they were ranked between journeymen and members of
their company's livery. *Yeomen* are almost always well-off farmers in
Shakespeare, which makes the city sense of the usage here stand out
all the more: the yeomanry was a social organization within a company below the elite livery members, and it also assumed some of the
practical tasks in company government.[66] Most company members
were yeomen; since many apprentices came from outside of London,
to be a yeoman's son was to be a real Londoner. Falstaff exchanges
these "toasts-and-butter," as he calls them, for the largely urban poor:
younger sons, dismissed or truant servants and apprentices, and the
"trade-fallen" (lines 20–21, 27–30). He admits, "you would think
that I had a hundred and fifty tattered prodigals lately come from
swine-keeping," an appropriate parable for a Bartholomew boar-pig
to cite (lines 27–30, 33–35). Falstaff's thorough familiarity with the
citizen and sub-citizen worlds he exploits is evident in his language in
1 Henry IV. The prince has learned his strategy of linguistic absorp-
tion at the knee of a great teacher. Now unable to see this knee for his
girth, Falstaff tells Hal that at his age "I could have crept into any
alderman's thumb-ring" (2.4.326–2.4.327). Where womanhood is
concerned, he tells Quickly, the transvestite morris-dancer Maid
Marian "may be the deputy's wife of the ward to thee"
(3.3.112–3.3.113). In these jests, the civic sublime is made low by
imaginary juxtaposition with the malleable, grotesque body.

Something similar happens in Hotspur's speech excusing his reten-
tion of the king's prisoners. He balked when approached by "a certain
lord" who "was perfumed like a milliner," and who blamed the soldiers for carrying the corpses upwind of his nobility (1.3.32, 1.3.35,
1.3.41–1.3.44). Finally,

> With many holiday and lady terms
> He question'd me, amongst the rest demanded
> My prisoners in your Majesty's behalf. (lines 45–46)

Familiarity with dead bodies defines the warrior's manliness and
separates him from the effeminate and, significantly, citified courtier.
The lord seems to have learned his manners and his weak oaths from

a milliner or haberdasher. Unlike Falstaff, however, Harry Percy is thoroughly opposed to London, not a knowledgeable and fond manipulator of city life. Hotspur is the complete provincial. He has no understanding of the urban rhythm of work and leisure that drives a culture of dilatory consumption. Thus, "holiday" terms are foreign and epicene to him, even when he is forced to rest from the battle upon his sword (line 31).

However teasing, Hotspur's censure of his wife for her delicate swearing in the Welsh scene is touched with genuine annoyance at imagined London ways:

> Heart, you swear like a comfit-makers wife—"Not you, in good sooth!", and "As true as I live!", and "As God shall mend me!", and "As sure as day!"—
> And givest such sarcenet surety for thy oaths
> As if thou never walk'st further than Finsbury.
> Swear me, Kate, like a lady as thou art,
> A good mouth-filling oath, and leave "In sooth",
> And such protest of pepper-gingerbread,
> To velvet-guards, and Sunday citizens. (3.1.241–3.1.250)

Hotspur's complaint is about class—great ladies are, oddly to our view, supposed to be great swearers—but also about region and religion. Puritan city leaders discouraged frank oaths. Finsbury fields were just north of the city; a place of holiday escape for Londoners, to a Percy they are a poor substitute for the north itself. Kate speaks sometimes as if she has traveled no further north than Finsbury. She makes him a confectioner by swearing like the wife of one. A sarcenet or silken surety is all she offers, milliners' ware rather than God's body or her salvation by it. She is a Sunday citizen on her weekly holiday, a velvet-guarded or trimmed friend, like the unfaithful mate who abandons the stricken deer in *As You Like It*.

Finsbury was also the setting for musters and martial display. When Vernon reports the prince's transformation into a knightly figure, he apparently includes many of Hal's city companions:

> All furnished, all in arms;
> All plum'd like estridges. . . .
> As full of spirit as the month of May,
> And gorgeous as the sun at midsummer;
> Wanton as youthful goats, wild as young bulls.
>   (4.1.97–4.1.98, 4.1.101–4.1.104)

The goatish lust and Falstaffian bullishness of the tavern world have briefly undergone conversion to chivalric spectacle. May and midsummer are holiday times, but also the period of military campaigns. Hotspur remains unimpressed by his southern enemies in their "trim." Common metaphors of butchery do not even occur to him— he will sacrifice them in the classical and aristocratic vein on the altar of Mars (lines 113–117).

In contrast to Hotspur, Hal grasps the rhythm of labor and rest, and he builds it into his planned reformation from the beginning:

> If all the year were playing holidays,
> To sport would be as tedious as to work;
> But when they seldom come, they wish'd-for come.

He will suddenly surprise the on-lookers by "Redeeming time when men least think I will" (1.2.199–1.2.201, 1.2.212). The prince's May-to-midsummer epiphany at the head of his London band is the culmination of this scheme. Hotspur's anti-citizen stance is not unlike that of the first tetralogy, in which Nashian burgomasters fearfully marvel at Duke Humphrey's anger or Richard's effrontery. In the Henriad, Shakespeare is skeptical about citizen culture, but like Falstaff he enjoys it. In Hal he creates a leader who takes over the city's cycle of labor and holiday. To Hal, Hotspur is someone who works too hard, and he sets out to make his northern rival toil for him. Proposing a play at the inn, he imagines an industrious borderer:

> the Hotspur of the north, he that kills me some six or seven dozen of
> Scots at a breakfast, washes his hands, and says to his wife, "Fie upon
> this quiet life, I want work." (2.4.100–2.4.103)

Percy will not take time out to break his fast or rest afterward. Hal takes rhetorical advantage of Hotspur's labors in defending himself to Henry IV:

> Percy is but my factor, good my lord,
> To engross up glorious deeds on my behalf,
> And I will call him to so strict account
> That he shall render every glory up,
> Yea, even the slightest worship of his time. (3.2.147–3.2.151)

The "northern youth" (line 145) is really the country factor or sales representative to the London prince. Making your enemy your agent is the other side of the holiday strategy that Hal's father also employed, in which he let others work for him while his state "Seldom, but sumptuous, show'd like a feast" (line 58).

The modern alternation of work and holiday is part of the play's larger attention to time, as the last substantial quotation shows. To redeem time, call in debts on time, keep time, and manage time are all citizen concerns. Even Falstaff claims to have "fought a long hour by Shrewsbury clock," at the end of which he killed Hotspur (5.4.147). It is in the scene where Falstaff makes this boast that Hal actually defeats Hotspur and completes his rival's final sentence. Time must have a stop for Percy, but it is a continuous process for the prince. Hotspur is now "food" for worms, and not for Time, or "time the eater of things" in the classic proverb that I would suggest Percy intended to cite (lines 81–86).[67] "Ill-weav'd ambition, how much art thou shrunk," Hal goes on, making the provincial rebellion a product of poor craftsmanship in a reminiscence of Jack Cade the clothier (line 87). Literalizing the metaphor in Hotspur's "And food for—," his master the prince insists that he is also so much wasted meat, to be consumed by vermin.

When Northumberland laments Hotspur's death at the start of *2 Henry IV*, the messenger reminds the grieving father that he knew the risks of the "bold enterprise" of rebellion: "You were advis'd . . . that his forward spirit / Would lift him where most trade of danger rang'd" (1.1.172–1.1.174, 1.1.178). Lord Bardolph expands the trope:

> We all that are engaged to this loss
> Knew that we ventur'd on such dangerous seas
> That if we wrought out life 'twas ten to one;
> And yet we ventur'd for the gain proposed,
> Chok'd the respect of likely peril fear'd,
> And since we are o'erset, venture again. (lines 180–185)

Northumberland, like Henry IV and the prince, has realized all along that war must now be understood in mercantile terms; only Hotspur fought vainly for honor while serving unwittingly as Hal's factor.[68] After the prince makes off with the crown, Henry, another mournful father, compares being a ruler and parent to the fruitless enterprise of an aging merchant:

> For this the foolish over-careful fathers
> Have broke their sleep with thoughts,
> Their brains with care, their bones with industry;
> For this they have engrossed and pil'd up
> The canker'd heaps of strange-achieved gold;
> For this they have been thoughtful to invest
> Their sons with arts and martial exercises. (4.5.67–4.5.73)

He is like a bee who gathers honey far and wide only to be murdered for his pains (lines 74–78). As with the elusive gains in Northumberland's sea-venture of rebellion, Henry's supposed profits are somehow "strange" or foreign. Hal demonstrates to him that he understands how this golden legacy brings care and self-destruction with it as well as profit (lines 156–164).

As the father was to the son, so the master was to the apprentice, and Hal remains in the frustrated position of an apprentice or journeyman to his merchant-like father through much of part 2. His situation is graphically realized in the trick he plays on Falstaff when he and Poins disguise themselves as drawers in the Eastcheap tavern. They put on aprons, symbols of the labor that went into citizen culture, and spy on the fat knight's dallying with Doll (2.4.231–2.4.290). "From a prince to a prentice?" Hal asks. "A low transformation, that shall be mine, for in everything the purpose must weigh with the folly" (2.2.167–2.2.169). Despite his excuses, his behavior bears out Falstaff's complaint elsewhere that "pregnancy is made a tapster, and his quick wit wasted in giving reckonings" (1.2.169–1.2.170). Northumberland had been said to "cast the'event of war . . . And summ'd the account of chance" (1.1.166–1.1.167). To thrive in what a character in *Richard II* called "this new world" (4.1.78), nobility has long since descended to the lowest forms of calculation in both pleasure and power. This may partly explain Hal's seemingly impractical joke on Francis the drawer in *1 Henry IV*. Tricked into demanding the thousand pounds the prince promised him "anon, anon" or right away, his habitual cry, Francis is told he will have to wait, as Hal himself will have to wait for the crown and the end of his apprentice or journeyman status as heir. Speaking of the sugar Francis gave him gratis, Hal badgers the tapster for stealing from his master the vintner: "Wilt thou rob this leather-jerkin, crystal-button, not-paited, agate-ring, puke-stocking, caddis-garter, smooth-tongue Spanish pouch"? (2.4.68–2.4.70). The volley of insults pairs contrasting attributes of citizen identity: for instance, leather work-wear with the crystal buttons that came into fashion in Elizabeth's reign, or the short hair of the humble Puritan with the agate rings favored by proud aldermen (lines 68, 69 note). The Vintner's Company was a wealthy one despite the lower-class milieu of some of its freemen, since it profited from the sale of food as well as drink in places like Eastcheap.[69] Hal's wit, the pregnancy of a tapster, is directed against his pious, industrious, and ruthless father as much as the civic authority-figures who stand in for him.

For the prince partly accepts the citizen translation of sovereign power that he mocks. In *2 Henry IV* it is Falstaff who takes on

Hotspur's role as scornful critic of the citizens and their ways, a sure sign of his downfall. The apparent difference between Hal and his companion had already been noted by the drawers in part 1, where they tell him "I am no proud Jack like Falstaff, but a Corinthian, a lad of mettle, a good boy" (2.4.11–2.4.12). After extorting money from householders in the first play, Falstaff abuses their financial demands in the second, posing as war hero and grandee. "What said Master Dommelton about the satin for my short cloak and my slops?", he asks his page (1.2.28–1.2.30). When told that Dommelton requests more security before sending the merchandise without payment, Falstaff calls him

> A rascally yea-forsooth knave, to bear a gentleman in hand, and then stand upon security! The whoreson smooth-pates do now wear nothing but high shoes and bunches of keys at their girdles. . . . Well, he may sleep in security, for he hath the horn of abundance, and the lightness of his wife shines through it. (lines 35–39, 45–47)

The passage echoes Hotspur's antipathy to devout city Protestants ("smooth-pates") and their weak swearing (like "yea-forsooth"). It also alludes to the familiar joke about tradesmen's wives cuckolding their husbands—throwing some retrospective "lightness" upon Percy's distaste for Lady Percy's citizen oaths. Falstaff continues to consort with rich townsmen, as he does in *Merry Wives*, although no mention is made of their spouses. Quickly sends officers to seek him for debt: "he is indited to dinner to the Lubber's Head in Lumbert Street to Master Smooth's the silkman" (2.1.26–2.1.28). Lombard Street, whose name preserves its association with Italian merchants, was one location for shops carrying luxury goods. *Indited* hints at the probable end of this transaction, too. Falstaff has of course been wooing Quickly herself (lines 83–101), now a widow and presumably the owner of her tavern.

Sent to the country in arms once more, this time to gather his troops there, Falstaff imposes his city methods of recruiting on Gloucestershire and its village types. Among the five potential conscripts, Bullcalf and Mouldy, evidently farmers by their names and speeches (for instance 3.2.113), buy out their services for a few pounds each, while Feeble, a woman's tailor, and Wart, who is probably a carpenter (3.2.142–3.2.144), are chosen, along with one Simon Shadow. A "shadow" was a false name on a muster-role (line 134 note), and also an actor—"Shadow will serve for summer," the season for battles and stage-plays (line 133). There may be a joke here about country boys with theatrical aspirations. In the country, it is the smallholders who have a bit of money and the tradesmen and their kin who are doing poorly, a situation not unfamiliar to Shakespeare. Defending his choices on military grounds, Falstaff tells Justice Shallow that spirit, not stature, makes the soldier:

> Here's Wart; you see what a ragged appearance it is—a shall charge you, and discharge you, with the motion of a pewterer's hammer, come off and on swifter than he that gibbets on a brewer's bucket. (lines 255–259)

It is unclear what the last phrase means, but the crafts referred to, especially brewing, were not among the richest. Falstaff declasses the military profession through trade analogies; it becomes the repository of the trade-fallen, not a pathway to middle-class honor. Observing Wart's exertions with the gun he has just been handed, Shallow worries that "He is not his craft's master, he doth not do it right" (line 273).

The Justice bases his judgment, typically, on memories of his youthful days at Clement's Inn in London. At the drill-ground in Mile-End Green he once saw a master-at-arms handle a caliver properly: "a would manage you his piece thus, and a would about, and about, and come you in, and come you in" (3.2.274–3.2.278). Shallow recalls that he played the fool Dagonet in the related show put on by The Ancient Order of Prince Arthur, which promoted archery. Like the apprentice plays and the Nine Worthies literature, the archers' Arthur-themed displays at Mile-End were intended to assure citizens that they could attain honor by acquiring skills for the defense of the realm.[70] The Gloucestershire muster scene precisely sends up such assurances, which were part of official Elizabethan propaganda.

Unintended sexual punning like that in the Mile-End maneuvers and a somewhat melancholy nostalgia characterize most of the rural JP's recollections of the great city. "Lusty" Shallow knew where the bona-robas or fashionable prostitutes could be found. He remembers young Falstaff as Mowbray's page, breaking someone's head at the court gate, and says "the very same day did I fight with one Samson Stockfish a fruiterer, behind Gray's Inn" (3.2.15, 3.2.28–3.2.32). Evidently a duel since they met in the fields beyond the inn, this encounter suggests yet another absurd or unsuitable single combat. That Stockfish was a fruiterer reflects complaints about "encroachers of handicrafts" who trade in occupations other than their own.[71] But given the student context, the dispute, whatever its outcome, was probably over debt. A little later, Shallow reminds Falstaff of a time "since we lay all night in the Windmill in Saint George's Field," one more field or green outside the city walls; the Windmill seems to be a tavern or brothel. "No more of that," his visitor repeats (lines 189–191). It is rare to see Falstaff embarrassed; even as he resolves to borrow money from Shallow, he is discomfited by memories of adventures in these places, neither rural nor urban, beyond the city's bars.[72] He abhors the past: "This same starved justice hath done nothing but prate to me of the wildness of his youth, and the feats he hath done about Turnbull Street, and every third word a lie" (lines 298–301). Turnbull Street was infamous for prostitution in both literature and contemporary law cases.[73] Falstaff concedes that Shallow was well known to the whores, who called him "mandrake" (line 306), the same epithet he applies to his little page (1.2.14). He bears out the legend of Shallow in part while passing over their farther-flung escapades.

Another character who is anxious about the past is Henry IV. After their final reconciliation, he counsels his son to adapt the plan of leading the country in a crusade when he becomes king:

> Be it thy course to busy giddy minds
> With foreign quarrels, that action hence born out
> May waste the memory of the former days. (4.5.213–4.5.215)

Memory is again the enemy. Henry's "by paths and indirect crook'd ways" to the crown, and not his son's days in Eastcheap, are what trouble the dying monarch (line 184). His "friends," and not his son's companions, are the danger, for the nobles "Have but their stings and teeth newly ta'en out" (line 205). As King Henry V, his son will follow this advice. And he will take care of his own former friends when he puts England on a war footing as well. Falstaff is rebuked and handed over to the Lord Chief Justice to be imprisoned. Not incidentally, the corrupt Shallow, whom he brought from Gloucestershire to London, is thrown in the Fleet with him, a disciplinary case of the city absorbing the country (5.5.91–5.5.92). Quickly and Doll Tearsheet are carried off for a whipping by the parish beadle (a "nut-hook" and "blue-bottle rogue" in the play's last burst of urban slang), accused of murder along with Pistol, who is presumably given a pass as a soldier (5.4.8, 5.4.16–5.4.21). As the disguised king of the Folio *Henry V* tells his men in a slightly different sense, criminals cannot escape God: "War is his beadle, war is his vengeance; so that here men are punished for before breach of the King's law in now the King's quarrel."[74] Prince John commends his brother's fair proceeding, and wagers that the English will convey their "civil swords" to France within the year (5.5.106).

Henry V, the final play of the tetralogies, appertains to forgetting as much as the making or remaking of memory. Henry defies the Dauphin's second-hand memory of his past, which is largely an urban past: tennis was a city sport, linked for instance to Poins and his shirts, and the mocking gift of the tennis balls alludes to Henry's reputation as a particular kind of city character, the young gallant-about-town (1.2.250–1.2.269; *2 Henry IV*, 2.2.16–2.2.20 and 18 note). An ancient and aristocratic lineage erases recent history with the onset of war. Henry is asked by his councilors to remember his conquering ancestors, and he charges his soldiers to attest that they are their forefathers' sons (1.2.115–1.2.124; 3.1.17–3.1.28). For all this, the language of the play often works against the overt shift to sovereignty and subjecthood. The picture of England and its displaced version, the English army in France, remains covertly urban. We are not, after all, in a world Talbot would recognize, although the historical time line seems to place us there.

Two classical commonplaces or *topoi* serve as bookends to *Henry V*'s subtle evocation of the city as a model for the nation: the beehive at the start of Act 1 and Rome as the seat of empire at the start of Act 5. In a comparison derived from Virgil, Canterbury says that honey-bees "by a rule in nature teach/The act of order to a peopled kingdom." They "have a king and officers of sorts," or of different degrees. Magistrates arbitrate at home, merchants venture abroad, and soldier-bees bring plunder to "The tent-royal of their emperor" (1.2.187–1.2.196). The bees are ruled by a king rather than a queen, as sixteenth-century natural history held, but the word *emperor* glances at the Roman model as well as contemporary apiology. The passage's urban connotations outweigh its sovereign context as it proceeds. The emperor-bee surveys

> The singing masons building roofs of gold,
> The civil citizens kneading up the honey,
> The poor mechanic porters crowding in
> The heavy burdens at his narrow gate,
> The sad-eyed justice, with his surly hum,
> Delivering o'er to executors pale
> The lazy yawning drone. (lines 197–204)

Masons, citizens, mechanicals, and the drone who serves as foil to set off their industry: for Canterbury, England becomes a metropolis dedicated to profitable order. In *The Book called The Governor*, Thomas Elyot had emphasized the royal nature of the bees' polity. Shakespeare acknowledges sovereign power but restores the *topos* to the urban scenes of Virgil's Carthage and the lawful city-state of bees in the *Georgics*.[75] The soldier-bee hints at the military qualification for civic participation in Machiavelli as well; in a sense, all members of apian society have a military role, and its command structure recalls that of a camp or fortified town, in which all labor for victory.

The play that follows repeatedly stresses the image of labor. Henry, who once consorted with apprentices and journeymen, apologizes for seeming "like a man for working days" until undertaking the serious task of the French war (1.2.278). Much later, he depicts war itself as labor in a homely but affirmative fashion: "Tell the Constable/We are but warriors for the working day" (4.3.108–4.3.109). Workmen's camaraderie lies behind Henry's best-known device in rallying his troops. At Agincourt he tells them "This day is called the feast of Crispian." The brothers Crispin and Crispianus, martyred shoemakers, were the patron saints of that occupation (4.3.40 and note). On their feast day every October 25, a play of St. Crispin was performed before the Cordwainers' Company of leather shoemakers; *Henry V* reminds the spectators that this was a date for national as well as company celebration. Crispin and his brother were originally Gallic saints with their own confraternity of shoemakers in Paris during the sixteenth century, although Crispin was supposed by the Cordwainers to have resettled in England. As the company was actively opposed to French and other alien cobblers in London during the 1590s, it is fitting that the anniversary of Agincourt also commemorates a victory of cultural appropriation.[76] The link between "Crispian" and shoemaking is not mentioned in the play, but would have been well known to workers in the audience from apprentices through to liverymen. Fluellen's suggestion that the common soldier Williams accept his gratuity to "mend your shoes" after the battle may mark the association (4.8.71).

Henry also adopts a workaday attitude in his wooing of Katherine of France. He is "a fellow of plain and uncoined constancy" (5.2.153–5.2.154) and must speak bluntly. Of course, his English plainness contrasts with Katherine's speeches in French in this scene and in 3.4, not to mention his own lapse into the alien tongue (5.2.181–5.2.183). If it was possible to win his love by fighting, "I could lay on like a butcher" (lines 141–142). Although crowded among a number of similar protestations, this simile stands out. At the siege of Harfleur, the king had warned the French that his men might defile their daughters and rampage like "Herod's bloody-hunting slaughtermen" (3.3.35–3.3.41). Henry's courtship of Katherine translates rape into marriage, the legitimate and domestic correlate of his provisional possession of France.

The royal suitor presents the match as a simple middle-class bargain (line 131). The French king prays that Henry's marriage with his daughter will "Plant neighbourhood" between the kingdoms (line 347). This word appears early in the play, in a slightly different sense, when Henry worries about England's "ill neighbourhood" next to the Scots (1.2.154). British anxieties are transferred to Europe when Henry sets up military camp next to the French emplacement, for "our bad neighbour makes us early stirrers,/Which is both healthful and good husbandry," as he quips (4.1.6–4.1.7). The English camp itself, of course, is riven by regional rivalries, with the Welsh, Irish, and Scot captains staking different loyalist claims (3.2). "Neighborhood" in all these examples is set against ethnic or national difference, as it often was within London and its suburbs. Henry's marriage to the French princess marks a dynastic alliance, but it is rendered affective or "romantic" by invoking the kind of neighborly intermarriage some Londoners claimed French and other communities resisted.[77]

In Henry's speech before the battle of Agincourt, in which he imagines the future and its memories of the present, the neighborhood is projected as unified and English:

> He that shall see this day and live old age
> Will yearly on the vigil feast his neighbors,
> And say "Tomorrow is Saint Crispian."
> Then will he strip his sleeve and show his scars,
> And say "These wounds I had on Crispin's day." (4.3.44–4.3.48)

The city will momentarily become the camp again, just as the camp refashioned the city and the idea of neighborhood. Fittingly, after all their working-day labor, the old soldiers will enjoy a special holiday: they will share in Hal's strategy of seldom-coming, wished for celebration. St. Crispin's is not for the Cordwainers' only, but has become a city-wide, in fact a national, feast day on the anniversary of Agincourt. But among the celebrants, Pistol survives as well. After his beating for poor discipline, "patches will I get unto these cudgelled scars,/And swear I got them in the Gallia wars" (5.1.89–5.1.90). Gower had already marked the fraudulent veteran as a specifically urban type, often to be met with: "a rogue, that now and then goes to the wars to grace himself at his return into London under the form of a soldier. And such fellows are perfect in the great commanders' names. . . . [;] what a beard of the General's cut and a horrid suit of the camp will do among foaming bottles and ale-washed wits is wonderful to be thought on" (3.6.66–3.6.69, 3.6.75–3.6.78). Despite Henry's royal transformation, Eastcheap abides.

The return to holiday time is also seen in the second classical *topos* of city and nation, the evocation of Rome in the depiction of Henry's London entry before Act 5:

> But now behold,
> In the quick forge and working-house of thought,
> How London doth pour out her citizens.
> The Mayor and all his brethren in best sort,
> Like to the senators of th'antique Rome
> With the plebeians swarming at their heels,
> Go forth and fetch their conquering Caesar in.

The Chorus compares Henry to a proleptic image of the Earl of Essex, "the General of our gracious Empress," returning victorious, as he was not to do, from Ireland (5.0.22–5.0.28, 5.0.30). Imperial Rome offers a panorama of the state in celebration, just as Virgil's bees suggest the nation at work. Again, the image is an urban one. Shakespeare compares the mayor and aldermen rather than the members of parliament to senators; the "swarming" plebeians recall the bees of the earlier set-piece, just as the bees' "emperor" looks forward to the queen as the empress of a city–state. The apiary and Roman models of the *civitas* are idealizing on the surface, but they each contain disquieting elements for the audience to interpret. The dying king of *2 Henry IV* had already compared himself to a worker bee who is murdered for his riches (4.5.74–4.5.78). If Essex is like Henry V, or worse, a conquering Caesar, how will his return to London sit with even so gracious an empress as Elizabeth?[78] The word *sort*, meaning degree and clothing suited to degree, appears in both passages. The speeches stop just short of recognizing "the middling sort," but it is the industrious spectators in the contemporary audience who form these images, good and bad, in the "working-house" of thought.[79]

In Shakespeare's history plays, the material language of everyday life in the city forges the link with the citizens in the audience. Work, production, holiday, and food—particularly in the considerable person of the second tetralogy's Falstaff—accompany references to charters, freedoms, and livery company tensions. The spectators' "thought" is the crucible of a specific kind of political subjectivity as well.

Their subjectivation through English history and public concerns extends the economic vision of romantic and domestic experience in the comedies. Passive, ridiculous, stubbornly silent, and occasionally in revolt, the citizen is a negative but persistent figure of nonsovereign and nonaristocratic political power in the tetralogies. As with the comedies, the negative manifestation of burgess freedom sometimes takes the form of resentment against strangers. But Shakespeare also represses antialien tensions in his historical material. It is the aristocrat, not the alien, who emerges as the prime noncitizen type in these plays. Unlike strangers, nobles are not excluded from economic subjectivation. Instead, they are incorporated, as their monopoly on violence is gradually taken over by demotic and trade-based images of conflict, aggression, and brutality. As a genre, then, the Shakespearean history play, like its Henslovian competitors, remains bound to the commoners in the audience, mostly through the material level of urban language rather than stage action.

In the first tetralogy, as we have seen, action centered upon London does accompany the urban vocabulary. Jack Cade's rebellion moves from the country to the city in *2 Henry VI*, bringing with it the imagery of butchery that overtakes aristocratic violence as well as popular revolt by *3 Henry VI*. Single combat between armorer and apprentice degrades the rituals of nobility as well as the low comic participants; Talbot's heroics in France have become a distant memory. The broken armor donned by Richard and Buckingham in *Richard III* recalls the mock-heroic encounter, yet at the Guildhall the Yorkists use fraud, not force, to manipulate an indeterminate and feminized citizenry. If aristocratic dignity is debased, citizen power is hardly elevated in consequence. The second section of the chapter traces different modes of urban language in *Richard II* and the Henriad. Bolingbroke manipulates both the citizens and the audience from within, employing the categories of citizen subjectivity to describe his own frustrated career before rising through demagogic flattery as well as force to the throne. His son the prince seems in turn subjected to Eastcheap, the center of London butchery, and its gross terms. By *2 Henry IV*, he asserts his mastery by throwing off Falstaff. Sir John confounds country and city through most of the action, but he turns against London and its inhabitants long before Hal turns against him. As Henry V, then, the erstwhile prince takes over the melding of urban and rural terms that Falstaff once represented.

Despite its fragmentary London frame, *Henry V* is mostly set in France. Its fighting monarch makes his camp into a mini-metropolis, however, turning ethnic, national, and finally international conflict and its marital resolution into neighborhood matters. Popular language subsumes aristocratic violence in the final history play too, but in the honorable form of "work." Holiday time is managed through events like Henry's return to London, where any loss of magnificence in his citified sovereignty is supplemented by the allusion to the eternal city of Rome. Yet the swarm of plebeians, not to mention the survival of the lazy drone Pistol, suggests an underside to classical images of civic glory. In *2 Henry IV*, Rumor had compared the people to "the blunt monster with uncounted heads," and the Archbishop decried the "fond many" as a "beastly feeder" that eats up its leaders only to spit them out (Induction, line 18, 1.3.91–1.3.96). These virulent images of the common people in the city lurk behind Henry V's triumphal entry and also look forward to the ambivalence of the Roman tragedies, the topic of chapter 3.

CHAPTER 3

TRAGEDY: WHAT ROME?

London's memory of the ancient city of Rome was built into its folkloric topography. Queen Isabel bemoans Richard II's imprisonment in "Julius Caesar's ill-erected tower."[1] The Tower of London was traditionally begun, if not quite built, by Caesar upon his short-lived conquest of the city, as Buckingham explains to the young prince in *Richard III*. Even if its origins are not attested by the historical record, the prince observes, "Methinks the truth should live from age to age,/As 'twere retail'd to all posterity."[2] London's true relation with Roman antiquity remained an uncertain and competitive one. Anti-Catholic feeling and suspicion of the Holy Roman Empire exacerbated London's insecure ambitions in the early seventeenth century. Supposedly founded by the Trojan Brute as a "New Troy," London claimed common roots with Rome but sought to become Rome's rival and, under James I, its proper heir.[3]

Early modern Londoners might have seen themselves in Philemon Holland's translation of Livy in 1600, particularly in the early books on the anxious beginnings of Rome. Here Rome is presented as a rapidly expanding and multiethnic town strategically placed on the banks of a river. Aeneas's Trojans soon mixed with the Latin "Aborigines" who lived by the Tiber. In common with other city founders, Romulus established the *Asylum* or sanctuary in Rome:

> Thither resorted (as to a place of refuge) out of the neighbor countries, a rable and confused medley of all sorts, tag and rag, bond and free, one with another; folke desirous of change and noveltie.

Romulus also encouraged the capture of the Sabine women, who called for unity between their fathers and the Romans; both peoples were known henceforth as "Quirites," from a Sabine word. Rome's fifth king, L. Tarquinius Priscus, was born of a Tuscan woman and a Corinthian father in Etruria.[4] These traditions preserve Rome's actual origins in the confluence of Latins, Etruscans, and Greek colonists. In later times, as Livy records, Rome secured its strength by conquering Italian towns and partly extending its privileges to their inhabitants. Within the city itself, communities of aliens or *cives sine suffragio*, "citizens without voting rights," existed from relatively early times. After 90 BC, following the unsuccessful Social War against the allies, full citizenship was extended to Italians in Rome and throughout the peninsula.[5]

Under the mature Republic and the Empire, to be a *civis* one no longer necessarily resided in the city, or even in a town; the *civitas* became the state beyond the walls of Rome as well as the city itself. The change in connotation had consequences for political theory much later. Even Thomas Hobbes used the word *civitas* to denote the entire commonwealth in his treatise *De cive*, or "On the citizen," despite his distaste for republican Rome and its rejection of monarchy. Machiavelli was somewhat before Hobbes, at times employing the word *città* for "state" in his *Discorsi* on Livy.[6] According to Machiavelli, Rome became a great city, and thus a great state, by granting conquered peoples access to certain civic rights in return for military service. Arguing against the use of alien mercenaries during his time, he exalted the Roman militia of citizen-soldiers.[7] Machiavelli's *Arte della guerra* outlined in full a militia roughly patterned after Rome's, and tied the improvement of the citizenry to the military discipline and the civic virtue it instilled.[8] The census and the militia it made possible were indeed the foundation of the Roman Republic's expanding civil society and military power. As Claude Nicolet, the historian of Roman citizenship, states, "In Roman eyes a soldier and a citizen were the same thing."[9] Machiavelli's exaltation of the Republican militia marks the high point of the classical republican tradition of the citizen-soldier traced by Quentin Skinner and J. G. A. Pocock.

There were three manuscript translations of the *Discorsi* in the sixteenth century, one complete, and Peter Whitethorne's 1560 translation *The Arte of War* was reissued in 1573 and 1588.[10] Despite the evident interest in Machiavelli among the later Elizabethans, however, the classical republican version of citizenship did not find much of a foothold in England. The reasons are to be found in Machiavelli himself. The *Arte della guerra* ends with a scathing attack on the modern professional soldier, for all its earlier glorification of the militia man. Its dedicatory letter contains a caricature of the soldier that must have seemed all-to-familiar in early modern London. Machiavelli acknowledges that most people think the civic and military lives are utterly opposed—that soldiers cannot in effect be citizens. What can one expect when the average soldier feels civility renders him weak, and that social encounters require a battery of oaths and a fearsome countenance?[11] According to Paul A. Jorgensen, soldiers in England were regularly typed as social failures whose poor manners and awkward behavior in peacetime placed them outside political participation.[12] Braggart soldiers of dramatic convention like Parolles in *All's Well That Ends Well*, and their imitators like Pistol and John Falstaff, bear this out. On the warriors' side, we have Nashe setting Talbot against the burghers, Hotspur's contempt for Sunday citizens, and the battling aristocrats of *1 Henry VI* whose exploits astonish the cowardly Mayor. The Elizabethan dislike of soldiers in general easily translated to suspicions of a different kind about the competency of citizen-soldiers in home-grown militias. The muster scene in *2 Henry IV* is enough evidence of this.

Shakespeare's Roman tragedies might be expected to tackle the relation between civic and military life in a sustained and serious manner. There are elements of classical republicanism in these plays. They put the Latinate term *citizen*, as opposed to *freeman*, into circulation in common English usage. But contemporary London, with its livery company vocabulary and economic conception of citizenship as the practice of a trade, keeps piercing the surface of Shakespeare's depiction of Rome. The freedom of the city frustrates the discipline of military citizenship in the Roman plays, in ways that are of considerable import to their tragic actions.

Titus Andronicus, Shakespeare's earliest tragedy, is set in a legendary version of late imperial Rome.[13] At the very beginning of the play, the Patricians and the people, somewhat surprisingly, seem to form a harmonious duo. Both their consents are necessary to elect the new emperor. "Noble patricians, patrons of my right," the claimant Saturninus appeals,

> Defend the justice of my cause with arms,
> And countrymen, my loving followers,
> Plead my successive title with your swords. (1.1.1–1.1.4)

Here, as in later plays, there may be a hint in the Shakespearean "countrymen" of the provincial origin of many ordinary citizens, in Rome as well as London. Patricians and people are asked to fight for a common cause, and it is soldiership that establishes citizen participation.

Titus, the Patrician warrior, is coupled with Marcus, who is both a tribune of the people and his brother. Bassianus, the rival candidate, proclaims: "let desert in pure election shine,/And, Romans, fight for freedom in your choice" (lines 16–17). The opening scene, however, traces the rapid falling off from social harmony, the purity of election, and the ideals of burgess and more abstract notions of political "freedom."

Tamora, captive queen of the Goths and intended consort of Saturninus, urges him to feign clemency to the old general, "Lest then the people, and patricians too,/Upon a just survey take Titus' part" (lines 450–451). People and Patricians are paired once again, although the people are the greater worry. As tribune, Marcus had presented his brother, not the rival claimants, with the candidate's robe, citing the authority of "the people of Rome." But Marcus prefaced the offer with an address to his surviving nephews, Titus's fighting sons, "That in your country's service drew your swords" (lines 182, 178). Only four of twenty-five sons remain alive. Military service hovers behind popular authority in Rome, as Tamora knows. Lavinia asks her father Titus to "bless me here with thy victorious hand,/Whose fortunes Rome's best citizens applaud" (lines 166–167). Titus's hand commands the commoners as well as the best citizens, as we see when he hands the emperorship to Saturninus. Later, when he agrees to let the villainous Aaron chop off his left hand to ransom two of his sons, Titus's hand is repeatedly cast as the ruined metonym of his and his family's service in warfare (for instance, 3.1.163–3.1.165; 5.3.101–5.3.102).

It is military service, represented by the Patricians but backed in *Titus Andronicus* by the common people, that implicitly grounds Roman citizenship in this early play. There are only a few artisanal metaphors in its language, although they alter its military ideals, as I shall show further on. A direct challenge to the citizen-soldier model arises in the action itself when Titus's son Lucius escapes from Rome and raises an army of Goths to invade the city. "We'll follow where thou lead'st," the First Goth promises him,

> Like stinging bees in hottest summer's day
> Led by their master to the flowered fields,
> And be avenged on cursed Tamora. (5.1.13–5.1.16)

The simile looks forward to the polity of bees in *Henry V*. It is appropriately Roman, yet the soldier-bees here are noncitizens. What will become of Rome's military ideals of service and political participation, preserved until now under the Empire in Shakespeare's fiction, if Goths and not Latins are the soldiers who restore its freedom? Of course, in Virgil's *Aeneid*, an early imperial epic, the apian simile is used to describe the Carthaginians and their growing city.[14] In returning the image to its non-Roman origin, Shakespeare opens an array of questions about citizens, enemies, and aliens in the late Roman Empire of his tragedy.[15]

It is difficult to align Shakespeare's Romans and Goths with the ethnic categories that cut across citizenship and alienage in sixteenth-century London. From one contemporary viewpoint, albeit the most distant and abstract one, the Goths are the forebears of both the English and the various groups known to them as "Dutch." In his marvelous book *The Goths in England*, Samuel Kliger shows how the Goths, a single Teutonic tribe, became common ancestors to a range of northern European peoples in Renaissance historiography. Their love of liberty and attacks on Rome in antiquity were taken as patterns for both burgess freedom and Protestant opposition to Catholic power in the present. Hugo Grotius claimed the Goths for Holland, and the Netherlands' resistance to Spain was cited as the latest example of Gothic courage.[16] In *Titus Andronicus*, the Goths may be seen as a Germanic or *Deutsch* threat that invades and infiltrates a Rome that is like London (founded, after all, by Brute), in warrior rather than merchant guise. But they simultaneously seem to stand for English and northern European vigor generally, pitted against a corrupt Rome that is London's antitype.

Neither of these interpretations gels, partly because of the multiple associations that swirl around Romans and Goths alike in the text. Titus wages war against "the barbarous Goths," "A nation strong" (1.1.28, 1.1.30). But when he mandates the human sacrifice of Tamora's son Alarbus, his brothers cry "Was never Scythia half so barbarous!" and "Oppose not Scythia to ambitious Rome" (lines 134–135). Rome should be compared and not contrasted with Scythia: in fact, the imperial center is no better than the mythical race on Europe's eastern and northern borders. The Scythians were the wellspring of the Goths as well, according to some authorities.[17] "Thou art a Roman, be not barbarous," Marcus asks his brother, and it is this plea that makes Titus relent and bury his cast-off son Mutius in the family tomb (line 383).

Romans, Goths, and Scythians; warfare, human sacrifice, and ritual interment. One reason the tragic clashes of *Titus Andronicus* should be held a little aloof from the small-scale ethnic conflicts of Shakespeare's London is that they form part of a larger, much older but still developing discourse of "race" in the period. Although they did not apply the word *race* in our modern sense, early modern Londoners were familiar with all of the elements that have gone toward its making, even if the elements did not always cohere. Geography and ancient history, and the common knowledge they gave rise to, suggested a contest of "nations," family-like agglomerations of distinct peoples with grand, half-legendary names and multiple descendants in the present. To geohistorical knowledge, one should add what we would call "culture," the sense of distinct practices, such as religion or burial rites, as well as ways of comporting and adorning the body. Finally, skin color and other bodily attributes form part of the list. Aaron the Moor's silent presence in the opening scene of sacrifice, betrothal, and betrayal is significant by virtue of the last two categories. Later, he refers to his "cloudy melancholy," a union of humoral and skin complexion, and his "fleece of wooly hair" (2.2.33–2.2.34). Others insult him for his color too many times to mention: he will make Tamora's honor "of his body's hue," he is like a raven, he is black and ill-favored, like a fly (2.2.73, 2.2.83; 3.2.67). Finally, he is a "misbelieving Moor" (5.3.142). Titus's later use of a verse from Horace that refers to the javelins of the Moor, *Mauri iaculis*, reminds us that, as with the Goths and Scythians, to be a Moor in the play is first of all to be part of a nation, not a religion (Horace wrote long before Islam) or a group stereotyped by color (4.2.21).

Color, more than religion, overtakes the geohistorical prehistory of racial discourse in *Titus* all the same. Marcus reflects the symbolic whiteness that covers Rome's sullied political process when he offers Titus the "palliament of white and spotless hue" that would make him *candidatus*, the wearer of the white robe who stands for office (1.1.185, 1.1.186). Saturninus renders the desire for whiteness literal. The Goth Tamora is "of the hue/That I would choose," the emperor says, and he asks this "fair" queen to clear up her momentarily cloudy countenance (1.1.265–1.1.267). Like Phoebe, the moon-goddess, she "Dost overshine" the Roman women (lines 321–322). It is as if Roman men, caught between the light Goths and dark Moors who are allied against them on their borders, want their women, and thus themselves, to be still whiter than they are. This is true of Saturninus in any case, and Tamora offers to be both a handmaid to his desires and "A loving nurse, a mother to his youth" (line 237). By mothering her husband she will Gothicize him, making him part of her lineage. It is with the language of nursing and motherhood that the sweeping concerns of color and nation suddenly speak to the original audience's quotidian anxieties about the northern European aliens who threatened to mix with the London population.

Tamora is rendered outwardly Roman even as Saturninus is subjected to her barbaric regime. As she tells her enemy: "Titus, I am incorporate in Rome,/A Roman now adopted happily" (1.1.467–1.1.468). Her off-stage marriage has made her one with Saturninus's body and the social body of his city, the corporation, in early modern terms, of Rome. Adoption, as Jonathan Bate glosses, is also a legal term in the period for the acceptance of someone as "heir, friend, citizen," or the like (line 468 note; OED 1). Tamora's sons Chiron and Demetrius turn out to have had a Roman education in the Latin classics, however poorly they have learned their lessons. The former recognizes the lines from Horace that Titus sends them along with the gift of some choice weapons from his armory. Young Lucius bears the scroll from his grandfather, calling the Gothic brothers "The hope of Rome, for so he bid me say" (4.2.13). With this odd episode, sixteenth-century notions of urban belonging meld with the classical and Machiavellian concept of military citizenship, albeit in an ironic fashion. The right use of Titus's weapons in battle would make Chiron and Demetrius Romans indeed. But the gift is actually intended to serve notice against the cowardly pair who raped and mutilated Lavinia. It is also aimed at Aaron, their setter-on. The Moor perceives the double meaning, but encourages his charges:

> And now, young lords, was't not a happy star
> Led us to Rome, strangers and, more so,
> Captives, to be advanced to this height? (lines 32–34)

The Goths and the Moors have turned from legendary beings to "strangers" or aliens who profit from the authorities' unjust protection.

Aaron is anxious to bind himself to the brothers by using the word "us" and reminding them of a shared history of alien status and captivity. The quotation from Horace that accompanies the weapons may be translated: "the man of upright life and free from crime does not need the javelins or bows of the Moor" (lines 20–21 note). These words would split Aaron from his Goth friends: Roman arms differ from African spears and arrows. Moreover, the sexual implication in *Mauri iaculis*, that is, the broad hint that Aaron has repeatedly "done" Tamora and dishonored Chiron and Demetrius through their mother, is immediately borne out when the horrified nurse brings in Tamora's black baby (line 78). Moorish antiquity, attested in Horace, is firmly marked by chromatic difference through this revelation. Both Moors and Goths are barbarians and strangers in the city, but color finally returns to separate Aaron and his kind from the partially assimilable Europeans. Aaron gleefully plays upon his difference once it becomes undeniable, even as he seeks to implicate the doltish brothers further in his fate:

> He is your brother, lords, sensibly fed
> Of that self blood that first gave life to you,
> And from that womb where you imprisoned were
> He is enfranchised and come to light. (lines 124–127)

All three brothers were freed from the same mother's body. If Chiron and Demetrius thought Titus's weapons symbolized one form of Roman enfranchisement, Aaron taunts them with his son's potential birthright as the emperor's supposed heir. Alas, the baby must be taken away for safekeeping, and a seemingly white child, the son of Aaron's countryman Muly and his fair wife, put in its place (lines 154–163). Race, in something like the modern sense, has become the limit to birth and birthright in the city, although the vagaries of color, culture, and geography make it an unreliable boundary. Alienage inherits the anxieties that attend the uneven coalescence of these grand categories, a legacy that generates ideas about ethnic difference on a small scale within European whiteness when economic and other forms of communal competition are added to the compound.

I wish to turn briefly to the economic sphere and the artisanal language it fosters even in *Titus Andronicus*, where there are many fewer references to trades than in the later Roman plays. The first handicraft allusion comes in a scene from the Folio text of the play, when the family dines frugally with the mute and handless Lavinia after her as yet undiscovered rape. Titus insists he can tell how Lavinia would speak could she do so: "She says she drinks no other drink but tears,/ Brewed with her sorrow, mashed upon her cheeks" (3.2.37–3.2.38). Mashing, the mixing of malt with hot water, was a step in the household and commercial brewing of beer. After Titus sends the emperor a knife wrapped in a letter, Saturninus uses a more familiar metaphor drawn from mealtime preparations. He complains that Titus accuses him as if his sons, rightfully executed for Bassianus's murder, "Have by my means been butchered wrongfully." The angry emperor avows he will indeed prove "slaughterman" to the old warrior for this charge (4.4.54, 4.4.57). Similarly, when Aaron reveals how Chiron and Demetrius violated Lavinia, he says she was "washed and cut and trimmed." "O barbarous villains," cries Lucius, punning despite his horror on barbarity and barbering (5.1.95, 5.1.97). But meat might also be washed and trimmed in butchery, so the vein of food preparation in these craft references is sustained.

Needless to say, the motif tends toward Titus's final revenge. "I'll play the cook," he explains as he cuts the Goths' throats so that Lavinia may catch their blood in a basin. His recipe for the crust of the "pasties" he will make of their heads has already been offered in quite technical terms (5.3.186–5.3.189, 5.3.204). Titus enters attired like a cook, as Saturninus notes, and exults at the brothers, "both baked in this pie,/Whereof their mother daintily hath fed"(lines 30, 59–60). Brewing, butchery, and baking are all skills that straddle the house-wife's domestic preserve and the professional incursions of the masculine victualing trades.[18] Dressed as a cook, Titus finally asserts the privilege of the craftsman; his feast would also recall for the audience the cere-monial dinners regularly mounted by the livery in crafts of every stripe. Nevertheless, there is a diminution in his final role, especially when it is compared with his turn as the victorious general of the first act. "Let housewives make a skillet of my helm," as Othello will say in doubting his own domestic dishonor.[19] That trade metaphors cluster around Lavinia's rape and her warrior-father's calculated revenge upon its perpetrators is significant. As in the English history plays, the proud violence of aristocratic warfare has been reduced to the demotic brutality of the kitchen or the butcher's shop.

As Jonathan Bate has noticed, "Tribunes and Others" are present at the banquet, but there are no Senators (5.3.SD 16 and note). The Patricians have virtually withdrawn from the late imperial scene—the actors who played them earlier may even be playing Lucius's Gothic soldiers now. Lucius is simply an acclaimed emperor, and despite assur-ances that "the common voice" is with him the earlier rituals of elections are now cast aside (line 139). Do the Goths join in the acclamation? To what extent has Lucius mounted a military *coup* with their alien support? The resolution of the action leaves these questions open. Lucius and his Goths restore the integrity of warrior violence after the scandal of Titus's spectacular and embarrassing revenge. But if they are accepted as Romans of a sort because of their military service to the Andronici, the Goths remain stranger-citizens as much as soldier-citizens. The later Roman tragedies in the Shakespeare canon will struggle with classical notions of Patrician leadership and military citizenship even as they rein-force the London experience of burgess freedom and alien competition most familiar to the early modern audience.

The military model of Roman citizenship is certainly relevant to *Julius Caesar*. It lies behind the many debates about honor, suicide, and precedence in leadership among the Patricians. Soldierly values, however, are pegged to an aristocratic version of civic identity. "If it be aught toward the general good," Brutus tell Cassius, "Set honour in one eye, and death i'th' other,/And I will look on both indifferently." Cassius replies that he knows that "virtue" to be in him (1.2.85–1.2.87, 1.2.90). Armed *virtù* for the general or common good and life-risking nobility appear to be at one. But "poor Brutus, with himself at war," is split (line 46). Military language is turned inward, as the citizen becomes the privileged site for philosophical as well as political subjectivity.[20] As Paul A. Cantor has noted, Brutus's second-act soliloquy on Caesar's necessary murder is prompted by public concerns and structured by a public logic.[21] The invention of inwardness as a response to, rather than a refuge from, the public sphere—this is the contribution of the citizen model of subjectivity to the tragic soliloquy as dramatic device on Shakespeare's stage. In the Roman tragedies themselves, however, the balance of outer and inner will prove difficult to sustain, and the soliloquy plays an increasingly diminished role.

As *Julius Caesar* proceeds, the military bases of public virtue are viewed with increasing ambivalence. Octavius defends Lepidus as "a tried and valiant soldier." "So is my horse," Antony rejoins,

> It is a creature that I teach to fight,
> To wind, to stop, to run directly on,
> His corporal motion governed by my spirit,
> And, in some taste, is Lepidus but so:
> He must be taught, and trained, and bid go forth;
> A barren-spirited fellow. (4.1.28–4.1.29, 4.1.31–4.1.36)

Like the soldiers in camp, who are bid to call "Stand" down the line in a dull display of order (4.2.32), Lepidus is a mere instrument without inward spirit, for all his Patrician blood. It is military leadership, not the bearing of arms, that determines what Antony calls "spirit." Brutus and Cassius argue about who is the better, or at least more experienced, soldier (4.3.30–4.3.56), just as Antony and Octavius clash over who will take the right flank (5.1.1–5.1.18). Caesar's rise from a military caste as the first citizen among supposed equals was inevitable in this culture of competition. And considerable irony attends Octavius's final tribute to Brutus, Caesar's republican opposite: "Within my tent his bones tonight shall lie,/Most like a soldier, ordered honourably" (5.5.79–5.5.80). The future Augustus has won the competition for Brutus's body, which is glorified, or reduced, to a soldier's, subject to order.

There are only two uses of the word *citizen* in *Julius Caesar*. Cassius plans to throw letters into Brutus's window,

> As if they came from several citizens,
> Writings all tending to the great opinion
> That Rome holds of his name. (1.2.316–1.2.318)

As in Plutarch, these imaginary citizens are presumably men whom Brutus would respect, members of the class of military leaders that constitutes the real "Rome." North's Cassius asks, "Thinkest thou that they be cobblers, tapsters, or suche like base mechanicall people, that wryte these billes and scrowles?"[22] Yet later in the play, when Antony reads Caesar's will to the people, he announces:

> To every Roman citizen he gives,
> To every several man, seventy-five drachmas. (3.2.234–3.2.235)

Here, at the symbolic realization of Caesar's death and his political afterlife, the citizenship of Rome's male population in general is suddenly confirmed. Called "Commoners" in the stage direction to the first chaotic scene of the play, and "Plebeians" when they are introduced in this episode by the direction to Act 3, Scene 2, the people have finally become the citizenry. Their status is marked in economic terms, with a cash gift, as well as Caesar's arbors and parks, now "common pleasures" (lines 238–241). Caesar's will is an antiquarian flourish derived from Plutarch, but it also had an appeal for contemporary Londoners. Bequests to city parishes or livery companies for the relief of the poor or apprentices were a customary feature in the wills of urban magnates.[23]

It is the economic or artisanal notion of citizenship native to London that dominates *Julius Caesar* from the outset. In Elizabethan England, "commoners" could mean "common soldiers" as distinct from officers, among other things, but the Commoners of Act 1, Scene 1 are occasional celebrants of Patrician victories, not combatants themselves. In the Roman plays, "commoners" and related terms connote something like the phrase "the commons of the city" does in *The Knight of the Burning Pestle*: the burghers of the town.[24] The familiar opening of *Julius Caesar* repays a careful rereading. The two tribunes berate the "idle creatures" in the streets, demanding "Is this a holiday?" and "wherefore art not in thy shop today?" (1.1.1–1.1.2, 1.1.28). The Cobbler finally tells Flavius that "we make holiday to see Caesar and to rejoice in his triumph" (lines 30–31). But Caesar's conquest over Pompey's sons makes spoil of Rome itself and contradicts the Commoners' own earlier allegiances, as Murellus declaims:

> O you hard hearts, you cruel men of Rome,
> Knew you not Pompey? Many a time and oft
> Have you climbed up to walls and battlements,
> To towers and windows, yea, to chimney-tops,
> Your infants in your arms, and there have sat

> The livelong day, with patient expectation,
> To see great Pompey pass the streets of Rome. (lines 37–43)

The passage brings to mind other descriptions of teeming streets and crowded windows in Shakespeare, like Bolingbroke's entry into London in *Richard II*. The set piece also echoes the Act 5 Chorus to *Henry V*, where Caesar's return itself is depicted as an orderly celebration of the conqueror by the "best sort" and the Plebeians. In the Roman play the Plebeians mill confusedly and are told by Flavius to "Assemble all the poor men of your sort" and fill the Tiber with their tears (lines 58–61). Perhaps he is "a strange republican" in Roman terms, as the most recent Arden editor remarks in the note to these lines, but the citizen hierarchy of contemporary London offers a clue to the tribunes' attitude.[25]

Shakespeare conceives of his tribunes as public officials who monitor the Commoners as much as represent them. They oppose not only Caesar, but the disruption of the cycle of work and holiday that his rise effects. Flavius begins his interrogation:

> What, know you not
> (Being mechanical) you ought not walk
> Upon a labouring day, without the sign
> Of your profession? Speak, what trade art thou? (1.1.2–1.1.5)

Mechanicals or craftsmen should know the calendar and the law that governs it—stage law in this case, since neither Romans nor Londoners bore mandated "signs" of their trades. Yet the question "what trade" comes up three more times: the tribunes are anxious to pin down the Carpenter and especially the Cobbler to their occupations despite the holiday attire that renders them all too "common" in the eyes of authority. "Where is thy leather apron and thy rule," Murellus asks the Carpenter, "What dost thou with thy best apparel on?" (lines 7–8). It is the absence of the leather apron, a traditional sign of craft identity and occasionally of its resistance to authority, that is rebellious here. The Cobbler's replies are especially troublesome because "to cobble" could mean to work poorly at any craft as well as to make or mend shoes (lines 10–11). Is he also a religious dissenter who mends "soles," or a bawd who offers to cobble or couple the outraged tribune with a mate (lines 14, 20)? Visibly and verbally, the citizen tradesmen of Act 1, Scene 1 are opaque to their own guardians.

The tribunes' concern to render artisans visible and regulate as much as represent their pursuits will play an even larger role in *Coriolanus*.

In *Julius Caesar* it may speak to a pressing issue in late sixteenth-century London, first raised by fourteen livery companies who proposed a law against "encroachers of handicrafts" in 1571. The measure was intended to prevent members of one company, say the Merchant Taylors, from practicing the craft of another company, like the Dyers, one of the petitioners. Nothing came of the proposal, or a similar bill before Parliament a few years later, because the Merchant Taylors and others argued it would undo "the custom of London," an unwritten principle that allowed any freeman to practice any trade within the city limits. The lords in parliament and the nobles at court also supported the encroachers; it was the hierarchy of the lesser guilds that urged increased regulation of company members. Numerous legal challenges to encroachers continued with little success into the early seventeenth century.[26] The wardens of each company, rather than a city official proper, were supposed to police the practitioners of their trade. Wardens were elite liverymen who undertook the judge's role in company courts, but they also had the power of "the search," the right to investigate shops and determine the company membership—or in the case of aliens, lack thereof—of its workers. Their role conflicted with the custom of London and the interests of large companies with many underemployed but versatile members. The tribunes in Shakespeare's Rome are part, if an equivocal part, of centralized city government, but in their in-betweenness they are similar to a given company's wardens in early modern London. "Thou art a cobbler, art thou?" an exasperated Flavius demands, that is, "so you do make shoes by trade rather than bungle others' occupations?" The reply? "Truly, sir, all that I live by, is with the awl: I meddle with no tradesmen's matters, nor women's matters" (1.1.21–1.1.24). The Cobbler ties down the inclusive "all" to the tool of his trade, albeit with another, bawdy pun, and claims to have no part in "tradesmen's matters" or company politics—like disputes over encroaching. As for coupling instead of cobbling, "women's matters" are also no concern of his.[27]

"You blocks, you stones, you worse than senseless things!" (1.1.36). Murellus's exclamation reduces the tradesmen to the materials upon which they work, or to the materials of the built city itself. They are made of "basest mettle" and may be easily molded despite their opacity and initial resistance (line 62). Caesar's secret opponents also express either disdain or fear of the changeable urban populace. Caska reports the refusal of the coronet: "the rabblement hooted, and clapped their chopped hands, and threw up their sweaty nightcaps, and uttered such a deal of stinking breath because Caesar refused the crown that it had almost choked Caesar" (1.2.243–1.2.247).

The physical presence of the Commoners threatens the elite with the contagion of citizenship from below, the citizenship of hands chapped from labor. Their commonness is also figured through bad breath and sweat, the latter on headgear that recall Elizabethan "statute caps" while confusing such diurnal "signs" of class with the bedroom. Behaving like an actor in the theater, Caska says, Caesar offered his life to the "common herd." "Three or four wenches where I stood cried, 'Alas, good soul,' and forgave him with all their hearts"—as they would have done had he "stabbed" their mothers, bawdily or otherwise (lines 263, 270–273). Shakespeare is careful to include susceptible women in the crowd, in a distant recollection of the "citizen's wife" type from city comedy. Their fickleness and bodily openness renders the herd of commoners feminine as well as bestial.

Women and stabbing appear together in the households of elite citizens as well in *Julius Caesar*. Questioning her husband after the conspirators leave, Portia doubts his claim of ill health except insofar as it comes from the "vile contagion of the night" with its "rheumy and unpurged air" (2.1.264–2.1.265). "Rome" could sound like "rheum" in sixteenth-century pronunciation. Brutus may not be wearing a nightcap, but he has caught a version of Rome's sickness from the secret society of the plotters, not its mob. (Fittingly, the supposedly ill Ligarius enters immediately after Portia departs: line 309.) Portia depicts her alienation from Brutus in legal language that also connotes the management of metropolitan space:

> Within the bond of marriage. . . .
>   Am I your self
> But as it were in sort or limitation,
> To keep with you at meals, comfort your bed
> And talk to you sometimes? Dwell I but in the suburbs
> Of your good pleasure? If it be no more,
> Portia is Brutus' harlot, not his wife. (lines 279, 281–286)

She claims she has been driven to the outskirts of her husband's public life even within her own home, like a (London) prostitute.

In using urban geography to map her domestic exclusion, Portia reveals that she already knows that Brutus's problems are about the city and its business. The corresponding scene between Caesar and Calphurnia contains a similar, if less recognized, reference to London places. Caesar recounts his wife's nightmare to Decius:

> She dreamt she saw my statue,
> Which, like a fountain with an hundred spouts,

Did run pure blood; and many lusty Romans
Came smiling and did bathe their hands in it. (2.2.76–2.2.79)

Decius, tempting Caesar to his doom at the Senate, insists that "Your
statue spouting blood in many pipes/ . . . Signifies that from you
great Rome shall suck/Reviving blood" (lines 85, 87–88). The vision
is Shakespeare's invention; in Plutarch, Calphurnia dreams that Caesar
was killed, or that a pinnacle fell from their house.[28] Fountains and
public statuary glance at Elizabethan images of ancient Rome and
modern Italy, but the spouting "pipes" and milling crowd suggest
the conduits found throughout early modern London. According to
Mark S. R. Jenner's recent historical study of water supply in the city,
conduits "were substantial stone structures covered with tiles, enclos-
ing large tanks that were filled by pipes coming from outside the city.
Smaller stopcocks or taps from which people received their supply
reached out into the street. The conduits' importance was emphasized
by architectural embellishment—some were crenelated or even painted
with oils."[29] Conduits were a regular resort of women and apprentices,
who were responsible for bringing water back to house and shop.
Crowds gathered to protest overuse of conduit water by aristocrats.
Thus, conduits were also an occasional site of public disruption, censure,
and punishment as well as the daily rituals of neighborhood social
life. As local centers, their placement made conduits geographically
the opposite of the suburbs, yet a similar carnivalesque atmosphere
seems to have attended them. It is suitable that Caesar's wife should
dream of a conduit-like statue in foretelling his multiple wounding,
for conduits were linked with both free speech by women and male
aggression.[30]

Caesar's body, flowing with blood in the prophecy and its fulfillment, suggests the menstruating female form to Gail Kern Paster and
a grim twist on nurturing motherhood to Coppelia Kahn.[31] Yet the
assassination is also a singular event, marked by dreams and portents
like a lioness whelping in the streets, also recounted by Calphurnia
(2.2.17). Caesar's "feminization" constitutes a crisis in the action, and
it kills him while bringing about a new half-life for Rome. As such it
resembles a fatal childbirth as well as menstruation or motherhood.
Yet to cast Caesar's violent death as the bloody birth of the Empire
is not casually to reaffirm supposedly natural affiliations between
women's bodies and openness, weakness, or procreation. The murder
replaces childbirth, masculinizing it as much as feminizing its victim.
Calphurnia's dream is part of a larger discourse that links population
and identity in *Julius Caesar*, and which ultimately disavows the female

role in all forms of social reproduction. At the beginning of the play, as in Plutarch and Roman custom, Caesar bids Antony touch his wife when he runs in the Lupercalia's footrace, to cure her supposed barrenness. "When Caesar says 'Do this,' " the athlete replies, "it is performed," by him if not by Calphurnia's body (1.2.6–1.2.10). A public and pious compact between men will generate a natural heir for the great man as the wife passively waits.

The play is full of references to birth: real, illegitimate, and figurative. Yet status and identity, not the natural process, are in question— birthright and its traditions rather than birth itself. In the temptation scene, Cassius asks Brutus:

> Upon what meat does this our Caesar feed
> That he is grown so great? Age, thou art shamed!
> Rome, thou hast lost the breed of noble bloods! (1.2.148–1.2.150)

Caesar has grown great because of his metaphorical diet, not because of his ancestry; Rome's decayed environment has fed him somehow, having abandoned its breeding. Cassius also puts it this way: "I was born free as Caesar, so were you;/We both have fed as well" (lines 97–98). Londoners would hear this as an assertion of citizenship by patrimony, rather than apprenticeship to some trade, and the antiquarians among them would appreciate how suitable such contemporary language was to Patricians in classical Rome. But the conspirators' equality with Caesar is really assured by their feeding, not their birthright, and by how they act: the stories of Caesar's neardrowning and his "sick girl" behavior while on military campaign follow. As their colloquy concludes, Cassius is assured that "Brutus had rather be a villager/Than to repute himself a son of Rome" in times like these (lines 171–172). Yet Brutus refuses to swear an oath in joining the conspiracy: every drop of Roman blood "is guilty of a several bastardy" if it breaks any promise whatsoever (2.1.137). He insists on the true Roman's essential integrity, as realized in deeds not words, even as he bemoans the decadence of the city as a community. In *Julius Caesar*, the title "Roman" is used overwhelmingly for the aristocrats, particularly the republican aristocrats, while ordinary citizens are called Commoners or Plebeians (e.g., 1.3.58; 4.3.186; 5.5.69). The famous exceptions are the introductory lines to the funeral orations, although Brutus and especially Antony are each out to enlist their hearers to serve elite interests.

The Plebeians, however, are not real Romans, at least according to the frequently repeated definitions of Brutus, Antony, and other nobles, which stress consistency, fortitude, and reason as Roman qualities rather than residence or even birth within the city walls. From the beginning, the men in the street are seen as breeders, literally "proletarians," another term with a classical pedigree. Recall Murellus's image of the Cobbler and the Carpenter, "Your infants in your arms," perched on chimney-tops to view the conquering Pompey (1.1.40). The Plebeians produce children rather than go to war; the traditional contribution of citizens' wives to the city becomes the general attribute of the common citizen. Antony's prophecy of civil war fuses spectacle, war, and child-bearing, finally revealing the obstructed maternal role, albeit in a hideous fashion:

> Blood and destruction shall be so in use,
> And dreadful objects so familiar,
> That mothers shall but smile when they behold
> Their infants quartered with the hands of war. (3.1.265–3.1.268)

Doomed mothers proliferate in the wake of Caesar's bloody death. Shakespeare pauses to devote the following lines to Cassius's mistaken suicide over Titinius's apparent capture:

> O hateful Error, Melancholy's child,
> Why dost thou show to the apt thoughts of men
> The things that are not? O Error, soon conceived,
> Thou never com'st unto a happy birth
> But kill'st the mother that engendered thee. (5.3.66–5.3.72)

Antony's prophecy is partly realized in such fatal acts. The death-in-birth presentation of Caesar's murder extends to the suicides that likewise herald the advent of the Empire.

Cassius's impulsiveness is prepared for in his dispute with Brutus in Act 4, when he excuses himself by "that rash humour which my mother gave me." Brutus replies that henceforth "He'll think your mother chides" when his friend is over-earnest (4.3.119, 4.3.121). A form of melancholy may well be the humor or substance they are talking about. Nevertheless, when Brutus sees Cassius and Titinius dead he says:

> The last of all the Romans, fare thee well:
> It is impossible that ever Rome
> Should breed thy fellow. (5.3.99–5.3.101)

It seems that Rome, not Cassius's mother, is finally credited with his breeding: the play has worked to occlude and then to stigmatize both the female and the communal roles in biological and social reproduction. Rome will not produce such children again. Or on another reading perhaps she never did: it is impossible that Rome should breed Romans at all. According to Livy, when Romulus opened the gates of Rome to foreign fugitives—implicitly creating the Plebeian class—he followed the common practice of city founders, "who by gathering about them the base multitude and obscure, feined that they were an offspring borne out of the earth."[32] It is the deeds of Titinius and Cassius, the one crowning the other between their suicides (line 98), that determine true *Romanitas*, at once Patrician and Republican.

A second look at the diptych of Portia and Calphurnia confirms the repression of concepts such as reproduction and population in the tragedy's understanding of urban identity.

Calphurnia's bleeding statue of her husband finds another parallel in Portia's "voluntary wound" in her thigh. "Can I bear that with patience/And not my husband's secrets?" she asks (2.1.299–2.1.301). Even if we discount the stage tradition that makes her "weak condition" (line 235) a sign of pregnancy, Portia's "bearing" of her wound supplants child-bearing. Before we see Caesar bleeding in one Roman wife's vision, we see another woman bleeding indeed, although like Caesar her bloody suffering accedes to a masculine compact. By a Patrician act, Portia would become "a Roman" like her husband and the plotters. It is true that she reminds us she is Cato's daughter, and as such "A woman well reputed" (line 294). But she stakes her claim to elite citizenship and its philosophical implications by creating a battlefield scar, not solely through birthright, and certainly not by giving birth in turn.[33] Aristocratic republican society is really reproduced through such deeds, she implies, not by producing children; Portia is Cato's child in as much as she emulates his reputation, not because she is the daughter of his unnamed wife. Her self-stabbing, which unlike parturition is completely voluntary, is a denial of the maternal. Similarly, the childless Calphurnia envisions her husband hemorrhaging among a perverse sort of brood, a male family or society generated through a violent event.

The ruler-as-fountain or conduit was a familiar symbol of munificence in Tudor-Stuart iconography, but the bloodbath vision turns out to be a literal prophecy when the successful conspirators wash themselves in their victim's gore at Brutus's sudden suggestion. They celebrate the rebirth of the republic rather than the baptism of an empire. Having demanded "enfranchisement" from exile for Publius Cimber, they now proclaim "Liberty, freedom and enfranchisement" in another sense that resonates—uneasily, for loyal subjects—with the burgess freedom sought by the apprentices and enjoyed by the citizens in the Globe audience (3.1.57, 3.1.81). The Patricians have embraced violence and the cry of liberty. Conversely, the Plebeians, as they are now called in the stage directions, begin to use reason and to use verse, however faulty their efforts are. Faced with Brutus and Cassius defending the assassination, "I will hear Brutus speak," says one, "I will hear Cassius speak," says another, "and compare their reasons/ When severally we hear them rendered" (3.3.8, 3.3.9–3.3.10). Of course, it is not long before they want to crown Brutus, and a little later still kill him, reasoning amidst Antony's speech that "If thou consider rightly of the matter,/Caesar has had great wrong" (lines 110–111). Cinna the poet is torn apart a few scenes later for sharing a conspirator's name. When we see the triumvirate similarly proscribing enemies by their names immediately afterward (4.1), it is clear that reason and debate have been abandoned by all Romans, elite citizens and tradesmen alike. As in the histories, a loose succession of battle scenes and episodes of recrimination and self-destruction follow.

"Shall Rome stand under one man's awe?" Brutus had asked himself, echoing the false messages thrown in his window. "What Rome?" is his answer, at least in the pointing of the Folio text. His ancestor Lucius Junius Brutus drove Tarquin from the streets, it is true, but Tarquin "was called a king" by someone in the first place (2.1.51–2.1.54 and note). Brutus suffers a flash of insight about his city's nature: Rome is not essentially republican or monarchical.[34] He soon resolves to uphold the Republic anyway, but his second question hangs over *Julius Caesar* and, tellingly, its near-sequel *Antony and Cleopatra*. What, or which, city is at stake, the Rome of citizen-soldiers or the Rome of citizen-commoners? What forms of government and political subjectivity, if any, does Rome inculcate?[35]

Antony and Cleopatra opens in Alexandria, where Rome is first mentioned as the source of grating news.[36] "Let Rome in Tiber melt," Antony declares, "and the wide arch/Of the ranged empire fall" (lines 34–35). The imaginary geography of the play is first sketched in these theatrical words: the end of the Republic means the separation of the city from the empire, as Octavius Caesar rules Rome and Italy while Antony and Lepidus take Asia and Africa. *Wide arch* and *ranged* begin a series of construction metaphors and suggest the artisanal foundation of empire-building; *ranged* also suggests the ranks of an army and the military resources necessary to maintain imperialism (line 35 note). Both types of Roman-ness are hinted at, but it is the artisanal mode that dominates, as in *Julius Caesar*. The Tiber, like London's Thames, carries with it a hint of commonness, of the everyday world of river traffic that ties the city together and to the outside world. Told of the Romans' gossip about her leadership in the war, Cleopatra later echoes her lover: "Sink Rome, and their tongues rot/That speak against us" (3.7.15–3.7.16). Antony complains of "Our slippery people" (1.2.192). When malcontents flock to the ports and Sextus Pompeius' navy, Octavius calls the Romans a "common body" that floats aimlessly on the stream "To rot itself with motion" (1.4.44–1.4.47). The language of instability and decay, joined to the evocations of rivers, ports, and seas, translates *Julius Caesar*'s unflattering portrait of the city populace to the imperial scene.

Octavius does not hesitate to make use of the qualities he denounces in the citizens. "Condemning Rome," Antony has enthroned himself and Cleopatra in Alexandria, according to Caesar, and "The people knows it" (3.6.1, 3.6.23). The Romans swear off Antony when he totally forsakes them for Cleopatra and another city. Although never present on stage, they are vividly imagined as Cleopatra's antagonists several times toward the play's end. Enraged at her second desertion, Antony implants the idea of Caesar's triumph in Cleopatra's imagination with the technical name for the common citizens: "Let him take thee/And hoist thee up to the shouting plebeians!" (4.12.33–4.12.34). Cleopatra's fear of "the shouting varletry/Of censuring Rome" incongruously yokes riot with the austere office of Censor (5.2.55–5.2.56). Finally, she tells Iras,

> Mechanic slaves
> With greasy aprons, rules and hammers shall
> Uplift us to the view. In their thick breaths,
> Rank of gross diet, shall we be enclouded
> And forced to drink their vapor. (5.2.208–5.2.212)

The aprons of craft revolt are joined to rules and hammers, tools of the building trades, appropriate to a mob that hoists or lifts its prizes to the view. Cleopatra had earlier been called a "piece of work" (1.2.151–1.2.152). The aprons are greasy, or sweaty, and once more bad breath serves as a metonymy for contagion from the common body and its diet.[37]

Antony's decline throughout the tragedy matches its increasingly debased picture of the Roman people. Paradoxically, perhaps, he loses the support of the artisans even as he degenerates as they have, by failing to sustain the other citizen model, that of the soldier. At one point, Antony, like Othello, combines the citizenship traditions, describing war as a trade ("Othello's occupation's gone," 3.3.360). "O love," Antony tells Cleopatra,

> That thou couldst see my wars today and knew'st
> The royal occupation, thou shouldst see
> A workman in't. (4.4.15–4.4.18)

Yet at the start of the action, Philo complains that "this dotage of our general's/O'erflows the measure," contrasting his military leadership with watery excess and laziness (1.1.1–1.1.2). Despite his sudden "Roman thought" (1.2.88), Cleopatra herself soon calls her champion the world's greatest liar as well as its greatest soldier (1.3.39–1.3.40). Octavius combines Roman and Alexandrian debauchery when he imagines Antony "To reel the streets at noon, and stand the buffet/ with knaves that smells of sweat" (1.4.20–1.4.21). At Modena, he says, Antony bore starvation "like a soldier" (line 71). At Actium, he ran after Cleopatra, violating experience, manhood, and honor (3.10.23). It is no wonder that he begs to live "A private man in Athens" after his defeat, as just another citizen in a city of the Empire (3.12.15).

Dying by his own hand, Antony claims that he remains "A Roman by a Roman/Valiantly vanquished" (4.15.59–4.15.60). Whether one thinks Antony's suicide absurdly botched or ultimately noble, it has undeniably consumed more stage-time than such a brief apothegm warrants.[38] Both "Roman" types are evoked in his slow death, in which the grotesque comedy of the artisan meets the violent tragedy of the soldier: one kills the other. When Octavius hears of Antony's death, he says:

> The breaking of so great a thing should make
> A greater crack. The round world
> Should have shook lions into civil streets
> And citizens to their dens. (5.1.14–5.1.17)

Antony's death marks the end of citizenship or "civil" life in the age of world empire. Townsfolk should exchange their haunts with lions, in the final fulfillment of the portents in *Julius Caesar*, and, it may be, a foretaste of the arena entertainments that will mar the time of universal peace (see 4.6.5).

For the most part, *Antony and Cleopatra* continues the Elizabethan dissociation of soldiership from citizenship. The one major character who is consistently linked with his military role is Antony's companion Enobarbus, who is called "soldier" again and again (e.g., 2.6.7, 2.7.106, and 3.2.22). Enobarbus is so traveled that he hardly seems an urban figure. His free speech does preserve something of the citizen-soldier's claim on public life. Yet Antony silences him during the conference with Octavius: "Thou art a soldier only. Speak no more" (2.2.113). The pattern reappears with variations. Ventidius is a self-silencing warrior who avoids angering Antony by boasting of his own conquests, writing a humble letter to his absent commander instead (3.1.11–3.1.35). And the soldier who warns Antony not to fight by sea is simply ignored, even though he insists he is in the right (3.7.61–3.7.67). This character may be the same as Scarus, who is later presented by Antony to Cleopatra and virtually ennobled for his bravery. But his elevation reflects the sovereign ceremonies of the court rather than the city's honors, complete with a Gloriana-like reference to Egypt's queen as "this great fairy" (4.8.11–4.8.13, 4.8.22–4.8.27). Scarus's rise also marks Enobarbus's fall. The old soldier he replaces has left Antony, and his desertion and guilt-ridden death, perhaps by suicide, are charted in the only proper soliloquies in the tragedy (3.13.200–3.13.206; 4.6.12–4.6.20, 4.6.31–4.6.40). In his final speech—overheard by the soldiers, yet a soliloquy in form—Enobarbus asks Antony to forgive him. "But let the world rank me in register," he concludes, "A master-leaver and a fugitive" (4.9.24–4.9.25). These words allude to the world of the livery companies as well as military and other forms of service: a "master-leaver" is someone who leaves his master, such as a wayward apprentice. The philosophical and political subjectivity of the citizen-soldier, embodied by Brutus in *Julius Caesar*, is merely glanced at in Enobarbus's character, and divorced entirely from Antony's central role.

In Shakespeare's final Roman tragedy, *Coriolanus*, the dissociation of military from artisanal citizenship is arguably the principal burden of the play. Set at a legendary moment of crisis early in the history of the Republic, *Coriolanus* assumes a Roman army largely composed of Plebeian soldiers who fight under Patrician commanders to enlarge the city's territory. But it also assimilates these "common" soldiers to the cowardly Plebeians from which they come, the "company of mutinous Citizens" who demand grain at the start of the play.[39] They are consumers and producers of a kind, but not fighters. When one demands the attention of his fellow "good citizens," another replies, "We are acounted poor citizens, the patricians good" (1.1.14–1.1.15). Patricians and citizens are increasingly opposed throughout the rest of the action. In the opening scene, the citizens are immediately pitched against the military leader Cauis Martius, and resolve to seek his death. Coriolanus, as he will later be renamed, enters to the rebellious crowd. War frightens them, Martius says: "He that trusts to you,/ Where he should find you lions, finds you hares;/Where foxes, geese" (lines 168–171). Menenius Agrippa, a wily old Patrician, confirms that the people are "passing cowardly" despite their lack of discretion (line 201). In the battle scene at Corioles, the retreating soldiers are similarly called "geese"; they refuse to enter the town, leaving their commander to fight alone inside the gates (1.4.34, 1.4.46–1.4.48). Nevertheless, the ingratiating Cominius praises the infantry:

> Breathe you, my friends; well fought; we are come off
> Like Romans, neither foolish in our stands
> Nor cowardly in retire. (1.6.1–1.6.3)

They are "like" Romans now, having proved themselves worthy to partake in the aristocratic and republican identity that adheres to the name of their birthplace. But Coriolanus is unmollified:

>   for our gentlemen,
> The common file—a plague! tribunes for them!—
> The mouse ne'er shunn'd the cat as they did budge
> From rascals worse than they. (lines 42–45)

The pretended gentlemen of the city, granted the tribunes as representatives after the recent mutiny, have once more shown themselves as cowards in the field, the opposite of soldiers. It is because of this, Coriolanus will later maintain, that they do not deserve the distribution of public grain (3.1.119–3.1.129).

Citizens already make bad soldiers in the early Republican Rome of *Coriolanus*. But a certain reciprocity between craftsmen and warriors has hitherto been maintained by leaders and followers. Volumnia brags of her son's wounds: "there will be large cicatrices to show the people when he shall stand for his place," in his bid for the office of Consul (2.1.146–2.1.148). Her language, as we shall see, might well be used of a seventeenth-century candidate standing for election to public office. But the display of battle scars, of course, purports to be an ancient Roman ritual that binds the common citizens, artisans and militia alike, to Patrician military rule.[40] The wound marks the border between elite and demotic citizenship. The Third Citizen explains that the Plebeians cannot customarily deny a wounded commander their "voice" for the consulship:

> We have power ourselves to do it, but it is a power that we have no
> power to do. For, if he show us his wounds and tell us his deeds, we
> are to put our tongues into those wounds and speak for them. So if he
> tells us his noble deeds, we must also tell him our noble acceptance
> of them. (2.3.4–2.3.9)

This passage incidentally throws retrospective light on Antony's
claim in soliloquy that Caesar's wounds are "dumb mouths" that "beg
the voice and utterance of my tongue," a claim he later reprises
before the people only to disavow (*Julius Caesar* 3.1.260–3.1.262;
3.2.218–3.2.219). At the dawn of the Empire, it is the vengeful and
ambitious Antony who assumes the people's voice through the
leader's wounds, converting it into a charismatic political power,
which he calls "Caesar's spirit" (line 270) but which Tudor jurists
would name the king's second body.[41]

  Coriolanus's own voice breaks the compact between military leaders and city-dwellers in his play and diffuses whatever charisma he still
enjoys. He tells a pair of citizens that he will not show them his
wounds, and frequently mocks the ceremony (2.3.105–2.3.108;
2.2.135–2.2.150). Menenius apologizes twice for his friend's angry
and contemptuous speeches to the Plebeians. He asks them to allow
for Coriolanus's upbringing, bred to warfare since he could draw
a sword and poorly schooled in "bolted" or refined language
(3.1.317–3.1.320). "Consider further," Menenius later pleads,

> That when he speaks not like a citizen,
> You find him like a soldier. Do not take
> His rougher accents for malicious sounds,
> But, as I say, such as become a soldier,
> Rather than envy you. (3.3.52–3.3.57)

His words are of no avail after Coriolanus rages against the tribunes
when they charge him with treason and he is banished the city. The
opposition of soldiers' and citizens' speech, as Jorgensen has shown in
his discussion of the play, was a commonplace of Elizabethan and
Jacobean discourse. The soldier, plainspoken to the point of being
antisocial, was a familiar figure for political failure on and off the public stage.[42] Conversely, "The tribunes are no soldiers," as the Volscian
leader Aufidius remarks (4.7.31). Coriolanus has defected to the
Volsces, the erstwhile possessors of Corioles, and offered to lead their
army against Rome. In a shrewd speech, Aufidius predicts his rival's

success, but notes his limitations as a politician, his inability to shift "From th'casque to th'cushion," or from war to the peaceful benches of the Senate (line 43; cushions are brought on as props in a Senate-scene, 2.2.SD 1). A victor at the gates of Rome, Coriolanus thinks he has finally found a warlike people to lead, telling his mother not to ask him to "Dismiss *my* soldiers, or capitulate/Again with Rome's mechanics" (5.3.82–5.2.83; emphasis added). But Aufidius, who is an adept politician, outflanks Coriolanus back in Volscian territory, accusing him of treason and provoking him to boast about his conquest of the town whose name he bears. Ironically, a crowd of Volscian citizen-soldiers join with Aufidius's conspirators as they surround Coriolanus and kill him in the play's final scene (5.6.120–5.6.130). Shakespeare expanded the role of the Volscian people in Plutarch's account of the conspiracy.[43]

In Rome itself, citizenship is imbued with the vocabulary of the livery companies and their rights throughout the play. As Theodore B. Leinwand has observed in his pathbreaking article on the middling sort, "while nearly every discussion of the politics of *Coriolanus* assumes that it is a drama of a nation . . . it may be instructive to tailor our reading of this play set in Rome to the city of London, not to England."[44] Like the nation–state approaches, however, Leinwand's interpretation stresses historical parallels between the play's plot and political events, in his case the career of Lord Mayor John Spencer. It is necessary once again to examine the language of the tragedy and the dispositions of power it presumes to understand the London sub-text to the full. For instance, Menenius Agrippa's fable of the belly, told to the citizens to pacify their hungry rage, reinforces their guild consciousness while subordinating it to the social body and Patrician interests. Accused by the other body parts of hoarding nourishment, the Belly has a ready reply:

> 'True it is, my incorporate friends,' quoth he,
> 'That I receive the general food at first
> Which you do live upon; and fit it is,
> Because I am the store-house and the shop
> Of the whole body. But if you do remember,
> I send it through the rivers of your blood
> Even to the court, the heart, to th'seat o'th'brain.' (1.1.129–1.1.135)

The word *incorporate* puns not only on the body politic but also on corporate or chartered towns and the corporations or chartered guilds that composed them from Medieval through Early Modern times in

England. The senatorial stomach claims an elite craft identity rather than an aristocratic one in Menenius's fiction. It is both a storehouse, where raw materials are conserved, and a shop, where they are made into goods. The Belly's goods are circulated throughout the common body. Earlier, Menenius has called the crowd "countrymen," "masters," and "honest neighbours," and assured them that "most charitable care/Have the patricians of you" (lines 54, 61, 64–65). The mandated charity of the great merchants as well as aristocratic *noblesse oblige* is suggested in these lines and the subsequent fable.[45]

Menenius's pretty tale is shattered when Coriolanus enters. The senatorial class now seems solely a military aristocracy, not a merchant elite. Shakespeare is playing with his audience's unstable sense of London hierarchy: at one moment, the Patricians are company members, lofty but charitable, at most others, they are a proud warrior caste that disdains the commercial inhabitants of the city. The play does not presume a fixed correspondence between social levels in ancient Rome and contemporary London. To Coriolanus's eyes, the citizens are "dissentious rogues" and, as we have noted, cowards, who carp at "the noble Senate" (lines 163, 185). "They'll sit by the fire, and presume to know / What's done in the Capitol," he wonders, "who's like to rise, . . . And feebling such as stand not in their liking/ Below their cobbled shoes" (lines 190–191, 194–195). The quibble on "cobbling" recalls the start of *Julius Caesar*—the shoes are both a metonymy for craft identity in general, and an example of poor and poorly regulated workmanship. Coriolanus tells Menenius that the Senate has granted five tribunes to the Plebeians, at which "they threw their caps" in the air (line 211). Much later, after we see the crowd throw up their caps on stage, Menenius blames them, "That made the air unwholesome when you cast/Your stinking greasy caps in hooting at/Coriolanus' exile" (3.3.137 SD; 4.6.131–4.6.133). Unwholesome citizen caps and infected air also recall the chaotic urban scene in *Julius Caesar* and the onset of Empire.

Guild language is sometimes echoed in Coriolanus's encounters with his fellow-Patricians. Cominius recalls young Martius's precocity in the battle against Tarquin: "His pupil age/Man-enter'd thus, he waxed like a sea" (2.2.98–2.2.99). To be "entered" was to pass from journeyman to householder status in a livery company.[46] As in Antony's time, warfare is a kind of craft with its own apprenticeship system. But the vestiges of burgess freedom in Shakespeare's conception of elite Roman citizenship are metaphorized and conflated with ideas about aristocratic lineage. Deflecting Cominius's compliments elsewhere in the play, Coriolanus says: "My mother,/Who has a charter to extol her blood,/When she does praise me, grieves me" (1.9.13–1.9.15). Even Volumnia's praise, chartered or authorized (by nature or the gods?) as a kind of self- or family-love, offends him. Memories of the Belly's "incorporate friends" haunt such metaphors. The tribune Brutus speaks of Plebeian rights as if they were grounded in early modern burgess status, saying that the citizens' great enemy would have "Dispropertied their freedoms" if given a chance (2.1.246). He eggs on the people to withdraw their initial support for Coriolanus's consulship:

> He was your enemy, ever spake against
> Your liberties and the charters that you bear
> I'th'body of the weal. (2.3.177–2.3.179)

The commonwealth's body apparently bears literal charters or documents in Shakespeare's shifting conflation of ancient Rome and Tudor-Stuart London. These incorporated liberties finally trump the bodily lineage of Volumnia or the Martii, and Coriolanus is banished.[47]

There are still other reminiscences of the city–company nexus in *Coriolanus*. Menenius calls the tribunes Brutus and Sicinius "a brace of unmeriting, proud, violent, testy magistrates (alias fools) as any in Rome" (2.1.42–2.1.44). In *Titus Andronicus*, too, the Clown says "I am going with my pigeons to the tribunal plebs to take up a matter of brawl betwixt my uncle and one of the emperal's men" (4.3.91–4.3.93). Commentators on the later play have noted that the historical tribunes did not have a judicial function, and have suggested that Brutus and his colleague resemble English Justices of the Peace (2.1.43 note). The nature of their duties, however, places them closer to the wardens of a livery company, or other members of a company's "court of assistants." Menenius mockingly tells the tribunes:

> you wear out a good wholesome forenoon in hearing a cause between
> an orange-wife and a faucet-seller, and then rejourn the controversy of
> threepence to a second day of audience. (lines 69–72)

A dispute between a seller of faucets and an orange-peddler, or perhaps a fruiterer's wife, suggests a particularly low, tavern-world version of commercial conflict. London city courts and even the local JPs were relatively weak in the early seventeenth century. The administration of justice was decentralized and shared among the chartered companies: many causes were judged by the assistants, or upper-level liverymen, of different companies, and especially the small number of wardens who were responsible for routine and petty matters. A company's court was appealed to when the defendant was a member of that company, and courts of assistants regularly judged matters that did not directly concern a given company's particular trade or skill.[48] For Machiavelli, the point of Livy's account of Coriolanus was not the general's betrayal of Rome, but the tribunes' use of due process to arraign him and thus diffuse Plebeian anger.[49] In Shakespeare, the tribunes' legal role reflects the judicial function of the guilds rather than classical republican policy.

In a slippage typical of the Roman plays, then, Shakespeare's tribunes are at once civic officials and livery company magistrates.[50] Furthermore, they represent tradesmen-citizens "from below," yet they also judge them as their superiors, like company elites. The courts of assistants were responsible for regulating trade practices in their guild. The wardens were granted the legal power of the search, the right to enter shops and look for violations of standards, encroachers, and alien laborers. Wardens and assistants employed the Mayor's sergeants to enforce their judgments: the tribunes use of the Aediles in *Coriolanus* partly alludes to this practice (3.1.181).[51] Routine attempts were made to employ the companies as a means of social control: for example, in 1571 they were enlisted by the Crown to search for sympathizers of the Ridolfi plot, and in 1584, the mayor had company leaders demand that their members refrain from attendance at stage plays in the city and its liberties.[52] The tribunes in *Coriolanus* are also linked with surveillance and social order. Menenius wishes they would "turn your eyes toward the napes of your necks, and make but an interior survey of your good selves" (2.1.37–2.1.39). It is at this point that they would see themselves as proud, violent, and testy magistrates. Brutus and Sicinius look outward instead, and what they see after Coriolanus's exile pleases them:

> His remedies are tame i'th'present peace
> And quietness of the people, which before
> Were in wild hurry. Here do we make his friends
> Blush that the world goes well; who rather had,
> Though they themselves did suffer by't, behold
> Dissentious numbers pest'ring streets, than see
> Our tradesmen singing in their shops and going
> About their functions friendly. (4.6.2–4.6.9)

Three or four citizens enter and greet the tribunes in a particularly mannerly fashion as Menenius looks on. "This is a happier and more comely time," Sicinius tells the Patrician, "Than when those fellows ran about the streets/Crying confusion" (4.6.27–4.6.29). Like the tribunes at the start of *Julius Caesar*, the first tribunes have already become the guardians of order, regulating the artisans they represent, albeit for their own purposes.[53] Their rise also betokens the status of company elites as competitors with the urban aristocracy at court, and perhaps with the Crown, at least where the management of "those fellows" in the shops and streets is concerned.

Coriolanus, with his steadfast refusal to display his wounds and thus gain the Plebeians' voice for the consulship, resists the regime of visibility now presided over by the tribunes. "I cannot/Put on the gown, stand naked," he says, "and entreat them/For my wounds' sake to give me their suffrage" (2.2.136–2.2.138). The business of the wounds obscures somewhat the ideal of political transparency shared by Roman and early modern English "suffrage." In a now classic comparison, Mark A. Kishlansky has shown how Shakespeare's antique ritual parallels the elections, or rather selections, of his own time: "these scenes so accurately portray the process by which officeholders were selected in the early seventeenth century that one must conclude that Shakespeare had first-hand experience, either of wardmote selections to the London Common Council or of parliamentary selections themselves."[54] Kishlansky's focus on *Coriolanus* and Parliament has been influential, but his first suggestion should not be passed over.[55] I would add that consensual selections to livery company posts like assistant, warden, or master operated along similar lines to Common Council and parliamentary voting. These principles are enumerated by Kishlansky: selections are not resolved by choice, they take place without a contest, and the voters are expected to give assent to designated (and cooperative) nominees. Participation, not decision, makes the ritual of suffrage, which is based on mutual honor and recognition between governors and governed. Any failure of the ritual is catastrophic: the city collapses in rebellion when Coriolanus balks and the Plebeians withdraw their tentative support of him, just as the unthinkable occasionally disrupted "elected" bodies in England, laying the groundwork for what we regard as democratic reform.[56]

In dismissing the transparent world of urban political ceremony in Rome, Coriolanus is refusing to be a citizen in either the artisanal or military-elite senses. Several critics have remarked upon his failure to uphold Aristotle's ideal of the participatory citizen: living apart from the *polis*, such an isolated man must be a god—or a beast.[57] "Where is this viper," demands Sicinius, "That would depopulate the city and/Be every man himself?" (3.1.261–3.1.263). The very nature of the *polis* is at stake during the scene of armed conflict in the streets in which these words are spoken. The Patricians are confronted by the tribunes and a crowd of Plebeians on the way to the marketplace. The tribunes would seize Coriolanus:

> *Men[enius].* This is the way to kindle, not to quench.
> *First Sen[ator].* To unbuild the city and to lay all flat.
> *Sic[inius].* What is the city but the people?
> *All Pleb[eians].*   True,
> The people are the city. (lines 195–198)

"The people are the city": this slogan may reflect a Latin legal maxim that translates as: "A city and town [*Civitas et urbs*] differ in this, that the inhabitants are called the city, but the town comprises the building" (3.1.197 note). The tribunes and Plebeians hold that Rome is its population—in effect, that its essence lies in the majority of its inhabitants, not with the Patricians, and not with their architecture.[58] Coriolanus declaims the contrary view a few lines later:

> That is the way to lay the city flat,
> To bring the roof to the foundation,
> And bury all which yet distinctly ranges
> In heaps and piles of ruin. (lines 202–205)

It is not that the city is its buildings, but that its buildings embody a hierarchy and order, a distinction, worth fighting for.

Soon, it is the banished Coriolanus who threatens to return and destroy both buildings and populace. Menenius blames the tribunes and their "apron-men," the forces of urban dissent, rather than the turncoat (4.6.97). Cominius says the exile leads his army like a "thing," not a man, made by some other deity than nature (lines 91–93), and imagines

> Your temples burned in their cement, and
> Your franchises, whereon you stood, confin'd
> Into an auger's bore. (lines 86–88)

The freedom of the city as an abstract political claim is reduced by Cominius to one of the craftsman's tools that provide its material foundation, or rather to a mere hole made by such a tool. Coriolanus, he says, will shake Rome about their ears (line 100). No longer Coriolanus, he has become an empty spot as well, an anticitizen, "a kind of nothing, titleless," until he forges himself a new name from the fires of Rome (5.1.13–5.1.15). In the Patricians' ironic view, if the people really are the city then they will not mind when their buildings are burnt to the ground. Is the city nothing more than a collection of houses and temples after all? Again, no: what is at stake is an aristocratic veneration of "place" in its topographical as well as social senses. The buildings massively embody the order, the hierarchy of places, that really constitutes the city and its inhabitants in Patrician eyes.[59]

Shakespeare's care in establishing the topography of Rome, from the Capitol, which is mentioned fifteen times, to the Tarpeian Rock, has been remarked.[60] Many scenes are set in the streets, and Coriolanus's confrontations with the people probably take place in the marketplace (2.2.159 and 2.2.3; 3.2.104). Once he leaves Rome—"Despising/ For you the city," as he tells them (3.3.133–3.3.134)—Coriolanus says he dwells "I'th'city of kites and crows" (4.5.45). He may mean the no-man's-land or battlefield between Roman and Volscian territory, but the kite was also "the common scavenger of Elizabethan London."[61] As the nineteenth-century editor W. A. Wright argued, the play's geography maps London as well as Rome.[62] The Capitol, a frequent object of gestures off-stage, stands in for the Tower of London. And at the end of Act I, the Volscian leader Aufidius retreats from Corioles to a cypress grove: " 'Tis south the city mills," he directs (1.10.30–1.10.31). Four grain mills were erected in Southwark not far from the Globe theater in 1588.[63] Corioles is meant to bring London to the spectators' minds just as Rome is, as a way of grounding their theatrical experience of each scene in the contemporary urban experience through neighborhood detail. Antium, the Volscian city Coriolanus visits in disguise, has citizens and "commons" as well as lords "o'th'city" (4.4.6 SD; 5.6.1–5.6.4). It is in Corioles that he is killed by the conspirators and the Volscian people, in a scene that echoes the mob violence in Roman public places earlier in the action. There is a sense in which Coriolanus never leaves Rome, or rather, London: present in almost every scene, he brings London with him wherever he goes, despite his ultra-aristocratic attitude.

So perhaps the people do indeed make up the city: the people in the audience. The well-attested fluidity of the early modern stage, the manner in which it suggests the Capitol as the Tower in one scene and the mills of Corioles as the Southwark mills in another, defies the aristocratic fetishization of place more effectively than the shouting Plebeians do. As in *Antony and Cleopatra*, the Roman people are linked with watery images throughout the play. Fleeing soldiers are said to stop and bend to Coriolanus "as weeds before/A vessel under sail" (2.2.105–2.2.106); earlier in the same scene, the Senators ask the Tribunes to offer a "loving motion toward the common body" (line 53), and together these images evoke Octavius's vagabond flag upon the stream. Later, however, Cominius fears the furious Plebeians, "Whose rage doth rend/Like interrupted waters, and o'er-bear/What they are us'd to bear" (3.1.246–3.1.248). The people are associated with freely flowing water, the aristocrats with attempts to control or channel it. In another vein, this contrast returns us to the conduit image of *Julius Caesar*. Coriolanus's family, as Plutarch notes, was linked with the construction of a key aqueduct. Shakespeare adapts his source by having Brutus recount his enemy's lineage: "Of the same house Publius and Quintus were,/That our best water brought by conduits hither" (2.3.239–2.3.240). Quintus Martius Rex built the Aqua Marcia in 144 BC, more than three centuries after Coriolanus's legendary time, but Shakespeare mixes the before and after in Plutarch's account for his own purposes.[64] He links Roman aqueducts with English pipes, and pipes with the conduit-buildings at their London termini. The Tribunes' anxiety to wrest control of the commons from the Patricians is cast in watery terms when Sicinius urges Brutus to head for the Capitol to witness their rejection of Coriolanus: "We will be there before the stream o'th'people;/And this shall seem, as partly 'tis, their own,/Which we have goaded onward" (lines 259–261).

The mention of conduits recalls their role as neighborhood gathering places for women and apprentices, and thus as sites of social protest over water usage between tradesmen and the urban nobility. According to Jenner, there was a "moral economy of the conduit" that echoed that of the grain market in London; although he does not cite *Coriolanus*, there is a similarity between the controversy over grain distribution in the play and its recurring imagery of water management. Both resources led to conflict in the early modern city: conduct at conduits and marketplaces was regulated by similar rules.[65] As Lawrence Manley has shown, London's conduits were also stations on the ceremonial routes of royal and mayoral processions, their crenellations often blending with the temporary castles or triumphal arches that served as speakers' platforms.[66] Conduits were also stages, then, and like the stage they implied a situational mobility that resisted the authorities' attempts to co-opt conduit culture and its theatricality. It is not coincidental that Rafe the apprentice is made to orate as the May-Lord from a conduit top in *The Knight of the Burning Pestle*, that most scenically opportunistic and unsettled of comedies.[67] Use of conduits for processions and public punishments alike failed to quiet protest over their practical function, the free allocation of water.

Eventually, aristocrats and the wealthy got around conduit equality by purchasing water from companies who raised water from the Thames or excavated their own systems of canals in the countryside; customers installed pipes that fed their houses off a main trunk. The privatization of the water supply, as Jenner explains, led to the decay of the public conduit system and its social role early in the seventeenth century.[68] A passage in *Coriolanus* may pertain to one projector's scheme for channeling water from Hertfordshire. Complaining of Sicinius's free speech, the Patricians' hero asks why,

> You grave but reckless senators, have you thus
> Given Hydra here to choose an officer,
> That with his peremptory "shall," being but
> The horn and noise o'th'monster's, wants not spirit
> To say he'll turn your current in a ditch
> And make your channel his? (3.1.91–3.1.96)

Hugh Myddleton, or Middleton, goldsmith, sought in 1609 to dig a canal in and around others' property to bring water to Londoners. Myddleton met with many objections before completing his "New River."[69] In infringing landed property rights for profit, he is like the citizens who would turn the Patricians' current to their own. Water comes to symbolize the indeterminacy and tumult that drives citizenship in general, and economic citizenship in particular. Shakespeare was probably aware that the Hydra was etymologically and mythographically a water beast. The people, a monster of many heads, threatens to fissure aristocratic territory into an artificial delta of competing interests and demands.

The conduit complex resurfaces once more in a manner that looks back to *Julius Caesar* and thus forward to Coriolanus's assassination. Excusing his friend's refusal to spare Rome at Cominius's petition, Menenius says:

> he had not din'd:
> The veins unfill'd, our blood is cold, and then
> We pout upon the morning, are unapt
> To give or to forgive; but when we have stuff'd
> These pipes and these conveyances of our blood
> With wine and feeding, we have suppler souls. (5.1.50–5.1.55)

Menenius's musings reprise his fable of the belly in a personal mode while speaking to greater anxieties about a body politic threatened by internal fragmentation and external invasion. Once again, a threat to the city is explained by diet, and blood flows in "rivers" and "cranks," or winding passages and ducts (1.1.134–1.1.136). Coriolanus is metaphorically a conduit system, and, like Calphurnia's dream of a fountain-Caesar, his blood will be let out when the assassins kill him in the final scene. After the murder, Aufidius commands that his body be carried through Corioles in procession, "Though in this city he/Hath widow'd and unchilded many a one" (5.6.150–5.6.151). As in *Julius Caesar*, masculine murder and its rituals displace wifehood, childbirth, and their claims. Caesar's death, a seeming rebirth of the Republic, was really the bloody nativity of empire and the spirit or second body of sovereignty. Coriolanus's much earlier murder in an enemy town is more ambiguous still: through his exile, which recalls Tarquin's (2.2.88), and his resulting death the Republic was indeed born again, but at the hands of alien men doomed to inevitable incorporation in the expanding Roman state.

Water management in *Coriolanus*, linked from the first mention of conduits with lineage and birthright, brings out a subtext in the initial belly fable: the belly can also be, perhaps should also be, the womb, as in Falstaff's "my womb undoes me" (*2 Henry IV*, 4.3.22–4.3.23). In their final encounter, Volumnia tells her son:

> thou shalt no sooner
> March to assault thy country than to tread—
> Trust to't, thou shalt not—on thy mother's womb
> That brought thee to this world. (5.3.122–5.3.125)

"Ay, and mine," his wife Virgilia uncharacteristically introjects, "That brought you forth this boy" (lines 125–126). It is the image of the polity as mother and womb that saves Rome, despite the way birth is made over into a masculine image of social reproduction through violence before and after this climactic moment.

As the son of Volumnia and of Rome itself, Coriolanus is the hub of the cycle of violent birth throughout the tragedy. In the opening scene, the First Citizen belittles his military record: "though soft-conscienced men can be content to say it was for his country, he did it to please his mother, and to be partly proud" (1.1.36–1.1.38). Volumnia's own memories of Caius Martius as a youth do not confirm the taunt, but they do show how it arose. Expostulating with the timid Virgilia, she says:

> When yet he was but tender-bodied, and the only son of my womb. . . . To a cruel war I sent him, from whence he returned, his brows wound with oak. I tell thee, daughter, I sprang not more in joy at first hearing he was a man-child, than now in first seeing he had proved himself a man. (1.3.5–1.3.6, 1.3.14–1.3.18)

Warfare was a second birth for the future Coriolanus, just as his victory over the enemy town renames him in the course of the action. At Corioles, in fact, "He was a thing of blood, whose every motion/Was tim'd with dying cries" (2.2.109–2.2.110). A truculent newborn once more, Coriolanus emerges alone from the town's gates, simultaneously inaugurating his identity in full and forecasting its bloody destruction in the assassination of the final scene.

Volumnia's contradictory relation to birth and childrearing is seen in the remainder of her opening scene with Virgilia. She imagines her son rallying his citizen troops:

> [Volumnia]. Methinks I see him stamp thus, and call thus:
> "Come on you cowards, you were got in fear
> Though you were born in Rome." His bloody brow
> With is mail'd hand then wiping, forth he goes
> Like to a harvest man that's task'd to mow
> Or all, or lose his hire.
> Vir[gilia]. His bloody brow? O Jupiter, no blood!
> Vol[umnia]. Away you fool! it more becomes a man
> Than gilt his trophy. The breasts of Hecuba
> When she did suckle Hector, look'd not lovelier
> Than Hector's forehead when it spit forth blood
> At Grecian sword contemning. (1.3.32–1.3.43)

As Janet Adelman has shown, the complex image of the lactating mother's breasts and the warrior-son's bleeding forehead encapsulates the sublimation of female nurture by masculine aggression in Shakespeare's account of Roman culture. Hector's forehead flaunts an offensive wound that spits blood against its assaulting enemy, like a weapon, as Kahn stresses; it channels the mother's love into the soldier's contempt, and justifies the woman's social existence by revealing her as the source and best custodian of the violence that defends the state.[70]

Warfare, not birth itself or birthright, grounds true citizenship under this Patrician regime, although women, childbirth, and early childhood education are essential to produce the military population and the Hectors that lead it. Blood becomes a man more than gold, and a man only becomes manly by bleeding. Moreover, it is not enough to be born in Rome if you were also begotten in fear, a fear like that of the weak mother Virgilia, or the Plebeian women who are almost invisible in the street scenes. In ventriloquizing her son's battle cry, Volumnia paradoxically employs a mother's authority to undo maternal authority pure and simple. She upholds military citizenship over the claim of birthright implicit in the tradesmen's slogan

"The people are the city." Her near-epic simile of Coriolanus as a mower completing his brutal task for hire speaks to the Plebeian's economic view of citizen privileges and demand for grain, the fruit of both the farmhand's and the soldier's labors. As Coriolanus says of his cowardly men at Corioles, "Even when the navel of the state was touch'd,/They would not thread the gates: this kind of service/Did not deserve corn gratis" (3.1.122–3.1.124). The phrase "navel of the state" recalls the belly fable's body-politic, converting a birthmark, the metonymy of Roman identity derived from the mother, into a metaphor for the centralized political order that must be protected at all costs.

Coriolanus, continuing to berate the common soldiers over the grain issue, adds: "Th'accusation/Which they have often made against the senate,/All cause unborn, could never be the native/Of our so frank donation" (3.1.126–3.1.129). Popular claims for sustenance are illegitimate, because they are founded upon a false charge of senatorial malice. The Plebeians' case, unborn—abortive, or without a proper lineage—is not a native of the Patricians' charitable regime. The play, no less than its title character, is obsessed with the language of birthright and legitimacy, if only to undermine it. Menenius commends the brave Lartius with the simple sobriquet "true-bred" (1.1.242). Outside Rome in alien territory, the Volscian servingmen confirm Coriolanus's cult of warfare, joking that peace breeds tailors and ballad-makers. Peace is "a getter of more bastard children than war's a destroyer of men," for if war "may be said to be a ravisher, so it cannot be denied but peace is a great maker of cuckolds" (4.5.227, 4.5.231–4.5.235). The scene of Roman tradesmen singing in their shops under tribunal supervision immediately follows. The complacent craftsmen are cast as cuckolds, victims of their city-wives, and their children may be Roman but are not rightfully theirs (see also 2.3.33–2.3.34 and note). In persuading her son to pretend compliance to electoral custom, Volumnia advises him to employ

> such words that are but rooted in
> Your tongue, though but bastards and syllables
> Of no allowance to your bosom's truth.
> Now, this no more dishonors you at all,
> Than to take in a town with gentle words. (3.2.55–3.2.59)

Here and elsewhere, the Martii regard the Plebeians as if they were enemies in an alien city.[71] Simply to speak their language is to use "bastard" words.

Although he attempts to follow Volumnia's counsel, Coriolanus detests the blending of Patrician truth with Plebeian bastardy. Referring tellingly to grain cultivation, he accuses the senate of nourishing the "cockle" or weed of rebellion in the political field, "Which we ourselves have plough'd for, sow'd and scatter'd,/By mingling them with us" (3.1.69–3.1.71). After he is expelled from Rome, he rejects the Plebeians and his former Patrician friends alike in the sole, otherwise unrevealing soliloquy he delivers in the play: "My birthplace hate I" (4.4.23). Coriolanus's total denial of birthright as the ground of citizenship in Rome has already reached a head in his enraged cry when the Plebeians reject him for the consulship:

> I would they were barbarians—as they are,
> Though in Rome litter'd; not Romans—as they are not,
> Though calv'd i'th'porch o'th'Capitol. (3.1.236–3.1.238)[72]

Coriolanus now speaks of claims for birth in the city precisely as his mother envisioned he would (1.3.33–1.3.34). He insists that the common people are barbarians, aliens in the extreme and implicitly enemies for the killing. Even if born in the Capitol itself, they are not Romans because they are not Patricians and are not fighters: the veneration of architecture and city places is suddenly set aside as well, in a foretaste of Coriolanus's later destructive intentions. The Plebeians at any rate are only littered or calved in the city of Rome. They have no more claim to citizenship for being born there than animals do. Birthright is biology, not destiny, or identity.

Coriolanus's claim that birth in the city does not confer communal identity was a familiar one in early modern London. In 1572, the common council of London had urged that "no citizen of this city . . . shall take as apprentice any person whose father is not the child of an Englishman born," in effect denying citizenship to children born in England of non-English parents. This measure was enforced in London for a while but a similar proposal failed in Parliament in 1581. James I looked favorably upon strangers, but toward the end of his reign he responded to continued concerns about them by charging Commissioners for Aliens to survey their population.[73]

Although they are often read as exclusively aristocratic characters, Coriolanus and the Patricians occasionally voice the anxieties of the upper echelons of the London citizenry, and even of the common tradesman or company member competing for work with recently arrived aliens.[74] Behind their backs, Cominius refers to the urban populace as "the tag" (3.1.246); like Caska's "rag-tag people" in *Julius Caesar* (1.2.257), the expression chimes with the "tag and rag" of Holland's Livy and its depiction of early Rome as a medley of fugitives. As Livy attests, Rome went on to consolidate its power by extending some privileges of citizenship to neighboring peoples and resident aliens. Shakespeare's Rome embodies the diversity of London as well. The First Citizen complains that Coriolanus calls the Romans a "many-headed multitude," and the Third Citizen punningly replies:

> We have been called so of many; not that our heads are some brown, some black, some abram [auburn], some bald, but that our wits are so diversely coloured. (2.3.16–2.3.21)

Unstable opinion is emphasized here, but the spectrum of hair colors betokens an emerging sense of ethnic difference; skin color may be part of the picture, too, despite the comically deflating reference to baldness. In one of this play's characteristic mixtures, the tradesmen of Rome are simultaneously London company members and the strangers who dwelt among them.

Earlier, a "windows" passage that recalls moments in *Julius Caesar* and *Henry V* presents an urban panorama with a similar import. Brutus enviously describes the people crowding to witness Coriolanus's victorious entry to the city:

> Your prattling nurse
> Into a rapture lets her baby cry
> While she chats him. The kitchen malkin pins
> Her richest lockram 'bout her reechy neck,
> Clamb'ring the walls to eye him; stalls, bulks, windows,
> Are smother'd up, leads fill'd and ridges hors'd
> With variable complexions, all agreeing
> In earnestness to see him. (2.1.204–2.1.211)

Women are suddenly visible in the crowded streets and their walls, and their role as mothers is underlined, as in *Julius Caesar*, by the infant held by the heedless nurse. The "lockram" sported by the scullery wench is a kind of linen brought from Breton. Foreignness and population are also combined in the "variable complexions" of the faces that pack every aperture. Like the different-colored heads of the multitude in the Third Citizen's joke, these faces hint at a surprisingly varied populace. "Complexion" can also mean humoral temperament, but the humors were linked to pigmentation and ethnicity, as in Aaron's "cloudy melancholy." It is hard to see how reference to phlegmatic and sanguine moods rather than pale and dark faces would be more natural in the rapid depiction of a teeming crowd. "Stalls" are shops and "bulks" are structures that jut out from them, just as windows pierce their fronts and upper stories. It is the commercial city that is jammed with faces and bodies of different genders, classes, and shades, all to see Coriolanus's short-lived triumph. It is ironic that this is the urban world he despises, and Brutus struggles to control. In passages such as these, Shakespeare attempts to visualize a community, picking out markers of difference as well as continuity, and tracing contemporary London divisions in a mobile and contradictory fashion on his otherwise quite accurate picture of early Republican Rome.

If the Plebeians are both citizens and aliens from an elite perspective, it is Coriolanus who is soon scapegoated for the strangeness that accrues to an expansive Rome. When he is exiled, Coriolanus is both "A strange one" in the Volscian city and "a foreign recreant" in Rome, even to his mother (4.5.21; 5.3.114). He revels in this reversal of fortune, of course, and attacks Rome with a Volscian army, just as Lucius did with his Goths (the comparison is already explicit in *Titus*, 4.4.67). But for a while, Coriolanus occupies the same position that More asks the Ill May Day rioters to imagine for themselves: an alien exile denied harbor in the city.[75] Editors have noted a number of parallels between the language of the supposed Shakespearean scene in the *More* play and *Coriolanus*. In both plays, for instance, the common people "Would feed on one another" if unchecked by their betters.[76] Moreover, early in each plot, an eloquent speaker, More and Menenius Agrippa, steps forth to quell a mob with wise and clever words in praise of social harmony in an urban setting. With our reading of *Coriolanus*, then, we have come full circle, back to the play of *Sir Thomas More* and the way citizenship and alienage are mutually constitutive categories on Shakespeare's stage.

In concluding with *Cymbeline*, I am turning finally to a Roman play that retreats from tragedy late in Shakespeare's career. Sophisticated contemporaries would have recognized this work as a tragicomedy, however, and one that preserves some affinities to the more accurate evocation of the ancient world in Shakespeare's tragic drama proper.[77] The hero, Posthumus, is British by birth and Roman by education. Praising Posthumus' behavior at Rome to his beloved Imogen, Iachimo uses words that summon up Coriolanus among the Volsces:

> He sits 'mongst them like a descended god;
> He hath a kind of honour sets him off,
> More than a mortal seeming.[78]

Posthumus, with his Latin name, woos Imogen illicitly, but their eventual union legitimates Britain's incorporation within the Roman empire. Distinctions among different models of citizenship, and the master distinction between citizenship and alienage itself, are compounded, or confounded, by the historical tragicomedy's end.

Temporal and geographical categories are mingled throughout *Cymbeline*, of course. Although Iachimo is an antique Roman, like the invading general Caius Lucius, he is depicted as a sort of Machiavellian merchant, and his Rome seems to be the "Romish" den of contemporary anti-Italian religious propaganda (1.7.152). His target at the British court is Imogen, whom he tries to seduce to win a bet with Posthumus. Much later, a cross-dressed Imogen will assert that she is "not so citizen a wanton as/To seem to die ere sick" (4.2.8–4.2.9). She distinguishes herself from the malingering wantonness or peevishness of the typical city-dweller. At court, Iachimo tries to treat the British princess as if she was a wanton citizen in another sense, like the stereotypical city-wife who cheats on her shopkeeping husband. The wager itself is described from the beginning as a financial transaction. Posthumus denies that his intended may be purchased like his ring (1.5.80–1.5.81). But Iachimo provokes him to lay his jewel against ten thousand ducats that she may be corrupted: "If you buy ladies' flesh at a million a dram, you cannot preserve it from tainting" (lines 131–132). In Shakespeare's sources for the scene, the wagerers and their witnesses are all merchants, not nobles and their guests in ancient Rome.[79] The mercantile roots of Iachimo's character are seen in his seduction attempt, in which he remarks upon her beauty ("All of her that is out of door most rich!," 1.7.15) and urges her to "Be reveng'd" on Posthumus's supposed unfaithfulness by sleeping with her visitor (line 126). Iachimo is a little like Justiniano in Dekker and Webster's *Westward Ho!*, an Italian merchant in London whose initial bitterness toward women inspires what turns out to be a playful vengeance as he brings his neighbors' wives to the brink of seduction.[80]

Iachimo's use of the stratagem of the trunk to gain entrance to Imogen's chamber at night and take "inventory" of its contents and her sleeping body also reflects his commercial sensibility (2.2.30). He describes her eyes as "enclosed lights, now canopied/Under these windows," where "windows" mean horizontal shutters not glass panes, such as covered openings in the front of shops (lines 20–21 and note).[81] In his Act 5 confession, Iachimo claims that "our loves of Italy" are likewise "A shop of all the qualities that man/Loves woman for" as well as beauty (5.5.161, 5.5.166–5.5.167). Iachimo is repeatedly characterized as an alien: Imogen calls him a "saucy stranger," Iachimo requests protection for his trunk because he is "strange," and the doltish Cloten marvels that he has not seen the new "stranger" at court (1.7.151, 1.7.191; 2.1.34). The Roman is a temporary visitor to Britain, but the word's connotations of resident alienage resonate with his merchant language. Justiniano again comes to mind. There were relatively few transplanted Italians in London compared with northern European immigrants. Yet the word *strange* occurs fourteen times in *Cymbeline*, and *stranger* eight times, more than in any other Shakespearean play. Iachimo comes to stand for alienage in general, despite the touristic intentions and Italian origins that mask his relation to contemporary anxieties about strangers closer to home. But Italian stereotypes do exaggerate the sexual aspect of these anxieties. Posthumus doubts that Imogen's servants were induced to steal the bracelet that serves Iachimo as proof of her infidelity: "And by a stranger? No, he hath enjoyed her" (2.4.126). Tellingly, he finds it easier to believe that a stranger could sleep with his beloved than corrupt her servants to a simple theft. And in his "woman's part" speech the fantasy of the potent alien soon shifts its derivation from south to north:

> Perchance he spoke not, but
> Like a full-acorn'd boar, a German one,
> Cried "O!" and mounted. (lines 167–169)

Iachimo, well-endowed and well-fed, becomes a German boar or "boer," a Germanic or Dutch peasant, his speech an inarticulate cry of lust rather than an Italian sonnet of seduction.

Not all the references to strangeness pertain to Iachimo, however. The exiled Posthumus is himself an alien, first in France, and then, as we see for ourselves, in Rome. Philario, he says, "makes no stranger of me" in the metropolis (1.5.98). But "none a stranger there,/So merry and so gamesome: he is called/The Briton reveller," Iachimo slyly tells Imogen (1.7.59–1.7.61). The crucial wager scene is set in Philario's house in Rome, where the stage directions specify the presence of a Dutchman and a Spaniard, both nonspeaking roles, along with the Frenchman who banters with Posthumus and Iachimo over their nations' women as their embarrassed host looks on (1.5.1 SD). This is the only time an unequivocally "Dutch" character appears on Shakespeare's stage. The scene echoes the meeting of the merchants in Boccaccio's tale from the *Decameron* and in *Frederyke of Jennen*, translated from a German version but originally Dutch. Rome is depicted as a cosmopolitan gathering pace, as London was increasingly coming to view itself. Spain had invaded the Netherlands, but here the Spanish and Dutch visitors revel together: England's traditional enemy and traditional guest are reconciled as many anti-Dutch Londoners secretly suspected was the case. The silent Dutchman foreshadows the German boar, as sexual competition brings the men together. Yet, in another example of the perspectivism implied in *Sir Thomas More*, the audience soon sees Posthumus abroad as subject to the same representations and misrepresentations as aliens in England. Iachimo teases Imogen with tales of her "jolly Briton" and his supposed liaisons with Italian women, hired "tomboys" and "diseas'd ventures" (1.7.67, 1.7.122–1.7.123). Unlike Iachimo, Posthumus would "Slaver with lips as common as the stairs/That mount the Capitol," which are free to all who approach (1.7.105–1.7.106).

The sudden mention of the Capitol reminds us that *Cymbeline* is set during the reign of Augustus, and that its Rome is still that of Julius Caesar and Antony. It even remains Coriolanus's city, where the porch of the Capitol was too common a birthplace in the eyes of that Patrician warrior. After Iachimo's adventures in Britain, the play gradually reasserts the antiquity of its Roman plot. Economic notions of urban identity, which find their nadir in prostitution and the "Romish stew" (1.7.152), are dislodged by the military ideals behind the classical understanding of citizenship. The Senators and Tribunes plan a campaign "against/The fall'n-off Britons," sending "the gentry" to supplement the legions in Gaul because "the common men" are fighting elsewhere in Europe (3.8.2–3.8.7: the military tribunes, not the *tribuni plebis*, are meant). This brings Iachimo and Posthumus, conscripted as a Patrician warrior, to Britain.

As the action unfolds, the tribute that Caius Lucius is sent to collect from King Cymbeline replaces the bracelet that Iachimo takes from Imogen and the ring he claims from Posthumus. Julius Caesar, the founder of the Tower in the history plays, imposed this economic obligation as well. A short-sighted British nationalism is associated with Cloten and the queen mother; Augustus's demand for the tribute comes to be seen as the legitimate entry fee for the privileges of empire.[82] The invasion is provoked by a just cause, although Rome also must be defeated by the hardy Britons before Cymbeline voluntarily concedes. Posthumus' career charts this paradox: a Briton, he becomes a Roman soldier, and then a British soldier on the Roman model, before he accedes to his status as Cymbeline's subject and son-in-law within Roman *imperium*. As Kahn argues, Posthumus, who already has a Latin name, bests the Romans at their own military discipline.[83] Alone on stage, he describes his guilt over his treatment of Imogen and longing for a warlike death in a series of speeches that fully return the soliloquy to Shakespeare's Rome. Thinking his man

Pisanio has killed Imogen, Posthumus questions servants' duty to their masters' behests and shames jealous husbands (5.1.2–5.1.7). Having killed Britain's mistress, he refuses to wound Britain itself, and it is this that provokes his disguise as a fighting British peasant: "Let me make men know/More valor in me than my habits show" (lines 29–30). While delivering his next soliloquy after the battle, he changes back to Roman garb so that he may be taken prisoner and executed. He decries a British lord for cowardice, maintaining Roman standards as he reassumes Roman armor (5.3.64–5.3.83). In prison, he soliloquizes about bondage and the freedom of death (5.4.1–5.4.29).

Posthumus's anger at his aristocratic countryman for fleeing the battle of the narrow lane marks his assertion of a new British subjectivity that appropriates Roman codes of military identity. At the lane itself, as Posthumus reports, old Belarius had threatened his fellow British fighters: "stand,/Or we are Romans, and will give you that/Like beasts which you shun beastly" (5.3.25–5.3.27). In other words, Belarius, the princes, and Posthumus will kill retreating cowards as if the four British heroes were Romans themselves. The "beastly" comparison recalls Coriolanus's contempt for his common soldiers. Together, Belarius and the sons are later said to be "the liver, heart, and brain of Britain," a reminiscence of the belly fable that brings out what Menenius represses: military courage is a requirement for full membership in the social body (5.5.14). Posthumus, who was once called a "leg of Rome" (5.3.92), is likewise praised as "the forlorn soldier that so nobly fought" alongside them (5.5.406). Revealed, he spares Iachimo's life in the final scene, displaying a Roman clemency that points the way to Cymbeline's general pardon at the end of the action.

The central character in *Cymbeline* is redeemed through his soldiership, which points the way to a form of subjectivity—or citizenship—that would not be realized in England until the Civil War and Interregnum.[84] Military heroism is itself rehabilitated by tragicomedy, then, although the degradation of the warrior in the Roman tragedies appears even sharper by contrast. We have seen how the artisanal and mercantile character of London citizenship repeatedly invades the classical territory of the Patrician citizen-soldier. In *Titus Andronicus*, where trade metaphors are few, Titus nevertheless ends his career not on the battlefield but at the dinner table, dressed as a cook. Lucius enters to reclaim Andronican military identity at the head of an invading army of Goths, supposed ancestors of the English audience but also of the "Dutch" aliens among them. The opening scene of *Julius Caesar* establishes an image of the citizen as craft-guild worker, although it is only with Caesar's testament that citizenship proper is symbolically extended from military leaders to commoners with the advent of a new, imperial model of Roman statehood. The "enfranchisement" promised by the conspirators melds this with the mindset of London citizenship, which also infuses the tribunes' earlier anxieties about holiday apparel and occupational mobility. Brutus and Antony each succumb to empty squabbling with their fellow generals among proscriptions and confused maneuvers that reveal their distant kinship with the violent Plebeians. But it is in *Antony and Cleopatra* that the military hero is most clearly debased by repeatedly abandoning his soldiership, which has largely become a mere trade. In this, Antony resembles the off-stage Roman citizens who await Caesar's triumph as mere spectators.

Coriolanus features these Plebeians as both onlookers and active participants in the republican politics of early Rome, "mutinous" subjects who, in rising up, become citizens. It seems that they are depicted in a negative and trivial light. Yet Menenius Agrippa feels he must appeal to their corporate and guild-inflected sense of public life through his corporal tale of the belly. Livery company consciousness in an elite vein is also evinced by the Patricians themselves, for whom war is again a craft, and the populace little better than aliens. Yet in Shakespeare's last Roman tragedy, the military citizenship of classical republicanism is finally divorced from the economic citizenship that actually existed in contemporary London. The terms *citizen* and *patrician* are recast as opposites in the play, and for Coriolanus, citizens cannot be true soldiers. Conversely, as the pure soldier, Coriolanus loses his citizenship. He refuses to participate in civic ritual and suffers expulsion from the city, like the vagabond of Homer and Aristotle, only to return as an alien and attack it. Insofar as he is a hero, he is a tragic one; military heroism and aristocratic identity, taken to the extreme, both fail in the play, for all the ignobility of the Plebeians. The people are the city, and their civic consciousness, based on production and consumption, wins by default.

The northern European conception of corporate citizenship prevails in Shakespeare's Rome, then. Once again, it is important to acknowledge that burgess freedom presupposes a form of political subjectivity, one that in the case of Roman tragedy directly rivals the classical model and its apogee in the citizen-soldier of Machiavelli. The Third Citizen claims that he and his fellows can defy Coriolanus's military service, "but it is a power that we have no power to do." As is typical in Shakespeare, citizen "power" manifests itself only in a negative form, canceling itself out in this passage or sparking catastrophe when the Plebeians eventually reject Coriolanus as candidate. Yet reject him they do, and the mediation of the warden-like tribunes hardly vitiates the exercise of their hard-won rights. Mostly, the subjectivity of the city is embodied in the language of material production and everyday life rather than political participation or abstract statements in these plays: shoes, aprons, stinking breath, and disputatious orange-sellers. But claims to freedom, charters, and liberty are also made, and these terms come from London citizenship, not from the aristocratic or classical traditions. Although they seem wholly positive taken out of their dramatic context, such words encode conflict, the constant struggle of citizens among themselves over exclusive rights to manufacture and trade goods, their struggle against aliens who threatened this preserve, and their struggle against aristocrats who asserted a still more hierarchical and exclusive order of political subjectivity.

Until the tragicomic transformation of Posthumus, Shakespeare sees the situation of the aristocratic classical republican hero as necessarily tragic within this citizen world. The medieval definition of tragedy as the fall from power of a person of high degree is still operative in the Roman plays. Whatever its origins and precise audience, medieval tragedy suited the burghers' religious perspective on their betters as well as aristocratic self-criticism. Brutus and Coriolanus are the central tragic figures in their plays because their attempts at public service or military honor fail to preserve aristocratic identity within the wider framework of economic citizenship. Titus Andronicus similarly fails when he tries to maintain the city's republican values amid a suddenly competitive imperial setting; Antony impersonates imperial values, but he continues to inhabit the shell of older soldierly ideals despite himself. Antony delivers no soliloquies: his lack of inwardness marks a falling-off from Brutus's acute citizen-subjectivity in *Julius Caesar* and foreshadows the empty subjectivity of Coriolanus, almost completely drowned out by city voices. The tragic soliloquy is a hallmark of Shakespeare's mature works in the genre, and its decline in the middle Roman plays suggests that an economic conception of citizenship may be incompatible with the tragic figure as hero. It is not until *Cymbeline* that the full-fledged soliloquy returns in a Roman play, spoken not by a Roman but by a Briton who would lay claim to Roman political subjectivity now that it has become detached from the city itself, under the Empire.

This book has shown how citizenship in Shakespeare cannot be understood apart from the city and the language of its material culture. *Cymbeline* is different from the other plays I have discussed. It augurs the return of the subject in the non- or rather poly-urban nation-state. According to Balibar, in the transition first to centralized sovereignty and then the revolutions against it, "the citizen is in fact liberated by the state from his dependency upon the 'absolute' religious community or pure 'corporative' economic and professional status (which we know had remained the obligatory condition of citizenship—'bourgeoisie'— in medieval cities and towns)."[85] The issue of religious community in England must be left to other studies. London freemen resisted any attempt to "free" themselves even further, since this meant loosening the corporate ties of the livery companies. Nevertheless, urban citizenship did expand in the seventeenth century among men if not women: many sons and grandsons of Flemish and other aliens *were* accepted into livery companies, but only through assimilation to the London populace through their perceived "whiteness" and the mainstream Protestantism of middle-class royalism—in a fitting irony, a Dutch monarch would eventually ascend the throne itself. As the citizen population adapted, the companies gradually faded in civic power during the later seventeenth and eighteenth centuries. Citizenship expanded, then, but it dissolved into subjecthood as it did so, freeing producers and merchants from the corporate bonds that had once sustained them.

It is the prospect of an expandable citizenship, "suspended between individuality and collectivity" yet also "revolutionary" in its assertion of equality, that leads Balibar to call the citizen "a *utopic* figure, which is not to say an unreal or millenarist figure projected into the future, but the elementary term of an 'abstract State'. "[86] When we consider Shakespeare's citizen, however, we are reminded forcefully of the exclusionary and conflictual character that continues to mark the post–Enlightenment citizen. Despite its basic stability, London citizenship was anything but utopic, not even in the etymological sense of Richard Helgerson's phrase "a noplace without meaning." Despite conflicts between and within companies, citizens strove to "place" themselves as a meaningful constituency by consolidating their identity against others, principally alien immigrants to London.[87] The "French" and the "Dutch" in particular were cast as anti-communities, whose separate ways of life menaced the enjoyment of citizen culture even as their industrial skills threatened the freemen's economic well-being. Yet if aliens occupied "the empty place of the *subject*, forming the shadow cast by the *citizen* in the space of sovereignty," this was because the sovereign and powerful aristocrats at court protected them.[88] Although their numbers were small, strangers became new urban subjects of the English monarch, vying with citizens for royal attention just as the citizens had feared.

Does a consideration of citizenship in Shakespeare merely perpetuate the notion that early modern sovereignty effortlessly conquered by dividing? The image of a defensive citizenship, defined by antagonism without and fractured by competition within, seemingly conforms to the top-down paradigm of political power. Yet, as I argued in the introduction to this book, *power* is a name for the unstable field of relationships among people; it proliferates new forms of relationship and identification without consistently serving the interests of either sovereignty or its subjects. In the early modern period, the sovereign had already commandeered much of the shifting field of power, but this should not blind us to the importance of the citizen, chartered by the monarch on the basis of a corporate economic and cultural identity. The imaginative works of the period were part of the sometimes difficult process by which power relations were negotiated among the sovereign and different social groups.

How then are we to explain Shakespeare's apparently derogatory attitude toward citizens in his plays? I cannot answer this question, but I do assert that his slighting references to citizen ways and the relative paucity of direct representations of freemen on his stage do not mean that citizenship was of little significance to Shakespeare. Shakespeare's opinion (if that is what it is) may reflect the self-criticisms of a city audience as well as the disdain of the aristocrats among them, voiced by an author who was both foreign to London and a working resident of the city and its suburbs. But in any case the representation of actions and attitudes in the plays is only part of the picture; language and its texture often tell a different story. However aristocratic his stance and loyalist his politics may have been, Shakespeare's investment in the language of everyday material life, of livery company status, of production, consumption, and economic exchange, demonstrates the playwright's profound involvement with citizenship as a form of subjectivity. For all this, it is true that the citizen in Shakespeare is a *dystopic* figure rather than the personification of utopian social fantasy. Negative, acquisitive, jealous, at once present and absent amid the play of speech and action, and ultimately delimited by the alien, the citizen embodies a lack at the symbolic center of the kingdom, in its metropolis. The negative "freedom" of early modern London created a need for another understanding of citizenship, one that looked forward but also backward to the example of Rome.

Late in the Shakespeare canon, as we have glimpsed, the tragicomic *Cymbeline* offers a provisionally utopian solution. Britain becomes one with Rome at the very end of the play. "My peace we will begin," the king announces,

> Although the victor, we submit to Caesar,
> And to the Roman empire; promising
> To pay our wonted tribute, from the which
> We were dissuaded by our wicked queen. (5.5.460–5.5.464)

Cymbeline's peace is also the *pax Romana* that heralded Christ's birth during his reign and that of Augustus. The Roman Empire, an earthly analogue and vehicle, however inadequate, of Augustine's *civitas Dei*, is a model for the modern state. Citizen and alien, relative categories in *Cymbeline* as in the *More* play, have now become one, as *subditi*. By a sort of contract, Britons in Rome and Romans in Britain will all experience the mutual convertibility of these terms just as Posthumus has. There are signs that Cymbeline's rule was already based on a social contract with the people, albeit a weak one. In his initial rebuff to Augustus's tribute demands, he tells Lucius:

> Our subjects, sir,
> Will not endure his yoke; and for ourself
> To show less sovereignty than they, must needs
> Appear unkinglike. (3.5.4–3.5.7)

Later, amazed at the Roman invasion, he misses the counsel of the absent Queen, only to blame her for his resistance to the Empire in his final submission. Hobbes would find Cymbeline an inadequate ruler who has received *imperium* from his people but who still feels bound to their standards and thus allows them a share in the sovereignty.[89]

Shakespeare's final exploration of Rome and of citizens wanton and warlike looks forward to the dissolution of urban citizenship in Hobbes's *De cive* in the mid-seventeenth century. Unlike the earlier plays, in *Cymbeline* it is the thought of Hobbes, not the influence of Machiavelli or the social role of the livery companies, that serves as the best index to citizen Shakespeare. As I noted earlier, Hobbes uses the word *civitas* to denote the state or commonwealth, not the city.[90] In his treatise, the *civis* or citizen is someone who dwells within a territory under sovereign authority, the usage that we loosely take for granted today. For all Hobbes's pronounced dislike of the Roman Republic, Roman *imperium* serves as his paradigm for political power. Similarly, *Cymbeline* is not a plea for Britain's membership in a foreign polity or even for an empire of its own, though it does flatter James I's internationalist and expansionist dreams. The play takes the Roman Empire as a model for a contractual yet somehow absolute sovereignty over the citizen-subject that supersedes the urban struggles of Cymbeline's capital. Divorced from the person of the monarch and invested in citizens who quickly forgot the metropolitan origins of their political identity, the new concepts of sovereignty and citizenship would long outlast attempts at absolutism itself. Eventually, every native or naturalized inhabitant of London became one more "British subject" within a growing but riven nation.

NOTES

INTRODUCTION

1. Patricia Parker, *Shakespeare from the Margins: Language, Culture, Context* (Chicago: University of Chicago Press, 1996), p. 1; Spitzer, "Development of a Method," in Alban K. Forcione et al., eds., *Representative Essays* (Stanford: Stanford University Press, 1988), pp. 433–434. Spitzer credits Hans Sperber with the concept as well.
2. Etienne Balibar, "Citizen Subject," in Eduardo Cadava, Peter Connor, and Jean-Luc Nancy, eds., *Who Comes After the Subject?* (New York: Routledge, 1991), p. 38.
3. Etienne Balibar, "Subjection and Subjectivation," in Joan Copjec, ed., *Supposing the Subject* (London: Verso, 1994), p. 13.
4. Balibar, "Subjection," pp. 6–7.
5. Aristotle, *The Politics*, trans. Carnes Lord (Chicago: University of Chicago Press, 1984), 1275b 16–20, 1277b 14–16, 1278a 35–39.
6. Balibar, "Citizen Subject," pp. 40–42.
7. Balibar, "Citizen Subject," pp. 43, 47.
8. Quentin Skinner, "The Republican Ideal of Political Liberty," in Gisela Bock, Quentin Skinner and Maurizio Viroli, eds., *Machiavelli and Republicanism* (Cambridge: Cambridge University Press, 1990), pp. 303–304.
9. J. G. A. Pocock, *The Machiavellian Moment: Florentine Political Thought and the Atlantic Republican Tradition* (Princeton: Princeton University Press, 1975), p. 203.
10. Skinner, "Machiavelli's *Discorsi* and the Pre-Humanist Origins of Republican Ideas," in Bock et al., pp. 121–134, 140.
11. Chantal Mouffe, "Democratic Citizenship and the Political Community," in Mouffe, ed., *Dimensions of Radical Democracy* (London: Verso, 1992), pp. 226–227.
12. Mouffe, "Democratic Citizenship," p. 227.
13. Slavoj Zizek, "Eastern Europe's Republics of Gilead," pp. 196–199, and Mouffe, "Preface: Democratic Politics Today," in Mouffe, ed., p. 3.
14. Mouffe, "Democratic Citizenship," p. 236.
15. Etienne Balibar, *We, the People of Europe? Reflections on Transnational Citizenship*, trans. James Swenson (Princeton: Princeton University Press, 2004), p. 40; author's emphasis.
16. Mouffe, "Preface," p. 13; Balibar, "Citizen Subject," pp. 51, 53.

17. Balibar, *Europe*, p. 76.
18. Mouffe, "Democratic Politics," pp. 231, 235 and "Preface," p. 13.
19. Pocock, *Machiavellian Moment*, pp. 334, 348.
20. Antony Black, *Guilds and Civil Society in European Political Thought from the Twelfth Century to the Present* (Ithaca: Cornell University Press, 1984), p. xii. Black's wide-ranging study spends little time in England, and considers political philosophy and guild history, not literature and culture.
21. Black, *Guilds*, pp. 96–109.
22. Susan Reynolds, *An Introduction to the History of English Medieval Towns* (Oxford: Clarendon, 1977), p. 71.
23. Ian W. Archer, *The Pursuit of Stability: Social Relations in Elizabethan London* (Cambridge: Cambridge University Press, 1991), p. 75.
24. Steve Rappaport, *Worlds Within Worlds: Structures of Life in Sixteenth-Century London* (Cambridge: Cambridge University Press, 1989), pp. 24–27; Archer, *Pursuit*, p. 100; Reynolds, *Medieval Towns*, pp. 123–125, 165–172.
25. Rappaport, *Worlds Within Worlds*, p. 53; the number, as opposed to the percentage, of freemen actually rose from about 14,800 to about 28,700, according to Rappaport.
26. Archer, *Pursuit*, p. 61.
27. Rappaport, *Worlds Within Worlds*, pp. 36–41.
28. Rappaport, *Worlds Within Worlds*, pp. 42–45; Archer, *Pursuit*, pp. 131–133. See also Andrew Pettegree, *Foreign Protestant Communities in Sixteenth-Century London* (Oxford: Clarendon, 1986), pp. 262–295.
29. The complete text is in: Arthur Freeman, "Marlowe, Kyd, and the Dutch Church Libel," *English Literary Renaissance* 3 (1973), 50–51.
30. Rappaport, *Worlds Within Worlds*, p. 59.
31. John Roche Dasent, ed., *Acts of the Privy Council of England* (London: Mackie & Co., 1902), n.s. Vol. 26, pp.16–21; Paul L. Hughes and James F. Larkin, eds., *Tudor Royal Proclamations* (New Haven: Yale University Press, 1969), Vol. 3, pp. 221–222.
32. On the perception of stranger communities, see Archer, *Pursuit*, p. 131, and Pettegree, *Foreign Protestant Communities*, pp. 262–295.
33. Montrose, *The Purpose of Playing: Shakespeare and the Cultural Politics of the Elizabethan Theatre* (Chicago: University of Chicago Press, 1996), pp. 198–199.
34. This is my conjecture. On apprenticeship and marriage, see Rappaport, *Worlds Within Worlds*, p. 236. For the school, see Park Honan, *Shakespeare: A Life* (Oxford: Oxford University Press, 1998), pp. 43–44. On John and William Shakespeare and the Stratford leather-trades, see Samuel Schoenbaum, *William Shakespeare: A Compact Documentary Life*, revised edn. (Oxford: Oxford University Press, 1987), pp. 16–17, 73–74.
35. Schoenbaum, *Compact Life*, pp. 33–40; Honan, *A Life*, pp. 25–38.

36. Honan, *A Life*, pp. 292–293.

37. Schoenbaum, *Compact Life*, pp. 279–280, 281–285.

38. Schoenbaum, *Compact Life*, p. 27. Gilbert Shakespeare is described as a haberdasher of St. Bride's parish, London, in a document that records his standing bail for a Stratford clock-maker. Scholars have not found his name in the Haberdasher's rolls, however (p. 331 note 6).

39. Gerald Eades Bentley, *Shakespeare: A Biographical Handbook* (New Haven: Yale University Press, 1961), p. 42.

40. Schoenbaum, *Compact Life*, pp. 227–230.

41. I have consulted the photographic reproduction of the indenture in Schoenbaum, *William Shakespeare: A Documentary Life* (New York: Oxford University Press and the Scolar Press, 1975), p. 221.

42. Honan, *A Life*, pp. 225, 321–322.

43. Honan, *A Life*, p. 322; on the Mountjoys, p. 325.

44. E. A. J. Honigman, "Shakespeare and London's Immigrant Community Circa 1600," in J. P. Vander Motten, ed., *Elizabethan and Modern Studies: Presented to Professor William Schrickx* (Gent: Seminaire voor Engelse en Amerikaanse Literatur, 1985), p. 148; Honan, *A Life*, pp. 322–324. Shakespeare's involvement with the Mountjoys is evidenced by his testimony in a legal case of 1612 about his role as an intermediary in their daughter's marriage negotiations (the facts are well known: see Schoenbaum, *Compact Life*, pp. 260–264). Honigman (pp. 149–150) and Honan (pp. 327–328) link the Mountjoy case to the treatment of marriage in *Measure for Measure* and *All's Well that Ends Well*, both written around 1604, when the marriage took place. I might add that Shakespeare resembled Paroles much more than Duke Vincentio. But situational parallels are of less interest in my study than the way language encodes citizen and alien encounters, and so I've eschewed reading these plays as biographical allegory here or in chapter 1.

45. Richard Helgerson, *Forms of Nationhood: The Elizabethan Writing of England* (Chicago: University of Chicago Press, 1992), p. 197.

46. Helgerson, *Nationhood*, pp. 238, 239, 240.

47. Helgerson, *Nationhood*, p. 206.

48. Helgerson, *Nationhood*, p. 240.

49. Leah S. Marcus, *Puzzling Shakespeare: Local Reading and its Discontents* (Berkeley: University of California Press, 1988), pp. 116–117.

50. Jean E. Howard, "Shakespeare and Genre," in David Scott Kastan, ed., *A Companion to Shakespeare* (Oxford: Blackwell, 1999), p. 308.

51. Theodore B. Leinwand, "Shakespeare and the Middling Sort," *Shakespeare Quarterly* 44 (1993), 284.

52. Leinwand, "Middling Sort," pp. 284–286. Leinwand also cites Annabel Patterson.

53. Leinwand, "Middling Sort," pp. 287–288.

54. Leinwand, "Middling Sort," p. 292.

55. Leinwand, "Middling Sort," pp. 289, 285 note 3. Wrightson is cited on p. 285 note 4, and pp. 290–291. Keith Wrightson's earlier work

on this topic has been superseded by his article on " 'Sorts of People' in Tudor and Stuart England," in Jonathan Barry and Christopher Brooks, eds., *The Middling Sort of People: Culture, Society and Politics in England, 1550–1800* (New York: St. Martin's Press, 1994), pp. 28–51, and esp. pp. 41–42.

56. Wrightson—who takes the Mulcaster passage into account as a somewhat isolated example—allows that the middling status of citizens before 1640 was taken for granted, if rarely enunciated, for they lacked the political identity the term "middling sort" would later confer (p. 44). In the same volume, Jonathan Barry remarks upon the fragmentation among the better-off workers but traces their gradual consolidation in cities through various associations and their values, a development in which livery companies played a large part. Barry, "Bourgeois Collectivism? Urban Associations and the Middling Sort," in Barry and Brooks, pp. 84–112.

57. Marx and Engels, *The Communist Manifesto* (London: Verso, 1998), p. 35 and Engel's note.

58. In other words, it is a discourse. On discourse, class, and antagonism, see Ernesto Laclau and Chantal Mouffe, *Hegemony and Socialist Strategy*, trans. Winston Moore and Paul Cammack (London: Verso, 1985), pp. 105–127.

59. Leinwand, "Middling Sort," p. 292.

60. Helgerson, *Nationhood*, p. 244.

61. Stephen Greenblatt, *Shakespearean Negotiations* (Berkeley: University of California Press, 1988), p. 54.

62. Michel Foucault, *The History of Sexuality*, Vol. 1: *An Introduction*, trans. Robert Hurley (New York: Vintage, 1980), pp. 10, 47, 92–96, 101.

63. Brian Gibbons, *Jacobean City Comedy: A Study of Satiric Plays by Jonson, Marston, and Middleton* (Cambridge: Harvard University Press, 1968), p. 17. Gibbons's emphasis.

64. Alexander Leggatt, *Citizen Comedy in the Age of Shakespeare* (Toronto: University of Toronto Press, 1973), pp. 150, 151–152.

65. Harry Berger, "Text against Performance in Shakespeare: The Example of *Macbeth*," in Stephen Greenblatt, ed., *The Power of Forms in the English Renaissance* (Norman, OK: Pilgrim Books, 1982), p. 77; Leinwand, *The City Staged: Jacobean City Comedy, 1603–1613* (Madison: University of Wisconsin Press, 1986), p. 13.

66. Steven Mullaney, *The Place of the Stage: License, Play, and Power in Renaissance England* (Chicago: University of Chicago Press, 1988); Leah Marcus, *Puzzling Shakespeare*, pp. 36–37 and chapter 4.

67. Douglas Bruster, *Drama and the Market in the Age of Shakespeare* (Cambridge: Cambridge University Press, 1992), pp. 30, 35–36. Bruster's emphasis.

68. Parker, *Margins*, pp. 2–3; Karl Marx, "Theses on Feuerbach," in *The Marx–Engels Reader*, 2nd edn., ed. Robert C. Tucker (New York: Norton, 1978), pp. 143–145.

69. Jean E. Howard treats citizens and aliens together in "Mastering Difference in *The Dutch Courtesan*," *Shakespeare Studies* 24 (1996), 105–117, and in "Women, Foreigners, and the Regulation of Urban Space in *Westward Ho*," in Orlin, ed., *Material London*, pp. 150–167. On aliens in the period's drama, see the standard work by A. J. Hoenselaars, *Images of Englishmen and Foreigners in the Drama of Shakespeare and His Contemporaries* (Toronto: Associated University Presses, 1992). Citizen and merchant types also appear in this study.
70. For these lexical matters, see the OED and Onions, *Oxford Dictionary of English Etymology*.

1 COMEDY: CIVIL SAYINGS

1. Howard, "Shakespeare and Genre," p. 308.
2. Leggatt, *Citizen Comedy*, p. 146.
3. See Gail Kern Paster's chapter on what she calls "Shakespeare's City Comedies," *The Idea of the City in the Age of Shakespeare* (Athens: University of Georgia Press, 1985), pp. 178–219.
4. Shakespeare, *Measure for Measure*, ed. J. W. Lever (London: Arden Shakespeare-Methuen, 1965), 3.2.1–4.
5. See *Measure for Measure*, ed. Lever, note to 3.2.3–4 and Shakespeare, *Measure for Measure*, ed. Mark Eccles (New York: New Variorum Shakespeare-Modern Language Association, 1980), note to line 1493.
6. Archer, *Pursuit*, p. 232.
7. Shakespeare, *All's Well That Ends Well*, ed. G. K. Hunter (London: Arden Shakespeare-Routledge, 1989), 2.2.16.
8. Paster, *Idea of the City*, p. 7.
9. Shakespeare, *The Comedy of Errors*, ed. R. A. Foakes (London: Arden Shakespeare-Methuen, 1963), 1.1.8.
10. *The Comedy of Errors*, ed. Foakes, p. xxix.
11. Ephesians 2: 12–15, 19–21. *The Geneva Bible: A Facsimile of the 1560 Edition* (Madison: University of Wisconsin Press, 1969). I have tacitly removed italics and abbreviations. On this passage and the play, see Barbara Freedman, "Egeon's Debt: Self Division and Self-Redemption in *The Comedy of Errors*," *ELR* 10 (1980), 381–382.
12. Patricia Parker, "Anagogic Metaphor: Breaking Down the Walls of Partition," in Eleanor Cook et al., eds. *Centre and Labyrinth* (Toronto: University of Toronto Press, 1983), pp. 38–58, and *Shakespeare from the Margins: Language, Culture, Context* (Chicago: University of Chicago Press, 1996), pp. 56–59.
13. On the liberties and the drama, Mullaney has been very influential. For a historian's less drastic view of their difference from the city, see Archer, *Pursuit*, pp. 234–235.
14. "Nativity," OED 5.a; William West, *Symbolaeography, which may be Termed the Art, Description, or Image of Instruments* (London: Jane Yetsweirt, 1597), I, section 46.

15. Shakespeare, *Love's Labour's Lost*, ed. H. R. Woudhuysen (Walton-on-Thames: Arden Shakespeare-Thomas Nelson and Sons, 1998), 5.1.13–5.1.14, 5.1.16–5.1.25.

16. Keir Elam, *Shakespeare's Universe of Discourse: Language-Games in the Comedies* (Cambridge: Cambridge University Press, 1984), pp. 262–263.

17. John Hart, *An Orthographie* (London: William Seres, 1569); William Bullokar, *Bullokars Booke at large, for the Amendment of Orthographie for English Speech* (London: Henrie Denham, 1580); Richard Mulcaster, *The First Part of the Elementarie* (London: Thomas Vautroullier, 1582; facsimile edn., Menston: Scolar Press, 1970); Peter Bales, *The Writing Schoolemaster* (London: Thomas Orwin, 1590). For a survey, see Jonathan Goldberg, *Writing Matter: From the Hands of the English Renaissance* (Stanford: Stanford University Press, 1990), pp. 190–207.

18. Ferdinand de Saussure, *Course in General Linguistics*, trans. Wade Baskin (New York: McGraw-Hill, 1966), p. 31.

19. François Rabelais, *The Histories of Gargantua and Pantagruel*, trans. J. M. Cohen (Harmondsworth: Penguin, 1955), p. 70.

20. John Drakakis, "Afterword," in John J. Joughin ed., *Shakespeare and National Culture* (Manchester: Manchester University Press, 1997), pp. 229–230.

21. Benedict Anderson, *Imagined Communities: Reflections on the Origin and Spread of Nationalism*, revised edn. (London: Verso, 1991), p. 44.

22. Hoenselaars, *Images of Englishmen*, pp. 46, 64.

23. Carla Mazzio, "The Melancholy of Print: *Love's Labour's Lost*," in Mazzio and Douglas Trevor, eds., *Historicism, Psychoanalysis, and Early Modern Culture* (New York: Routledge, 2000), p. 203.

24. Hart, *Orthographie*, pp. 4 recto-verso; Bullokar, *Bullokars Booke*, pp. 1, 19, 38.

25. Bales, *Schoolemaster*, E1 recto, R3 recto.

26. Hart, *Orthographie*, p. 15 verso.

27. Francis Yates, *A Study of Love's Labour's Lost* (Cambridge: Cambridge University Press, 1936), pp. 60–61. Many of her specific conclusions linking characters to historical personages are less helpful.

28. Freeman, "Marlowe, Kyd," p. 50. The poem is signed "per. Tam-berlaine," and as Freeman points out this may have lead to the implication of Marlowe and Kyd in the libel.

29. James Shapiro, *Shakespeare and the Jews* (New York: Columbia University Press, 1996), p. 185.

30. Yates, *A Study*, p. 66.

31. Archer, *Pursuit*, pp. 1–9.

32. Shakespeare, *Love's Labour's Lost*, ed. Woudhuysen, note to 3.1.3.

33. Archer, *Pursuit*, p. 134.

34. On Goldsmith's Row in the 1590s, see Paul Griffiths, "Politics Made Visible: Order, Residence and Uniformity in Cheapside, 1600–45," in Griffiths and Mark S. R. Jenner, eds., *Londinopolis: Essays in the Cultural and Social History of Early Modern London* (Manchester: Manchester University Press, 2000), pp. 176–177.

35. Pettegree, *Foreign Protestant Communities*, p. 12.

36. John Michael Archer, *Old Worlds: Egypt, Southwest Asia, India, and Russia in Early Modern English Writing* (Stanford: Stanford University Press, 2001), pp. 124–130.

37. John Michael Archer, "Love's Labour's Lost," in Richard Dutton and Jean E. Howard, eds., *A Companion to Shakespeare's Works*, Vol. 3: *The Comedies* (Oxford: Blackwell, 2003), pp. 320–337.

38. Shakespeare, *Love's Labour's Lost*, ed. Richard David (London: Methuen, 1956), note to 5.2.247.

39. Marston, *The Dutch Courtesan*, 3.3.27–3.3.29, in Russell A. Fraser and Norman C. Rabkin, eds., *Drama of the English Renaissance*, Vol. 2: *The Stuart Period* (New York: Macmillan, 1976).

40. Shakespeare, *Love's Labour's Lost*, ed. David, note to 5.2.281.

41. Meredith Skura, *Shakespeare the Actor and the Purposes of Playgoing* (Chicago: University of Chicago Press, 1993), pp. 88–95, 89 note 9.

42. William Carroll, *The Great Feast of Language in Love's Labour's Lost* (Princeton: Princeton University Press, 1976), p. 233.

43. Shakespeare, *Love's Labour's Lost*, ed. David, note to 5.2.610.

44. Shakespeare, *Love's Labour's Lost*, ed. Horace Howard Furness (Philadelphia: New Variorum Shakespeare-J. B. Lippincott), note to 5.1.79–5.1.80.

45. Archer, *Pursuit*, pp. 82–92. On the parish power-structures in general, see Keith Wrightson, "The Politics of the Parish," in Paul Griffiths, Adam Fox, and Steve Hindle, eds., *The Experience of Authority in Early Modern England* (Basingstoke: Macmillan, 1996), pp. 10–46. On London parishes, see Michael Berlin, "Reordering Rituals: Ceremony and the Parish, 1520–1640," in Griffiths and Jenner, eds., *Londinopolis*, pp. 47–60.

46. Joan R. Kent, *The English Village Constable, 1580–1642: A Social and Administrative Study* (Oxford: Clarendon, 1986), p. 62.

47. Anthony Munday et al., *Sir Thomas More*, eds. Vittorio Gabrieli and Giorgio Melchiori (Manchester: The Revels Plays-Manchester University Press, 1990), 2.3.17–2.3.19.

48. The examples in Tilley suggest that the proverb mainly pertains to class and religious differences. But it is applied to Jenkins the Welshman in *Northward Ho!*, one of his examples (4.1.11–4.1.12). Tilley does not cite the *More* passage: Morris P. Tilley, *A Dictionary of the Proverbs in England in the Sixteenth and Seventeenth Centuries* (Ann Arbor, MI: University of Michigan Press, 1950), M162.

49. Freeman, "Marlowe, Kyd," p. 51.

50. Shakespeare, *The Merchant of Venice*, ed. John Russell Brown (London: Arden Shakespeare-Routledge, 1988), 1.2.53. And on sovereign power in Belmont, see for instance 3.2.49–3.2.50, 5.1.94–5.1.97.

51. On the expulsion orders and the play, see Kim F. Hall, "Guess Who's Coming to Dinner? Colonization and Miscegenation in *The Merchant of Venice*," *Renaissance Drama* 23 (1992), 90–91.

52. Pocock, *The Machiavellian Moment*, pp. 321, 324–325.

53. Tretiak, "*The Merchant of Venice* and the 'Alien' Question," *RES* 5 (1929), 402–409.

54. Shapiro, *Shakespeare and Jews*, pp. 186–187.

55. Shakespeare, *The Merchant of Venice*, ed. Brown, note to 3.3.27. Thomas, *The History of Italy*, in M. Lindsay Kaplan, ed., *The Merchant of Venice: Texts and Contexts* (Boston: Bedford/St. Martin's, 2002), pp. 133, 137.

56. Aristotle's compound definition of justice is of course more complex than this. The good citizen is at stake in his approach; distributive justice concerns "those who have a stake in the constitution," and reciprocal justice draws its examples from exchanges among artisans: *The Nicomachean Ethics*, trans. David Ross (Oxford: Oxford University Press, 1980), pp. 111, 117–122. The Aristotelian view may have been familiar to Shakespeare from Book 5 of Spenser's *Faerie Queene*, among other sources. The Egalitarian Giant with his balance, emblem of an unjust because disproportionate equality, stands behind Shylock and his scales: *The Faerie Queene*, ed. Thomas P. Roche (Harmondsworth: Penguin, 1978), 5.2.30–5.2.32. The Giant may embody fears of a leveling Anabaptism associated with London's Dutch immigrants.

57. "Proclamation Ordering Peace Kept in London" and Coke, *Reports*, in *The Merchant of Venice*, ed. Kaplan, pp. 159–160, 161–162.

58. Freeman, "Marlowe, Kyd," p. 50.

59. Shapiro, *Shakespeare and Jews*, p. 185.

60. Archer, *Pursuit*, pp. 24, 100–101. Archer argues that it is a mistake to overstress either conflict or cooperation between artisans or merchants; the evidence is uneven, and companies should be judged on a case by case basis.

61. Archer, *Pursuit*, p. 102 and passim.

62. Rappaport, *Worlds Within Worlds*, pp. 39, 372–373.

63. Archer, *Pursuit*, pp. 5–7.

64. Shakespeare, *The Merry Wives of Windsor*, ed. H. J. Oliver (London: Arden Shakespeare-Methuen, 1971), 1.1.32, 2.3.103–2.3.104. For Shallow as a Garter guest, see 2.3.53.

65. Rosemary Kegl, *The Rhetoric of Concealment: Figuring Gender and Class in Renaissance Literature* (Ithaca: Cornell University Press, 1994), pp. 96–100.

66. *A Most Pleasaunt and Excellent Conceited Comedie, of Syr Iohn Falstaffe, and the Merrie Wiues of Windsor*, A3 recto. The Quarto is reproduced in facsimile in Giorgio Melchiori, ed., *The Merry Wives of Windsor* (Walton-on-Thames: Arden Shakespeare-Thomas Nelson and Sons, 2000). Further citations from this facsimile.

67. In the Quarto, it is true that Slender later says he is "as good as any is in *Glostershire*" (F1 recto). But in the scene where the false duel is explained, Shallow seems quite familiar with "Doctor *Cayus* and

sir *Hu*" in Q, less so in F (2.1.191–2.1.192). Q's Shallow and his fighting past is already familiar to Page (C2 recto), where in F, Shallow volunteers the information to counter Page's praise of Caius's dueling skill (2.1.211–2.1.218).

68. Leah Marcus, *Unediting the Renaissance: Shakespeare, Marlowe, Milton* (London: Routledge, 1996), p. 88.

69. *The Merry Wives of Windsor*, ed. Oliver, p. xxxvii.

70. Marcus, *Unediting the Renaissance*, pp. 84–88.

71. Peter Erickson, "The Order of the Garter, the Cult of Elizabeth, and Class–Gender Tension in *The Merry Wives of Windsor*," in Jean E. Howard and Marion F. O'Connor, eds. *Shakespeare Reproduced: The Text in History and Ideology* (New York: Methuen, 1987), pp. 116–130; Marcus, *Unediting the Renaissance*, pp. 69–81.

72. Rappaport, *Worlds Within Worlds*, p. 13; Archer, *Pursuit*, p. 3.

73. Marcus, *Unediting the Renaissance,* p. 93.

74. Shakespeare, *The First Part of King Henry IV*, ed. A. R. Humphreys (London: Arden Shakespeare-Routledge, 1988), 1.2.25–1.2.29; 2.2.81.

75. Shakespeare, *The Second Part of King Henry IV*, ed. A. R. Humphreys (London: Arden Shakespeare-Methuen, 1966), 5.4.7.

76. Shakespeare, *The Merry Wives of Windsor*, ed. Oliver, note to 1.1.271.

77. C. J. Sisson, "Shakespeare's Helena and Dr. William Harvey," *Essays and Studies* (1960), 1–20; Pettegree, *Foreign Protestant Communities*, pp. 176, 206–207, 230.

78. Gertrude Annan, "John Caius," in Elizabeth M. Nugent, ed., *The Thought and Culture of the English Renaissance* (The Hague: Martinus Nijhoff, 1969), pp. 289–290. Caius died in 1573.

79. Pettegree, *Foreign Protestant Communities*, p. 13.

80. In John Webster's *The White Devil* (New York: Norton, 1996), Francisco disguises himself as a Moor: could this have affected the 1623 Folio?

81. Archer, *Pursuit*, p. 131.

82. Rappaport, *Worlds Within Worlds*, pp. 44, 57.

83. Pettegree, *Foreign Protestant Communities*, pp. 12, 82.

84. Patricia Parker, *Literary Fat Ladies: Rhetoric, Gender, Property* (London: Methuen, 1987), pp. 20–21; Valerie Traub, *Desire and Anxiety: Circulations of Sexuality in Shakespearean Drama* (London: Routledge, 1992), pp. 56–64.

85. Zizek, "Republics of Gilead," in Mouffe, pp. 196–197.

86. Parker, *Margins*, pp. 121–122.

87. M. J. Power, "East London Housing in the Seventeenth Century," in Peter Clark and Paul Slack, eds., *Crisis and Order in English Towns, 1500–1700: Essays in Urban History* (Toronto: University of Toronto Press, 1972), p. 241.

88. Pettegree, *Foreign Protestant Communities*, p. 82.

89. Rappaport, *Worlds Within Worlds*, p. 54; Pettegree, *Foreign Protestant Communities*, pp. 283–285. The complaint is prominent in the Dutch Church Libel: Freeman, "Marlowe, Kyd," p. 50.

90. Rappaport, *Worlds Within Worlds*, p. 66. The number of aliens in London had probably decreased during the latter part of the sixteenth century *relative* to the entire population (p. 105).

91. Deanne Williams, " 'Will you go, Anhhers?' *The Merry Wives of Windsor*, II. i. 209," *Notes and Queries* (June 1999), 233–234.

92. Shakespeare, *The Merry Wives of Windsor*, ed. Oliver, pp. xlvi–xlviii; and the edition by Melchiori, pp. 26–27.

93. Barbara Freedman, "Shakespearean Chronology, Ideological Complicity, and Floating Texts: Something is Rotten in Windsor," *Shakespeare Quarterly* 45 (1994), 203–205; *Calendar of State Papers, Domestic Series, of the Reign of Elizabeth, 1598–1601*, ed. M. A. Everett Green (1869; rpt. Nendeln, Liechtenstein: Kraus, 1967), pp. 5–6.

94. Parker, *Margins*, p. 130.

95. Shakespeare, *The Merry Wives of Windsor*, ed. Oliver, note to 4.6.30.

96. Pettegree, *Foreign Protestant Communities*, pp. 36–37.

97. I am building on William Empson's classic definition of pastoral in general: *Some Versions of Pastoral* (New York: New Directions, 1974), p. 22.

98. Richard Wilson, *Will Power: Essays on Shakespearean Authority* (Detroit: Wayne State University Press, 1993), pp. 73–74.

99. Mario DiGangi, *The Homoerotics of Early Modern Drama* (Cambridge: Cambridge University Press, 1997), pp. 56–57.

100. Shakespeare, *As You Like It*, ed. Agnes Latham (London: Arden Shakespeare-Methuen, 1975), 1.3.122–1.3.124.

101. Shakespeare, *As You Like It*, ed. Richard Knowles (New York: New Variorum Shakespeare-Modern Language Association, 1977), note to line 1326.

102. Shakespeare, *As You Like It*, note to 2.1.23; and New Variorum edition, ed. Knowles, note to line 629.

103. Thomas Nashe, *Pierce Penilesse his Supplication to the Divell*, in R. B. McKerrow, ed., *The Works of Thomas Nashe*, 2nd edn., revised by F. P. Wilson (Oxford: Blackwell, 1958), 1.223.

104. On the type of the citizen's wife, see Ian W. Archer, "Material Londoners?", in Lena Cowen Orlin, *Material London, ca. 1600* (Philadelphia: University of Pennsylvania Press, 2000), p. 186. In addition to his examples, see Anonymous, "A Tale of a Citizen and his Wife," in C. A. Patrides, ed., *The Complete English Poems of John Donne* (London: Dent-Everyman's Library, 1985), and the characters of "A Very Woman," "A Purveyor of Tobacco," "A Handsome Hostess," and "A Gull Citizen" (the last two by John Earle) in Thomas Overbury, *A Wife now the Widow of Sir T. Overburye* (1616), ed. James E. Savage (Gainesville: Scholars Facsimiles, 1968).

A. Stuart Daly argues that both the city-woman and city-deer references are mere satirical commonplaces and do not alter the play's overwhelmingly rural character: "We can only conclude that city life has no relevance to the drama." In providing a broad context for these allusions within the play and Shakespearean comedy at large in this chapter, I hope to show the opposite. See Daly, "The Dispraise of the Country in *As You Like It*," *Shakespeare Quarterly* 36 (1985), 305.

105. Howard, "Shakespeare and Genre," p. 308; on *Edward IV*, pp. 303–304.

106. Shakespeare, *Measure for Measure*, ed. Lever, p. xxxii.

107. Archer, *Pursuit*, p. 214. On Henslowe and other citizen brothelowners, see John L. McMullan, *The Canting Crew: London's Criminal Underworld, 1550–1700* (New Brunswick: Rutgers University Press, 1984), p. 193. On Henslowe's rise, see Andrew Gurr, *The Shakespearean Stage, 1574–1642*, 3rd edn. (Cambridge: Cambridge University Press, 1992), p. 58.

108. On "evils" and "houses of office," see the New Variorum edition, ed. Eccles, note to line 935.

109. See Marcus, *Puzzling Shakespeare*, p. 177, for (roughly) citizen magistrate parallels to Angelo's hypocrisy in contemporary London. My reading of Angelo compliments hers, but I do not think that Angelo is a "local" figure for the Lord Mayor's function (p. 170). It is possible that Isabella's silence at the Duke's marriage proposal registers nostalgia for Queen Elizabeth's chastity and her supposed protection of London's freedoms. Isabella-Elizabeth resists the Duke much as London passively withstood James I's royal entry, an attempted penetration of the city in more ways than one (p. 184).

110. McMullan, *The Canting Crew*, p. 87; Archer, *Pursuit*, pp. 223–224.

111. Archer, *Pursuit*, p. 230.

112. Shakespeare, *Much Ado About Nothing*, ed. A. R. Humphreys (London: Arden Shakespeare-Methuen, 1981), 3.5.19; 3.3.73–3.3.74.

113. Kent, *The English Village Constable*, pp. 19–20, 62, 74.

114. Rappaport, *Worlds Within Worlds*, p. 259.

115. From the title page of the first Quarto: *Midsummer Night's Dream*, ed. Brooks, p. xxi.

116. Shakespeare, *A Midsummer Night's Dream*, ed. Harold F. Brooks (London: Arden Shakespeare-Methuen, 1979), 5.1.72.

117. On artisanal contexts for acting companies in the play, see Montrose, *Playing Shakespeare*, pp. 179–205. Montrose links the mechanicals' names to medieval guilds, such as those that mounted the Corpus Christi plays (p. 185).

2   HISTORY: CIVIL BUTCHERY

1. Helgerson, *Forms of Nationhood*, pp. 234, 240, 244–245.

2. See Ronald Knowles, "Introduction," in Shakespeare, *Henry VI, Part 2*, ed. Knowles (Walton-on-Thames: Arden Shakespeare-Thomas Nelson and Sons, 1999), pp. 116–120.

3. The Q text of part 2 is entitled *The First part of the Contention betwixt the two famous Houses of York and Lancaster* (1594), and the Octavo text of part 3, its earliest published version, *The true Tragedie of Richard Duke of Yorke, and the death of good King Henrie the Sixth* (1595). Q *Richard III* was printed in 1597, followed by Q2 in 1598 and later editions.

4. Knowles, "Introduction" to Shakespeare, *2 Henry VI*, pp. 111–116.

5. Shakespeare, *2 Henry VI*, 1.1.155–1.1.156, 1.1.161.

6. In this, she is somewhat like Simcox's wife in the false miracle scene. Here the husband joins with his wife in using a sham supernatural claim to fool the villagers of St. Albans. It is Gloucester who exposes the husband (2.1).

7. See Ian W. Archer, "Material Londoners?" p. 186.

8. On women as aliens in history plays, see Phyllis Rackin, "Foreign Country: The Place of Women in Shakespeare's Historical World," in Richard Burt and John Michael Archer, eds., *Enclosure Acts: Sexuality, Property, and Culture in Early Modern England* (Ithaca: Cornell University Press, 1994), pp. 68–95. As Jean E. Howard and Rackin point out in a separate study, Eleanor unwittingly assumes an alien air herself before the Elizabethan audience if not her pre-Reformation enemies, since in late sixteenth-century England, Roman Catholic priests were linked with the Continent: *Engendering a Nation: A Feminist Account of Shakespeare's English Histories* (London: Routledge, 1997), p. 76.

9. Bertram Wolffe, *Henry VI* (New Haven: Yale University Press, 2001), p. 126.

10. Knowles, "Introduction" to Shakespeare, *2 Henry VI*, pp. 85–86.

11. On the apron and its later appearances in Shakespeare and seventeenth-century political tracts, see Charles Hobday, "Clouted Shoon and Leather Aprons: Shakespeare and the Egalitarian Tradition," *Renaissance and Modern Studies* 23 (1979), 69–70.

12. Shakespeare, *2 Henry VI*, ed. Andrew S. Cairncross (London: Arden Shakespeare-Methuen, 1957), 3.1.357 note; R. A. Griffiths, *The Reign of Henry VI*, 2nd edn. (Stroud, Gloucestershire: Sutton Publishing, 1998), pp. 617, 653–654 note.

13. Wolffe, *Henry VI*, p. 232; for the Kentish commons' complaint, see *2 Henry VI*, ed. Knowles, p. 443; Suffolk's murder is depicted in 4.1.

14. Paul Griffiths, "Politics Made Visible: Order, Residence and Uniformity in Cheapside, 1600–45," pp. 176–196.

15. *Contention*, in *1 Henry VI*, ed. Knowles, p. 400.

16. Griffiths, *Henry VI*, p. 615.

17. *2 Henry VI*, ed. Knowles, 4.2.69 note, and p. 372.

18. Griffiths, *Henry VI*, pp. 615, 628.

19. Spurgeon, *Shakespeare's Imagery and What It Tells Us* (Cambridge: Cambridge University Press, 1935), pp. 227–228; Knowles, "Introduction" to *2 Henry VI*, pp. 72, 99–100.

20. Under Queen Elizabeth, "Lenten butchers" were generally banned unless a license was granted to consumers who required meat for medical reasons. This helped support the fishery and so it was treated as a public as well as religious good. Butchers often ignored the law, however, and were fined by the Butchers' Company. Such fines were common in the 1590s, and in 1607 the Company reiterated the prohibition on Lenten butchery in its formal ordinances: Arthur Pearce, *The History of the Butchers' Company* (London: Meat Traders' Journal Company, 1929), pp. 81, 237.

21. Pearce, *Butchers' Company*, pp. 31–32, 48, 230.

22. See the doubling chart in *2 Henry VI*, ed. Knowles, pp. 434–437.

23. Shakespeare, *King Henry VI, Part 3*, ed. John D. Cox and Eric Rasmussen (London: Arden Shakespeare-Thompson Learning, 2001), 1.1.67, 1.1.70–1.1.71.

24. Pearce, *Butchers' Company*, p. 144.

25. Shakespeare, *2 Henry VI*, ed. Knowles, 5.2.51–5.2.59, and line 52 note.

26. In a different mode, the queen had earlier steeled her troops by describing how the Yorkists have made her husband's kingdom a "slaughterhouse" (5.4.78).

27. Hall, *The Union of the Two Noble and Illustre Famelies of Lancastre and Yorke*, in Shakespeare, *King Henry VI, Part 3*, ed. Andrew S. Cairncross (London: Arden Shakespeare-Routledge, 1989), p. 170.

28. Shakespeare, *King Henry VI, Part 1*, ed. Edward Burns (London: Arden Shakespeare-Thomson Learning, 2000), 2.3.22, 2.3.60–2.3.71.

29. *Pierce Penilesse his Supplication to the Divell*, in Nashe 1.212–213.

30. Edward Burns, "Introduction," in *1 Henry VI*, ed. Burns, p. 21.

31. I am dependent upon Wolffe, pp. 39–41, and especially Griffiths, *Henry VI*, pp. 73–81, for the historical overview of these paragraphs.

32. Raphael Holinshed, *Holinshed's Chronicles of England, Scotland, and Ireland*, Vol. 3 (London: J. Johnson, 1808; rpt. New York: AMS, 1965), p. 148.

33. Griffiths, *Henry VI*, pp. 74–75; "Gregory's Chronicle," in James Gairdner, ed., *The Historical Collection of a Citizen of London in the Fifteenth Century* (London: Camden Society, 1876), pp. 157–158.

34. The *Brut* chronicle, available in a sixteenth-century edition based on Caxton's version, records that Winchester bore a "hevy herte" against the citizens without mentioning his support of aliens: *The Brut, or The Chronicles of England*, Vol. 2, ed. F. W. D. Brie (London: Early English Text Society, 1908), p. 432.

35. Shakespeare, *Richard III*, ed. Antony Hammond (Walton-on-Thames: Arden Shakespeare-Thomas Nelson and Sons, 1997), 3.1.1.

36. John Stow, *A Survey of London*, "Reprinted from the text of 1603," ed. Charles Lethbridge Kingsford, 2 vols. (Oxford: Clarendon, 1908), I.85.

37. Henry Wright, *The First Part of the Disqvisition of Truth, Concerning Political Affairs* (London: Nicholas Okes, 1616), p. 68.

38. OED 1. By the late sixteenth century, the recorder of the city of London had become an important magistrate who sat on the commission of the peace and had other legal duties: Archer, *Pursuit of Stability*, p. 18.

39. Phyllis Rackin argues that Shakespeare's histories often invite the contemporary audience to compare their situation with the political action on stage: *Stages of History: Shakespeare's English Chronicles* (Ithaca: Cornell University Press, 1990), pp. 119–120; on *Richard III*, see pp. 95–96.

40. Shakespeare, *King John*, ed. E. A. J. Honigmann (London: Arden Shakespeare-Thomson Learning, 1998), 3.3.146–3.3.159.

41. Quotation altered from "Kings of our fear." "King'd" is the reading in the Folio, the only early text (2.1.371 collation). The Arden edition also makes the Citizen into Huberd, following speech prefixes after line 325: it is possible the SP indicates that the same actor played two roles, although the conflation of Huberd with the wily Argierian is tempting.

42. In addition to the passages cited below, Jane Shore is mentioned at 1.1.93 and 3.5.31.

43. For the exclusion of Jane Shore as the exclusion of the "common people" and a "people's history," see Helgerson, *Forms of Nationhood*, pp. 237–238.

44. Howard and Rackin, *Engendering a Nation*, p. 107.

45. Examples include 1.2.54, 1.2.102, 1.3.276, 3.5.86–3.5.90, 4.4.393, and 5.3.123.

46. Shakespeare, *King Richard II*, ed. Peter Ure (Bungay: Arden Shakespeare-Methuen, 1961), 1.3.128.

47. Rappaport, *Worlds Within Worlds*, p. 55.

48. Shakespeare, *The Life and Death of King Richard the Second*, ed. Matthew W. Black (Philadelphia: New Variorum Shakespeare-J. B. Lippincott, 1955), 1.3.266a–z, and *Richard II*, 1.3.271–1.3.274 note. The recent Third Series Arden edition also misses the citizen connotation of "freedom" and adds little to the tense crux discussed below: *Richard II* ed. Charles R. Forker (London: Arden Shakespeare-Thomson Learning, 2002), 1.3.271–1.3.274.

49. Rappaport, *Worlds Within Worlds*, p. 29. On length of apprenticeships, see pp. 320–321.

50. Rappaport, *Worlds Within Worlds*, pp. 241, 294, 333–334.

51. On apprenticeship, see Ilana Krausman Ben-Amos, *Adolescence and Youth in Early Modern England* (New Haven: Yale University Press, 1996), chapters 4, 5, and 9 ("Rites of Passage"). Around 10% of the

London population were apprentices in the mid-sixteenth century and the proportion was higher by the 1590s (p. 84); most citizens in the audience had passed through apprentice status.

52. Shakespeare, *The Merchant of Venice*, ed. Brown, 4.1.39. See chapter 1 of this book.

53. Shakespeare, *The First Part of Henry IV*, ed. Humphreys, 1.2.126, 2.4, location note.

54. John Dover Wilson, *The Fortunes of Falstaff* (Cambridge: Cambridge University Press, 1943), pp. 25–27. And see Stow, I.216–217. Stow also recounts how Henry IV's other sons John and Thomas engaged in a brawl while dining in Eastcheap.

55. Pearce, *Butchers' Company*, pp. 144–152.

56. No satisfactory explanation for the link to highwaymen appears to have been offered: *Henry the Fourth Part I*, ed. Samuel Burdett Hemingway (Philadelphia: New Variorum Shakespeare-J. B. Lippincott, 1936), 3.2.58, 3.2.59 note.

57. On the church and the Boar's Head, see Pearce, pp. 59, 73. A boar's head appeared on one version of the Butchers' Company's arms: p. 51. Pearce mentions the play on p. 148.

58. Shakespeare, *The Second Part of King Henry IV*, ed. Humphreys, 1966), 2.1.90–2.1.93.

59. OED: Civil 1, 4; Intestine, a., Intestine sb., and Intestinal.

60. OED 2. The word also appears in *King John*, in the context of tearing apart morsels and bones (4.3.146), and soon after a "slaughter-house" reference (line 112).

61. Many of the following examples are discussed in a somewhat different context by Wilson, *Fortunes of Falstaff*, pp. 27–31.

62. Compare *Henry VIII*, ed. R. A. Foakes (London: Methuen-Arden Shakespeare, 1964), 1.1.55, 1.1.120, where Wolsey is called a "keech" and "This butcher's cur." In a retrospective glance at the history world near the end of his career, Shakespeare emphasizes the tradition that Wolsey was a butcher's son.

63. *1 Henry IV*, 2.2.97 and note; Wilson, *Fortunes of Falstaff*, p. 30; OED "Martinmass."

64. Edward Burns makes this point amusingly in glossing *1 Henry VI*, 1.2.9.

65. *1 Henry IV*, ed. Humphreys, 2.4.1–2.4.19. On "recording," see Stephen Greenblatt, *Shakespearean Negotiations: The Circulation of Social Energy in Renaissance England* (Berkeley: University of California Press, 1988), pp. 21–65.

66. Rappaport, pp. 219–232. The term *bachelor* was reserved in special cases for the elite of the yeomanry, well-established and probably married men, so its usage in the passage is not particularly urban in connotation (pp. 221, 226).

67. For *tempus edax rerum*, or "time the eater of things," see Ovid, *Metamorphoses* 15.234. As an English proverb, it is recorded by

Tilley (T 326). Shakespeare also alludes to it in *Love's Labour's Lost* 1.1.4, *Measure for Measure* 5.1.13, and Sonnet 19, lines 1–2.

68. The same metaphor appears in the Epilogue: "Be it known . . . I was lately here in the end of a displeasing play, to pray your patience for it, and to promise you a better. I meant indeed to pay you with this; which if like an ill venture it come unluckily home, I break, and you, my gentle creditors, lose" (lines 7–13). A second play, like a second rebellion, is a worthwhile but doubly risky investment. Northumberland, faking his illness, is like an actor–dramatist; unlike the player, he promises a second performance but lacks the nerve to go through with it.

69. Sara Pennell, " 'Great quantities of gooseberry pie and baked clod of beef': Victualling and Eating Out in Early Modern London," in Griffiths and Jenner, pp. 235–236.

70. Ian W. Archer, "Popular Politics in the Sixteenth and Early Seventeenth Centuries," in Griffiths and Jenner, p. 33.

71. Rappaport, *Worlds Within Worlds,* pp. 110–117. The "custom of London," it was often said, allowed such cross-over trading and this frustrated attempts to legislate against it: see chapter 3 of this book. There is some evidence that grocers were especially liable to change trades (p. 110). Stow, as it happens, describes the amalgamation of the Stockfishmongers and Saltfishmongers into a single company in 1536 and recounts their litigious history (I.214–215).

72. The fields about London were notorious as places for sexual encounters, as well as places for military exercises and holiday escape from the city. See Laura Gowing, " 'The Freedom of the Streets': Women and Social Space, 1560–1640," in Griffiths and Jenner, pp. 144–145.

73. Laura Gowing, "The Freedom of the Streets" in Griffith and Jenner, p. 146.

74. Shakespeare, *King Henry V,* ed. T. W. Craik (London: Arden Shakespeare-Routledge, 1995), 4.1.168–4.1.170.

75. Virgil, *Aeneid* 1.430–1.435 and *Georgics* 4.148–4.227, in *Eclogues, Georgics, Aeneid I–IV*, ed. H. Rushton Fairclough and G. P. Good (Cambridge: Loeb Classical Library-Harvard University Press, 1999); Thomas Elyot, *The Book called The Governor*, ed. S. E. Lehmberg (London: Dent, 1962), pp. 7–8. The lazy drone appears in *Georgics* and Elyot. Shakespeare's version of the commonplace anticipates Milton, who argues in the *First Defense of the English People* that the *Georgics*'s bees are law-abiding, and thus cannot be used as evidence for the legitimacy of absolute (oriental) monarchies: *Pro populo Anglicano defensio*, in *The Works of John Milton* (New York: Columbia, 1932), 7.85–7.87.

76. Charles C. H. Waterland Mander, *A Descriptive and Historical Account of the Guild of Cordwainers of the City of London* (London: Williams, Lea & Company for the Cordwainers' Company, 1931), pp. 11, 196. He mentions *Henry V* on p. 12. On the Cordwainers'

demand to search the shops of alien shoemakers in 1593, see Rappaport, p. 35.

77. On intermarriage, see Archer, *Pursuit*, p. 131. On ideas of neighborhood, see Wrightson, "The Politics of the Parish," in Griffiths, Fox, and Hindle, *The Experience of Authority in Early Modern England* (Basingstoke: Macmillan, 1996), pp. 18–22.

78. See Annabel Patterson, who also notes that bees were thought to "swarm" when they followed a new leader out of the hive, abandoning their ruler: *Shakespeare and the Popular Voice* (Oxford: Blackwell, 1989), p. 86. On swarming, see Elyot, p. 7.

79. On the Folio version and London performances, see *Henry V*, ed. Craik, "Introduction," p. 25.

3   TRAGEDY: WHAT ROME?

1. Shakespeare, *Richard II*, ed. Ure, 5.1.2.

2. Shakespeare, *Richard III*, ed. Hammond, 3.1.70, 3.1.75– 3.1.77.

3. Jonathan Goldberg, *James I and the Politics of Literature* (Baltimore: Johns Hopkins University Press, 1983), pp. 33–50.

4. Livy, *The Romane Historie written by T. Livius of Padva*, trans. Philemon Holland (London: Adam Islip, 1600), pp. 4, 7, 8–10, 25.

5. Claude Nicolet, *The World of the Citizen in Republican Rome*, trans. P. S. Falla (Berkeley: University of California Press, 1980), pp. 23–30.

6. Machiavelli, *The Discourses*, ed. Bernard Crick, revised trans. Leslie J. Walker (London: Penguin, 1998), p. 109 and passim.

7. Machiavelli, *Discourses*, pp. 281–282, 302, 330–331.

8. Machiavelli, *The Art of War*, ed. Neal Wood, revised trans. Ellis Farnsworth (Cambridge, MA: Da Capo Press, 2001), pp. 22–23, 40–41.

9. Nicolet, *Republican Rome*, p. 93. On the census and the militia, see chapters 2 and 3.

10. Felix Raab, *The English Face of Machiavelli: A Changing Interpretation, 1500–1700* (London: Routledge & Kegan Paul, 1964), pp. 52–53.

11. Machiavelli, *The Art of War*, pp. 3–4, 208–210.

12. Paul Jorgensen, *Shakespeare's Military World* (Berkeley: University of California Press, 1956), pp. 214–314.

13. As Jonathan Bate argues in his introduction to the third Arden edition of the play, a range of historical periods from the early Republic to the fall of the Empire is implied in its eclectic plot. In my opinion, fixing the setting in the later Empire—the default setting, after all—is nevertheless important if we are to understand alienage and the weakening of Patrician citizenship in the action: see Shakespeare, *Titus Andronicus*, ed. Bate (London: Arden Shakespeare-Routledge, 1995), pp. 16–17.

14. Virgil, *Aeneid*, 1.430–1.435.

15. The echo of Virgil in this passage may be another example of the depletion of this author in *Titus* noted by Heather James, whose discussion of Roman degeneration in the play has influenced my reading

of it: "Cultural Disintegration in *Titus Andronicus*," *Themes in Drama* 13 (1991), 123–140.

16. Samuel Kliger, *The Goths in England: A Study in Seventeenth and Eighteenth Century Thought* (Cambridge: Harvard University Press, 1952), pp. 7–33, 83, 124.

17. Kliger, *Goths in England*, p. 92. Of course, attributions of Scythian lineage were extremely opportunistic in the period: Tartars, Russians, Scandinavians, Scots, and Irish were all implicated. However, there is a consistent pattern here in the form of a backwards crescent, swooping over central Europe from the southeast to the northwest.

18. On household butchery in particular, see Wendy Wall, *Staging Domesticity: Household Work and English Identity in Early Modern Drama* (Cambridge: Cambridge University Press, 2002), pp. 192–195.

19. Shakespeare, *Othello*, ed. E. A. J. Honigmann (Walton-on-Thames: Arden Shakespeare-Thomas Nelson, 1997), 1.1.273.

20. For a somewhat different view of a Brutus divided between "citizenship" and "friendship," see Sharon O'Dair, " 'You cannot see yourself so well as by reflection': Social Role and the Making of Identity in *Julius Caesar*," *SEL* 33 (1993), 289–307.

21. Paul Cantor, *Shakespeare's Rome: Republic and Empire* (Ithaca: Cornell University Press, 1976), pp. 114–115.

22. Plutarch, "The Life of Marcus Brutus," in Shakespeare, *Julius Caesar*, ed. David Daniell (London: Arden Shakespeare-Thomson Learning, 2000), p. 335.

23. Rappaport, *Worlds Within Worlds*, pp. 195–196, 337, 368 (on the example of Dick Wittington). Archer, *Pursuit* (pp. 189–190), provides examples of bequests of land to parishes for poor relief: the purpose was to provide rents from the property, not recreation.

24. Francis Beaumont, *The Knight of the Burning Pestle*, Induction, line 28, in Fraser and Rabkin, eds., *Drama of the English Renaissance*, Vol. 2 (New York: Macmillan, 1976). And see OED I. 1. b.

25. Daniell, ed., in Shakespeare, *Julius Caesar* 1.1.59–1.1.61 note. On the disrupted rhythm of holiday-time and the everyday in the play and in London, see Paster, *The Idea of the City*, p. 61. Paster mostly deals with Shakespeare's image of the ancient city in her discussion of the Roman plays, rather than situational or linguistic parallels with London.

26. George Unwin, *The Gilds & Companies of London* (London: George Allen & Unwin, 1938), pp. 262–264; Rappaport, *Worlds Within Worlds*, pp. 91, 110–117.

27. On the bawdy here, see Jonathan Bate, "The Cobbler's Awl: *Julius Caesar* 1.1.21–1.1.24," *Shakespeare Quarterly* 35 (1984), 461–462.

28. Plutarch, "The Life of Julius Caesar," in Shakespeare, *Julius Caesar*, ed. Daniell, p. 326.

29. Mark S. R. Jenner, "From Conduit Community to Commercial Network? Water in London, 1500–1725," in Paul Griffiths and Jenner, p. 252.

30. And they are likewise associated with female speech, or its violent curtailment, and masculine aggression in *Titus Andronicus*, where Marcus calls the wounded Lavinia "a conduit with three issuing spouts" (2.3.30).

31. Paster, *The Body Embarrassed: Drama and the Disciplines of Shame in Early Modern England* (Ithaca: Cornell University Press, 1993), p. 93; Coppelia Kahn, *Roman Shakespeare: Warriors, Wounds, and Women* (London: Routledge, 1997), pp. 103–104.

32. Livy, *Romane Historie*, p. 7.

33. Kahn, *Roman Shakespeare*, p. 101, sees the wound as a sign of castration. It exposes masculine wounds as inadequate fetishes that fail to cover the origin of Roman masculinity in castration and its complicity with its own images of the feminine.

34. As Richard Burt argues, politics and discourse, or the manipulation of signs, do not coincide in the play or elsewhere: " 'A Dangerous Rome': Shakespeare's *Julius Caesar* and the Discursive Determination of Cultural Politics," in Marie-Rose Logan and Peter L. Rudnystsky, eds., *Contending Kingdoms: Historical, Psychological, and Feminist Approaches to the Literature of Sixteenth Century England and France* (Detroit: Wayne State University Press, 1991), pp. 109–127, esp. p. 118.

35. On the related issue of Rome as a composite construction in a racial sense in *Antony and Cleopatra*, see John Michael Archer, *Old Worlds: Egypt, Southwest Asia, India and Russia in Early Modern English Writing* (Stanford: Stanford University Press, 2001), pp. 46–53.

36. Shakespeare, *Antony and Cleopatra*, ed. John Wilders (Arden Shakespeare-Routledge, 1995), 1.1.18–1.1.19.

37. Nicolet sees triumphs, funeral orations (such as we see in *Julius Caesar*), and other occasions for public display in the late Republic as the institutions of an "alternative city" (pp. 345–346, 352–356). Cleopatra deliberately conflates demotic demonstrations of opinion with the traditional institutions of the Republic.

38. Kahn (pp. 121–133) argues that Antony's suicide is neither botched nor ridiculous.

39. Shakespeare, *Coriolanus*, ed. Philip Brockbank (London: Arden Shakespeare-Routledge, 1976), 1.1.SD 1.

40. In fact, wounds were not shown during Roman elections. Canvassing of voters did take place in a manner that approaches modern election-eering: Nicolet, pp. 297–310.

41. Ernst H. Kantorowicz, *The King's Two Bodies: A Study in Mediaeval Political Theology* (Princeton: Princeton University Press, 1957). Annabel Patterson overstates the case for a populist Shakespeare who invests the people's speech with unmediated integrity and power in *Coriolanus: Shakespeare and the Popular Voice* (Oxford: Blackwell, 1989), pp. 127–128, 132–133. Patterson does offer a useful correction to what she calls "conservative" readings that assume

Shakespeare shares Coriolanus's contempt for the often canny citizens in the play.

42. Jorgensen, pp. 214–314; on Menenius's excuse, see p. 302.

43. Plutarch, "The Life of Caius Martius Coriolanus," in Shakespeare, *Coriolanus*, ed. Brockbank, p. 367.

44. Leinwand, "Shakespeare and the Middling Sort," p. 296. The "drama of a nation" studies he mentions include Zeeveld, Kishlansky, and Patterson, cited later.

45. The belly fable comes mostly from Plutarch, but the claim that blood circulates nourishment through the body is based on Livy, p. 65. See Plutarch, "Coriolanus," in Shakespeare, *Coriolanus*, ed. Brockbank, p. 320.

46. Rappaport, *Worlds Within Worlds*, p. 328. The term appears in this sense in Dekker's "The Shoemaker's Holiday," in Peter G. Lawrence, ed., *Early Seventeenth Century Drama* (London: Dent, 1963), 1.1.159.

47. As Marcus points out, London had been granted a new charter by James in 1608, one that extended its control over certain liberties. Coriolanus's banishment parallels the renewal of the city's corporation (pp. 208–209). As is typical in representational readings, she hardly cites the language of the play text and misses the several appearances of "charter."

48. Rappaport, *Worlds Within Worlds*, pp. 201–206, 264.

49. Machiavelli, *The Discourses*, pp. 124–125; Livy, *Romane Historie*, p. 67.

50. They may also reflect the parliamentarians of the royal purveyance crisis of 1606: see W. Gordon Zeeveld, "*Coriolanus* and Jacobean Politics," *Modern Language Review* 57 (1962), 321–334. James I himself referred to his opponents in the House of Commons as "tribunes," but the structural role of the tribunes in the play seems closer to that of livery company officials to me, however overdetermined their political meaning may have been to audiences early in James's reign.

51. Rappaport, *Worlds Within Worlds*, p. 268; Archer, *Pursuit*, pp. 110, 134, 138. On sergeants, see Rappaport, *Worlds Within Worlds*, p. 208.

52. Rappaport, *Worlds Within Worlds*, pp. 189–190; Archer, *Pursuit*, p. 258.

53. Cantor *Shakespeare's Rome* (p. 62) notes their new conservatism.

54. Mark A. Kishlansky, *Parliamentary Selection: Social and Political Choice in Early Modern England* (Cambridge: Cambridge University Press, 1986), p. 5.

55. Without referring to *Coriolanus*, Archer (*Pursuit*, p. 30) cites Kishlansky but notes that common council elections had more than one selected candidate. He stresses that consensus was still the goal as in parliamentary selection, however. For *Coriolanus* and parliamentary politics in 1606, see Zeeveld.

56. Kishlansky, *Parliamentary Selection*, pp. 5–9.

57. Cantor, *Shakespeare's Rome*, p. 101; Michael Platt, *Rome and Romans According to Shakespeare* (Salzburg: Institute fur Englishe Sprache und Literatur, 1983), pp. 91–92. Aristotle, *Politics*, 1253a 1–5.

58. The same maxim, or quibble, may lie behind an exchange in *Titus Andronicus*, 4.4.77–4.4.78.

59. In his Roman plays, Shakespeare anticipates Nicolet on the relation among tradition, urban geography, and architecture. According to Nicolet (p. 11), "A striking feature [of citizen experience in the Republic] is the importance of the monumental setting which the Roman city . . . came to create as a framework to its collective activity. . . . It is not only a question of 'placing' the cardinal features and key points of civic life, of estimating space and distance, but also of recognizing the constant interrelation and mutual influence between this topographical and monumental setting, in its permanence or its modifications, and the actions and events which took place there." On Coriolanus's identification with the built city, see Paster, *The Idea of the City*, pp. 80–81.

60. Shakespeare, *Coriolanus*, ed. Brockbank, p. 17 and 1.1.46 note, and Robert S. Miola, *Shakespeare's Rome* (Cambridge: Cambridge University Press, 1983), p. 181. Shakespeare might have glanced at Marlianus's detailed *Topographie of Rome in Ancient Time*, a lengthy description of buildings and public places that is appended to Holland's 1600 translation of Livy (pp. 1347–1403).

61. Shakespeare, *The Second Part of King Henry VI*, ed. Cairncross, 3.1.249 note. Incidentally, "carrion kites and crows" appear again in the same play (5.2.11). Kites and crows are mentioned in a battlefield context in *Julius Caesar*, 5.1.84.

62. Shakespeare, *Coriolanus*, ed. W. A. Wright (Oxford: Clarendon, 1879), 1.1.41 note.

63. Shakespeare, *Coriolanus*, ed. W. A. Wright, 1.10.31 note.

64. Plutarch, "Coriolanus," in Shakespeare, p. 313; and see 2.3.236–2.2.243 note.

65. Jenner, pp. 254–255. On the grain conflicts, see Marcus, *Puzzling Shakespeare*, pp. 203–204.

66. Lawrence Manley, *Literature and Culture in Early Modern London* (Cambridge: Cambridge University Press, 1995), p. 225.

67. Beaumont, *Knight*, Act 4, pp. 386–388, 404–407.

68. Jenner, "*Water in London*," pp. 256–265.

69. Shakespeare, *Coriolanus*, ed. Brockbank, p. 25 and 3.1.95–3.1.96 note. The suggestion is G. B. Harrison's. See also Jenner, "Water in London," p. 257. Leinwand (p. 298) mentions that Spencer was involved in a dispute about renovations to his estate that would have blocked the supply of water to St. Bartholomew's hospital in 1599, but he does not relate this to the conduit complex in the play.

70. Janet Adelman, *Suffocating Mothers: Fantasies of Maternal Origin in Shakespeare's Plays* (London: Routledge, 1992), p. 132; Kahn, *Roman Shakespeare*, p. 151.

71. Cantor, *Shakespeare's Rome*, p. 88.

72. The Folio's assignment of this speech to Menenius, while an intriguing option, is belied by Menenius's subsequent words, which are clearly addressed to a Coriolanus who has just spoken in anger.

73. Rappaport, *Worlds Within Worlds*, p. 55; Pettegree, *Foreign Protestant Communities*, p. 290; Laura Hunt Yungblut, *Strangers Settled Here Amongst Us: Policies, Perceptions and the Presence of Aliens in Elizabethan England* (London: Routledge, 1996), p. 105. On James I, see Pettegree, p. 295, and Yungblut, p. 116.

74. For an exclusively Stuart reading of Coriolanus, see Marcus, *Puzzling Shakespeare*, pp. 206–207.

75. Munday et al., *The Play of Sir Thomas More*, 2.3.133–2.3.144.

76. *Sir Thomas More*, 2.3.93; *Coriolanus*, 1.1.187. See also the people as "the number" in *More*, 2.3.56, and "numbers" in *Coriolanus*, 4.6.7, and the exhortation to beg mercy by walking on knees: *More*, 2.3.118–2.3.121, *Coriolanus*, 5.1.5–5.1.6. The rioters are also compared to overflowing water in *More*, 2.3.43–2.3.44.

77. See Robert S. Miola, *Shakespeare's Rome*, p. 207.

78. Shakespeare, *Cymbeline*, ed. J. M. Nosworthy (London: Arden Shakespeare-Routledge, 1988), 1.7.169–1.7.171 and note. Compare Shakespeare, *Coriolanus*, 4.6.91–4.6.93: "He is their god. He leads them like a thing/Made by some other deity than nature,/That shapes man better." This is Nosworthy's observation; he cites similar passages from other Roman tragedies.

79. "Introduction," in Shakespeare, *Cymbeline*, ed. Nosworthy, pp. xxi–xxv.

80. Thomas Dekker [and John Webster], *Westward Ho!*, in Fredson Bowers, ed., *The Dramatic Works of Thomas Dekker*, Vol. 2 (Cambridge: Cambridge University Press, 1964), 1.1.220–1.1.229; for the revenge theme, see 5.4.51.

81. On windows and shutters, see Kathleen Tillotson, in Geoffrey Tillotson, *Essays in Criticism and Research* (Cambridge: Cambridge University Press, 1942), pp. 204–207. On pentices ("penthouse lids") and shop boards as horizontal shutters, see Peter W. M. Blayney, "John Day and the Bookshop that Never Was," in Orlin, p. 332.

82. See Jodi Mikalachki, "The Masculine Romance of Roman Britain: Cymbeline and Early Modern English Nationalism," *Shakespeare Quarterly* 46 (1995), 301–322.

83. Kahn, *Roman Shakespeare*, p. 162.

84. On the slow emergence of the citizen-soldier, see Pocock, *Machiavellian Moment*, pp. 374–389.

85. Balibar, *Europe*, pp. 158–159.

86. Balibar, "Citizen Subject," pp. 54–54. He borrows the term from the political philosopher Pierre-François Moreau.

87. Helgerson, *Forms of Nationhood*, p. 206. On stability and conflict, see Archer, *Pursuit*, pp. 17, 257–260.

88. Balibar, *Europe*, p. 40; author's emphasis.

89. Hobbes, *On the Citizen*, ed. Richard Tuck and Michael Silverthorne (Cambridge: Cambridge University Press, 1998), p. 96.

90. Hobbes, *On the Citizen*, p. 73.

WORKS CITED

Adelman, Janet. *Suffocating Mothers: Fantasies of Maternal Origin in Shakespeare's Plays*. London: Routledge, 1992.

Anderson, Benedict. *Imagined Communities: Reflections on the Origin and Spread of Nationalism*. Revised edn. London: Verso, 1991.

Anonymous. "A Tale of a Citizen and his Wife." In C. A. Patrides, ed. *The Complete English Poems of John Donne*. London: Dent-Everyman's Library, 1985.

Annan, Gertrude. "John Caius." In Elizabeth M. Nugent, ed. *The Thought and Culture of the English Renaissance*. The Hague: Martinus Nijhoff, 1969.

Aristotle. *The Nicomachean Ethics*. Trans. David Ross. Oxford: Oxford University Press, 1980.

———. *The Politics*. Trans. Carnes Lord. Chicago: University of Chicago Press, 1984.

Archer, Ian W. *The Pursuit of Stability: Social Relations in Elizabethan London*. Cambridge: Cambridge University Press, 1991.

———. "Popular Politics in the Sixteenth and Early Seventeenth Centuries." In Griffiths and Jenner, pp. 26–46.

———. "Material Londoners?" in Orlin, pp. 174–192.

Archer, John Michael. *Old Worlds: Egypt, Southwest Asia, India, and Russia in Early Modern English Writing*. Stanford: Stanford University Press, 2001.

———. "Love's Labour's Lost." In Richard Dutton and Jean E. Howard, eds. *A Companion to Shakespeare's Works*. Vol. 3: *The Comedies*. Oxford: Blackwell, 2003.

Bales, Peter. *The Writing Schoolemaster*. London: Thomas Orwin, 1590.

Balibar, Etienne. "Citizen Subject." In Eduardo Cadava, Peter Connor, and Jean-Luc Nancy, eds. *Who Comes After the Subject?* New York: Routledge, 1991, pp. 33–57.

———. "Subjection and Subjectivation." In Joan Copjec, ed. *Supposing the Subject*. London: Verso, 1994, pp. 1–15.

———. *We, the People of Europe? Reflections on Transnational Citizenship*. Trans. James Swenson. Princeton: Princeton University Press, 2004.

Barry, Jonathan. "Bourgeois Collectivism? Urban Associations and the Middling Sort." In Barry and Brooks, pp. 84–112.

Barry, Jonathan and Christopher Brooks, eds. *The Middling Sort of People: Culture, Society and Politics in England, 1550–1800*. New York: St. Martin's Press, 1994.

Bate, Jonathan. "The Cobbler's Awl: *Julius Caesar* 1. 1. 21–24." *Shakespeare Quarterly* 35 (1984), 461–462.

Beaumont, Francis. "The Knight of the Burning Pestle." In Fraser and Rabkin, *Drama of the English Renaissance*, Vol. 2. New York: Macmillan, 1976.

Ben-Amos, Ilana Krausman. *Adolescence and Youth in Early Modern England*. New Haven: Yale University Press, 1996.

Bentley, Gerald Eades. *Shakespeare: A Biographical Handbook*. New Haven: Yale University Press, 1961.

Berger, Harry. "Text against Performance in Shakespeare: The Example of *Macbeth*." In Stephen Greenblatt, ed. *The Power of Forms in the English Renaissance*. Norman, OK: Pilgrim Books, 1982, pp. 49–79.

Berlin, Michael. "Reordering Rituals: Ceremony and the Parish, 1520–1640." In Griffiths and Jenner, pp. 47–60.

Black, Antony. *Guilds and Civil Society in European Political Thought from the Twelfth Century to the Present*. Ithaca: Cornell University Press, 1984.

Blayney, Peter W. M. "John Day and the Bookshop that Never Was." In Orlin, ed., pp. 322–343.

Bock, Gisela, Quentin Skinner, and Maurizio Viroli, eds. *Machiavelli and Republicanism*. Cambridge: Cambridge University Press, 1990.

Brie, F. W. D., ed. *The Brut, or The Chronicles of England*. Vol. 2. London: Early English Text Society, 1908.

Bruster, Douglas. *Drama and the Market in the Age of Shakespeare*. Cambridge: Cambridge University Press, 1992.

Bullokar, William. *Bullokars Booke at large, for the Amendment of Orthographie for English Speech*. London: Henrie Denham, 1580.

Burt, Richard. " 'A Dangerous Rome': Shakespeare's *Julius Caesar* and the Discursive Determination of Cultural Politics." In Marie-Rose Logan and Peter L. Rudnystsky, eds. *Contending Kingdoms: Historical, Psychological, and Feminist Approaches to the Literature of Sixteenth Century England and France*. Detroit: Wayne State University Press, 1991, pp. 109–127.

Calendar of State Papers, Domestic Series, of the Reign of Elizabeth, 1598–1601. Ed. M. A. Everett Green. London, 1869; rpt. Nendeln, Liechtenstein: Kraus, 1967.

Cantor, Paul. *Shakespeare's Rome: Republic and Empire*. Ithaca: Cornell University Press, 1976.

Carroll, William C. *The Great Feast of Language in Love's Labour's Lost*. Princeton: Princeton University Press, 1976.

Daly, A. Stuart. "The Dispraise of the Country in *As You Like It*." *Shakespeare Quarterly* 36 (1985), 300–314.

Dasent, John Roche, ed. *Acts of the Privy Council of England*. New series. Vol. 26. London: Mackie & Co., 1902.

Dekker, Thomas. "The Shoemaker's Holiday." In Peter G. Lawrence, ed. *Early Seventeenth Century Drama*. London: Dent, 1963.

Dekker, Thomas and John Webster. "Westward Ho!" In Fredson Bowers, ed. *The Dramatic Works of Thomas Dekker*. Vol. 2. Cambridge: Cambridge University Press, 1964.

DiGangi, Mario. *The Homoerotics of Early Modern Drama*. Cambridge: Cambridge University Press, 1997.

Drakakis, John. "Afterword." In John J. Joughin, ed. *Shakespeare and National Culture*. Manchester: Manchester University Press, 1997, pp. 326–337.

Elam, Keir. *Shakespeare's Universe of Discourse: Language-Games in the Comedies*. Cambridge: Cambridge University Press, 1984.

Elyot, Thomas. *The Book called The Governor*. Ed. S. E. Lehmberg. London: Dent, 1962.

Empson, William. *Some Versions of Pastoral*. New York: New Directions, 1974.

Erickson, Peter. "The Order of the Garter, the Cult of Elizabeth, and Class-Gender Tension in *The Merry Wives of Windsor*." In Jean E. Howard and Marion F. O'Connor, eds. *Shakespeare Reproduced: The Text in History and Ideology*. New York: Methuen, 1987.

Foucault, Michel. *The History of Sexuality*. Vol. 1: *An Introduction*. Trans. Robert Hurley. New York: Vintage, 1980.

Freedman, Barbara. "Egeon's Debt: Self Division and Self-Redemption in *The Comedy of Errors*," *ELR* 10 (1980), 360–383.

———. "Shakespearean Chronology, Ideological Complicity, and Floating Texts: Something is Rotten in Windsor." *Shakespeare Quarterly* 45 (1994), 190–210.

Freeman, Arthur. "Marlowe, Kyd, and the Dutch Church Libel." *English Literary Renaissance* 3 (1973), 50–51.

Gairdner, James, ed. *The Historical Collection of a Citizen of London in the Fifteenth Century*. London: Camden Society, 1876.

The Geneva Bible: A Facsimile of the 1560 Edition. Madison: University of Wisconsin Press, 1969.

Gibbons, Brian. *Jacobean City Comedy: A Study of Satiric Plays by Jonson, Marston, and Middleton*. Cambridge: Harvard University Press, 1968.

Goldberg, Jonathan. *James I and the Politics of Literature*. Baltimore: Johns Hopkins University Press, 1983.

———. *Writing Matter: From the Hands of the English Renaissance*. Stanford: Stanford University Press, 1990.

Gowing, Laura. " 'The freedom of the streets': Women and Social Space, 1560–1640," in Griffiths and Jenner, pp. 130–151.

Greenblatt, Stephen. *Shakespearean Negotiations: The Circulation of Social Energy in Renaissance England*. Berkeley: University of California Press, 1988.

Griffiths, Paul. "Politics Made Visible: Order, Residence and Uniformity in Cheapside, 1600–45." In Griffiths and Jenner, pp. 176–196.

Griffiths, Paul and Mark S. R. Jenner, eds. *Londinopolis: Essays in the Cultural and Social History of Early Modern London*. Manchester: Manchester University Press, 2000.

Griffiths, R. A. *The Reign of Henry VI*. 2nd. edn. Stroud, Gloucestershire: Sutton Publishing, 1998.

Gurr, Andrew. *The Shakespearean Stage, 1574–1642*. 3rd ed. Cambridge: Cambridge University Press, 1992.

Hart, John. *An Orthographie*. London: William Seres, 1569.

Hall, Kim F. "Guess Who's Coming to Dinner? Colonization and Miscegenation in *The Merchant of Venice*." *Renaissance Drama* 23 (1992), 87–111.

Helgerson, Richard. *Forms of Nationhood: The Elizabethan Writing of England*. Chicago: University of Chicago Press, 1992.

Hobbes, Thomas. *On the Citizen*. Ed. Richard Tuck and Michael Silverthorne. Cambridge: Cambridge University Press, 1998.

Hobday, Charles. "Clouted shoon and leather aprons: Shakespeare and the egalitarian tradition." *Renaissance and Modern Studies* 23 (1979), 63–78.

Hoenselaars, A. J. *Images of Englishmen and Foreigners in the Drama of Shakespeare and His Contemporaries*. Toronto: Associated University Presses, 1992.

Holinshed, Raphael. *Holinshed's Chronicles of England, Scotland, and Ireland*. Vol. 3. London: J. Johnson, 1808; rpt. New York: AMS, 1965.

Honan, Park. *Shakespeare: A Life*. Oxford: Oxford University Press, 1998.

Honigman, E. A. J. "Shakespeare and London's Immigrant Community Circa 1600." In J. P. Vander Motten, ed. *Elizabethan and Modern Studies: Presented to Professor William Schrickx*. J. Gent: Seminaire voor Engelse en Amerikaanse Literatur, 1985, pp. 143–153.

Howard, Jean E. "Mastering Difference in *The Dutch Courtesan*." *Shakespeare Studies* 24 (1996), 105–117.

———. "Shakespeare and Genre." In David Scott Kastan, ed. *A Companion to Shakespeare*. Oxford: Blackwell, 1999, pp. 97–310.

———. "Women, Foreigners, and the Regulation of Urban Space in *Westward Ho*." In Orlin, pp. 150–167.

Howard, Jean E. and Phyllis Rackin. *Engendering a Nation: A Feminist Account of Shakespeare's English Histories*. London: Routledge, 1997.

Hughes, Paul L. and James F. Larkin, eds. *Tudor Royal Proclamations*. Vol. 3. New Haven: Yale University Press, 1969.

James, Heather. "Cultural Disintegration in *Titus Andronicus*." *Themes in Drama* 13 (1991), 123–140.

Jenner, Mark S. R. "From Conduit Community to Commercial Network? Water in London, 1500–1725." In Paul Griffiths and Jenner, pp. 250–272.

Jorgensen, Paul A. *Shakespeare's Military World*. Berkeley: University of California Press, 1956.

Kahn, Coppelia. *Roman Shakespeare: Warriors, Wounds, and Women*. London: Routledge, 1997.

Kantorowicz, Ernst H. *The King's Two Bodies: A Study in Mediaeval Political Theology*. Princeton: Princeton University Press, 1957.

Kaplan, M. Lindsay, ed. *The Merchant of Venice: Texts and Contexts*. Boston: Bedford-St. Martin's, 2002.

Kegl, Rosemary. *The Rhetoric of Concealment: Figuring Gender and Class in Renaissance Literature*. Ithaca: Cornell University Press, 1994.

Kent, Joan R. *The English Village Constable, 1580–1642: A Social and Administrative Study*. Oxford: Clarendon, 1986.

Kishlansky, Mark A. *Parliamentary Selection: Social and Political Choice in Early Modern England*. Cambridge: Cambridge University Press, 1986.

Kliger, Samuel. *The Goths in England: A Study in Seventeenth and Eighteenth Century Thought*. Cambridge: Harvard University Press, 1952.

Laclau, Ernesto and Chantal Mouffe. *Hegemony and Socialist Strategy*. Trans. Winston Moore and Paul Cammack. London: Verso, 1985.

Leggatt, Alexander. *Citizen Comedy in the Age of Shakespeare*. Toronto: University of Toronto Press, 1973.

Leinwand, Theodor B. *The City Staged: Jacobean City Comedy, 1603–1613*. Madison: University of Wisconsin Press, 1986.

———. "Shakespeare and the Middling Sort." *Shakespeare Quarterly* 44 (1993), 284–303.

Livy. *The Romane Historie written by T. Livius of Padva*. Trans. Philemon Holland. London: Adam Islip, 1600.

Machiavelli, Niccolo. *The Discourses*. Ed. Bernard Crick. Trans. Leslie J. Walker. London: Penguin, 1998.

———. *The Art of War*. Ed. Neal Wood. Trans. Ellis Farnsworth. Cambridge, MA: Da Capo Press, 2001.

Mander, Charles C. H. Waterland. *A Descriptive and Historical Account of the Guild of Cordwainers of the City of London*. London: Williams, Lea & Company for the Cordwainers' Company, 1931.

Manley, Lawrence. *Literature and Culture in Early Modern London*. Cambridge: Cambridge University Press, 1995.

Marcus, Leah S. *Puzzling Shakespeare: Local Reading and Its Discontents*. Berkeley: University of California Press, 1988.

———. *Unediting the Renaissance: Shakespeare, Marlowe, Milton*. London: Routledge, 1996.

Marston, John. "The Dutch Courtesan." In Russell A. Fraser and Norman C. Rabkin, eds. *Drama of the English Renaissance*. Vol. 2: *The Stuart Period*. New York: Macmillan, 1976.

Marx, Karl. "Theses on Feuerbach." In Richard C. Tucker, ed. *The Marx-Engels Reader*. 2nd edn. New York: Norton, 1978. pp. 143–145.

Marx, Karl and Frederick Engels. *The Communist Manifesto*. London: Verso, 1998.

Mazzio, Carla. "The Melancholy of Print: *Love's Labour's Lost*." In Mazzio and Douglas Trevor, eds. *Historicism, Psychoanalysis, and Early Modern Culture*. New York: Routledge, 2000, pp. 186–227.

McMullan, John L. *The Canting Crew: London's Criminal Underworld, 1550–1700*. New Brunswick: Rutgers University Press, 1984.

Mikalachki, Jodi. "The Masculine Romance of Roman Britain: Cymbeline and Early Modern English Nationalism." *Shakespeare Quarterly* 46 (1995), 301–322.

Milton, John. "Pro populo Anglicano defensio." In *The Works of John Milton*. New York: Columbia, 1932.

Miola, Robert S. *Shakespeare's Rome*. Cambridge: Cambridge University Press, 1983.

Montrose, Louis. *The Purpose of Playing: Shakespeare and the Cultural Politics of the Elizabethan Theatre*. Chicago: University of Chicago Press, 1996.

Mouffe, Chantal, ed. *Dimensions of Radical Democracy: Pluralism, Citizenship, Community*. London: Verso, 1992.

———. "Preface: Democratic Politics Today." In Mouffe, ed., pp. 1–14.

———. "Democratic Citizenship and the Political Community." In Mouffe, ed., pp. 225–239.

Mulcaster, Richard. *The First Part of the Elementarie*. London: Thomas Vautroullier, 1582. Facsimile edn. Menston: Scolar Press, 1970.

Mullaney, Steven. *The Place of the Stage: License, Play, and Power in Renaissance England*. Chicago: University of Chicago Press, 1988.

Munday, Anthony et al., *Sir Thomas More*. Eds. Vittorio Gabrieli and Giorgio Melchiori. Manchester: The Revels Plays—Manchester University Press, 1990.

Nashe, Thomas. "Pierce Penilesse his Supplication to the Divell." In R. B. McKerrow, ed. *The Works of Thomas Nashe*. 2nd ed., revised by F. P. Wilson. Oxford: Blackwell, 1958.

Nicolet, Claude. *The World of the Citizen in Republican Rome*. Trans. P. S. Falla. Berkeley: University of California Press, 1980.

O'Dair, Sharon. " 'You cannot see yourself so well as by reflection': Social Role and the Making of Identity in *Julius Caesar*." *SEL* 33 (1993), 289–307.

Orlin, Lena Cowen, ed. *Material London, ca. 1600*. Philadelphia: University of Pennsylvania Press, 2000.

Overbury, Thomas. *A Wife now the Widow of Sir T. Overburye*. Ed. James E. Savage. Gainesville: Scholars Facsimiles, 1968.

Parker, Patricia. "Anagogic Metaphor: Breaking Down the Walls of Partition." In *Centre and Labyrinth*. Ed. Eleanor Cook et al. Toronto: University of Toronto Press, 1983, pp. 38–58.

———. *Literary Fat Ladies: Rhetoric, Gender, Property*. London: Methuen, 1987.

———. *Shakespeare from the Margins: Language, Culture, Context*. Chicago: University of Chicago Press, 1996.

Paster, Gail Kern. *The Idea of the City in the Age of Shakespeare*. Athens: University of Georgia Press, 1985.

———. *The Body Embarrassed: Drama and the Disciplines of Shame in Early Modern England*. Ithaca: Cornell University Press, 1993.

Patterson, Annabel. *Shakespeare and the Popular Voice*. Oxford: Blackwell, 1989.

Pearce, Arthur. *The History of the Butchers' Company*. London: Meat Traders' Journal Company, 1929.

Pennell, Sara. " 'Great quantities of gooseberry pie and baked clod of beef': Victualling and Eating Out in Early Modern London." In Griffiths and Jenner, pp. 228–249.

Pettegree, Andrew. *Foreign Protestant Communities in Sixteenth-Century London*. Oxford: Clarendon, 1986.

Platt, Michael. *Rome and Romans According to Shakespeare*. Salzburg: Institute fur Englishe Sprache und Literatur, 1983.

Pocock, J. G. A. *The Machiavellian Moment: Florentine Political Thought and the Atlantic Republican Tradition*. Princeton: Princeton University Press, 1975.

Power, M. J. "East London Housing in the Seventeenth Century." In Peter Clark and Paul Slack, eds. *Crisis and Order in English Towns, 1500–1700: Essays in Urban History*. Toronto: University of Toronto Press, 1972, pp. 237–262.

Raab, Felix. *The English Face of Machiavelli: A Changing Interpretation, 1500–1700*. London: Routledge & Kegan Paul, 1964.

Rabelais, François. *The Histories of Gargantua and Pantagruel*. Trans. J. M. Cohen. Harmondsworth: Penguin, 1955.

Rackin, Phyllis. *Stages of History: Shakespeare's English Chronicles*. Ithaca: Cornell University Press, 1990.

———. "Foreign Country: The Place of Women in Shakespeare's Historical World." In Richard Burt and John Michael Archer, eds. *Enclosure Acts: Sexuality, Property, and Culture in Early Modern England*. Ithaca: Cornell University Press, 1994, pp. 68–95.

Rappaport, Steve. *Worlds Within Worlds: Structures of Life in Sixteenth-Century London*. Cambridge: Cambridge University Press, 1989.

Reynolds, Susan. *An Introduction to the History of English Medieval Towns*. Oxford: Clarendon, 1977.

Saussure, Ferdinand de. *Course in General Linguistics*. Trans. Wade Baskin. New York: McGraw-Hill, 1966.

Schoenbaum, Samuel. *William Shakespeare: A Documentary Life*. New York: Oxford University Press and the Scolar Press, 1975.

———. *William Shakespeare: A Compact Documentary Life*. Revised edn. Oxford: Oxford University Press, 1987.

Shakespeare, William. *All's Well That Ends Well*. Ed. G. K. Hunter. London: Arden Shakespeare-Routledge, 1989.

———. *Antony and Cleopatra*. Ed. John Wilders. London: Arden Shakespeare-Routledge, 1995.

———. *As You Like It*. Ed. Agnes Latham. London: Arden Shakespeare-Methuen, 1975.

———. *As You Like It*. Ed. Richard Knowles. New York: New Variorum Shakespeare-Modern Language Association, 1977.

———. *The Comedy of Errors*. Ed. R. A. Foakes. London: Arden Shakespeare-Methuen, 1963.

———. *Coriolanus*. Ed. W. A. Wright. Oxford: Clarendon, 1879.

———. *Coriolanus*. Ed. Philip Brockbank. London: Arden Shakespeare-Routledge, 1976.

———. *Cymbeline*. Ed. J. M. Nosworthy. London: Arden Shakespeare-Routledge, 1988.

———. *King Henry the Fourth Part I*. Ed. Samuel Burdett Hemingway. Philadelphia: New Variorum Shakespeare-J. B. Lippincott, 1936.

———. *The First Part of King Henry IV*. Ed. A. R. Humphreys London: Arden Shakespeare-Routledge, 1988.

Shakespeare, William. *The Second Part of King Henry IV*. Ed. A. R. Humphreys. London: Arden Shakespeare-Methuen, 1966.

———. *King Henry V*. Ed. T. W. Craik. London: Arden Shakespeare-Routledge, 1995.

———. *King Henry VI, Part 1*. Ed. Edward Burns. London: Arden Shakespeare-Thomson Learning, 2000.

———. *King Henry VI, Part 2*. Ed. Andrew S. Cairncross. London: Arden Shakespeare-Methuen, 1957.

———. *King Henry VI, Part 2*. Ed. Ronald Knowles. Walton-on-Thames: Arden Shakespeare-Thomas Nelson and Sons, 1999.

———. *King Henry VI, Part 3*. Ed. Andrew S. Cairncross. London: Arden Shakespeare-Routledge, 1989.

———. *King Henry VI, Part 3*. Eds. John D. Cox and Eric Rasmussen. London: Arden Shakespeare-Thompson Learning, 2001.

———. *King Henry VIII*. Ed. R. A. Foakes. London: Methuen-Arden Shakespeare, 1964.

———. *King John*. Ed. E. A. J. Honigmann. London: Arden Shakespeare-Thomson Learning, 1998.

———. *Julius Caesar*. Ed. David Daniell. London: Arden Shakespeare-Thomson Learning, 2000.

———. *Loues Labour's Lost*. Ed. Horace Howard Furness. Philadelphia: New Variorum Shakespeare-J. B. Lippincott, 1904.

———. *Love's Labour's Lost*. Ed. Richard David. London: Methuen, 1956.

———. *Love's Labour's Lost*. Ed. H. R. Woudhuysen. Walton-on-Thames: Arden Shakespeare-Thomas Nelson and Sons, 1998.

———. *Measure for Measure*. Ed. J. W. Lever. London: Arden Shakespeare-Methuen, 1965.

———. *Measure for Measure*. Ed. Mark Eccles. New York: New Variorum Shakespeare-Modern Language Association, 1980.

———. *The Merchant of Venice*. Ed. John Russell Brown. London: Arden Shakespeare-Routledge, 1988.

———. *The Merry Wives of Windsor*. Ed. H. J. Oliver. London: Arden Shakespeare-Methuen, 1971.

———. *The Merry Wives of Windsor*. Ed. Giorgio Melchiori. Walton-on-Thames: Arden Shakespeare-Thomas Nelson and Sons, 2000.

———. *A Midsummer Night's Dream*, Ed. Harold F. Brooks. London: Arden Shakespeare-Methuen, 1979.

———. *Much Ado About Nothing*. Ed. A. R. Humphreys. London: Arden Shakespeare-Methuen, 1981.

———. *Othello*. Ed. E. A. J. Honigmann. Walton-on-Thames: Arden Shakespeare-Thomas Nelson, 1997.

———. *The Life and Death of King Richard the Second*. Ed. Matthew W. Black. Philadelphia: New Variorum Shakespeare-J. B. Lippincott, 1955.

———. *King Richard II*. Ed. Peter Ure. Bungay: Arden Shakespeare-Methuen, 1961.

————. *King Richard II.* Ed. Charles R. Forker. Arden Shakespeare-Thomson Learning, 2002.

————. *King Richard III.* Ed. Antony Hammond. Walton-on-Thames: Arden Shakespeare-Thomas Nelson and Sons, 1997.

————. *Titus Andronicus.* Ed. Jonathan Bate. London: Arden Shakespeare-Routledge, 1995.

Shapiro, James. *Shakespeare and the Jews.* New York: Columbia University Press, 1996.

Sisson, C. J. "Shakespeare's Helena and Dr. William Harvey," *Essays and Studies* (1960), 1–20.

Skinner, Quentin. "Machiavelli's *Discorsi* and the Pre-Humanist Origins of Republican Ideas." In Bock et al., pp. 121–141.

————. "The Republican Ideal of Political Liberty." In Bock et al., pp. 293–309.

Skura, Meredith. *Shakespeare the Actor and the Purposes of Playgoing.* Chicago: University of Chicago Press, 1993.

Spenser, Edmund. *The Faerie Queene.* Ed. Thomas P. Roche. Harmondsworth: Penguin, 1978.

Spitzer, Leo. "Development of a Method." In Alban K. Forcione et al., eds. *Representative Essays.* Stanford: Stanford University Press, 1988, pp. 425–448.

Spurgeon, Caroline F. E. *Shakespeare's Imagery and What It Tells Us.* Cambridge: Cambridge University Press, 1935.

Stow, John. *A Survey of London.* Ed. Charles Lethbridge Kingsford. 2 vols. Oxford: Clarendon, 1908.

Tilley, Morris P. *A Dictionary of the Proverbs in England in the Sixteenth and Seventeenth Centuries.* Ann Arbor, MI: University of Michigan Press, 1950.

Tillotson, Geoffrey and Kathleen Tillotson. *Essays in Criticism and Research.* Cambridge: Cambridge University Press, 1942.

Traub, Valerie. *Desire and Anxiety: Circulations of Sexuality in Shakespearean Drama.* London: Routledge, 1992.

Tretiak, Andrew. "*The Merchant of Venice* and the 'Alien' Question." *Review of English Studies* 5 (1929), 402–409.

Unwin, George. *The Gilds & Companies of London.* London: George Allen & Unwin, 1938.

Virgil. *Eclogues, Georgics, Aeneid I–IV.* Eds. H. Rushton Fairclough and G. P. Good. Cambridge: Loeb Classical Library-Harvard University Press, 1999.

Wall, Wendy. *Staging Domesticity: Household Work and English Identity in Early Modern Drama.* Cambridge: Cambridge University Press, 2002.

West, William. *Symbolaeography, which may be Termed the Art, Description, or Image of Instruments.* London: Jane Yetsweirt, 1597.

Williams, Deanne. " 'Will you go, Anhhers?' *The Merry Wives of Windsor,* II. i. 209." *Notes and Queries* (June 1999), 233–234.

Wilson, J. Dover. *The Fortunes of Falstaff.* Cambridge: Cambridge University Press, 1943.

Wilson, Richard. *Will Power: Essays on Shakespearean Authority.* Detroit: Wayne State University Press, 1993.

Wolffe, Bertram. *Henry VI.* Yale English Monarchs Series. New Haven: Yale University Press, 2001.

Wright, Henry. *The First Part of the Disqvisition of Truth, Concerning Political Affairs.* London: Nicholas Okes, 1616.

Wrightson, Keith. " 'Sorts of People' in Tudor and Stuart England." In Barry and Brooks, pp. 28–51.

———. "The Politics of the Parish." In Paul Griffiths, Adam Fox and Steve Hindle, eds. *The Experience of Authority in Early Modern England.* Basingstoke: Macmillan, 1996, pp. 10–46.

Yates, Francis. *A Study of Love's Labour's Lost.* Cambridge: Cambridge University Press, 1936.

Yungblut, Laura Hunt. *Strangers Settled Here Amongst Us: Policies, Perceptions and the Presence of Aliens in Elizabethan England.* London: Routledge, 1996.

Zeeveld, W. Gordon. "*Coriolanus* and Jacobean Politics." *Modern Language Review* 57 (1962), 321–334.

Zizek, Slovoj. "Eastern Europe's Republics of Gilead." In Mouffe, ed., pp. 193–207.

INDEX

WS stands for William Shakespeare.